The story of British Forces Broadcasting began officially on 1st January 1944 in North Africa. Mobile stations were used in the advance northwards through Italy, and followed closely behind the troops after D-Day as they fought their way across Europe into Germany. However, this approach was not suitable for the war east of Suez. The India and South-East Asia Commands (SEAC) covered such a huge area that other means were needed to deliver programmes to the forces in that theatre. A start had been made in Delhi in 1944, where a station had been set up which used air time provided by All-India Radio on one of its transmitters. Efforts to improve welfare facilities were made by Vice-Admiral Mountbatten, soon after he arrived to take up his appointment as Supreme Allied Commander, South East Asia. He set up a forces newspaper, and started experimental radio transmissions, but found there were financial constraints on what could be achieved. Friends and relatives back home became unhappy about the forces' living conditions, and articles appeared in the English press. These came to Churchill's notice, and he was persuaded to send Lord Munster on a fact-finding tour to establish what improvements were needed. His report was made available to MPs just before Christmas 1944, when Churchill addressed the Commons on the situation. Lord Munster had noted the station in Delhi, but wrote that transmitters were needed for forces broadcasting, and that many more receiving sets were required. Discussions involving the War Office and the BBC reached the conclusion that the best option was a powerful short wave transmitter, supported by another with less power. This was approved by the War Cabinet, along with most of Munster's recommendations. What was much more difficult to resolve was the disagreement between those who wished to have the station in Delhi, and Mountbatten who wanted it under his command, in Ceylon. The text of a signal is included in which he set out his reasons. The furious argument was decided in his favour, and the result was Radio SEAC.

Early estimates of targets for when the station might go on the air proved to be optimistic. They underestimated the difficulty of shipping, from England to Ceylon, the components of a big transmitter, complete with its own power supply. Several aerial towers (300 feet high) had to be dismantled, shipped and re-erected. In order to provide some broadcasting as soon as possible, the small transmitter was used for about a year before the powerful one went on the air in May 1946 - long after the war was over. Even readers with some knowledge of the technical details of radio receivers may be surprised by photographs showing the sheer size of the components used in the big transmitter.

One could justify the huge expense of the transmitting station on the grounds that when it was not longer needed for forces broadcasting it could serve as a relay station for the BBC. This would mean, for example, that the BBC Overseas Service would be received well in Australia. It was used in this way for a short time, but independence for Ceylon led to the station being handed over to the country's new government.

The story of Radio SEAC, and Mountbatten's pivotal involvement in it, has remained untold until now. Eric Hitchcock presents a balanced and fascinating account, blending military, social, political and scientific history together to produce an important account.

Eric Hitchcock was fortunate in having a physics master at school who made electricity and magnetism fascinating. On leaving school he went to work for a high street bank, and took up radio construction as a hobby. Second-hand components were bought from junk shops in wartime London, and a simple shortwave receiver was eventually made to work. He was called up in the summer of 1944, and was fortunate in being sent on a six-month wireless mechanics course in the Royal Signals, followed by nine weeks' experience at the BBC transmitting station at Skelton, in what is now Cumbria. With eleven other similarly trained men he was introduced to the same model Marconi shortwave transmitter that was being installed in a purpose-built transmitter about twenty miles from Colombo in Ceylon. The men were flown to India in a Dakota, to operate and maintain this and other transmitters which carried Radio SEAC's programmes. In 1947 he was demobilised, after sailing up the Mersey on SS *Devonshire*. He returned to the bank, but was moved in the 1960s to a department where he helped design computer systems for early applications such as payroll and personnel records. Several of his SEAC friends became radio amateurs, but listening to the monitor speaker in the transmitter hall for many hours on most days encouraged his interest in playing popular music and jazz on piano. In retirement he decided to find out what record of the station existed in the Public Record Office, now National Archives. This book and his contact with many like-minded individuals is the result.

Making Waves

Admiral Mountbatten's Radio SEAC 1945-49

Eric Hitchcock

Helion & Company

Helion & Company Limited
26 Willow Road
Solihull
West Midlands
B91 1UE
England
Tel. 0121 705 3393
Fax 0121 711 4075
email: info@helion.co.uk
website: www.helion.co.uk
Twitter: @helionbooks
Visit our blog http://blog.helion.co.uk/

Published by Helion & Company 2014

Designed and typeset by Great White Designs, Stroud, Gloucestershire
Cover Design by Farr out Publications, Wokingham, Berkshire
Printed by Lightning Source, Milton Keynes, Buckinghamshire

ISBN 978-1-906033-95-8

British Library Cataloguing-in-Publication Data
A catalogue record for this book is available from the British Library

We always welcome receiving book proposals from prospective authors working in military history.

Contents

List of Illustrations

Photographs

All the above photographs were taken by men working on the station.

Those marked 'C' featured in the October 2000 edition of *Short Wave Magazine*. P.W. Publishing Limited has given permission for their use in the book.

Diagrams

Preface

A desirable feature of the twentieth century was a 'job for life'. I had one in a branch bank, but have observed recently the great reduction in such jobs. My career was interrupted by three years in the army, most of which time was spent on the Radio SEAC transmitting station near Colombo in Ceylon, as Sri Lanka was called then. In retirement I had time to reflect on that unusual occupation, and wondered what record might exist of the station, and where to start looking for it.

For someone living in a London suburb, the Imperial War Museum was an obvious choice. I obtained permission to visit their library, where I was able to see a month's editions of the forces daily newspaper which Admiral Mountbatten arranged to have produced for his forces in South East Asia Command. This included a report of the opening of the Marconi 100 kW short wave broadcasting transmitter. Enquiries made at the Museum revealed that there were records and photographs of other forces broadcasting stations, but there was nothing about Radio SEAC in the picture or sound archives.

Had anyone written a book? A search in the library of the National Army Museum produced Doreen Taylor's book *A Microphone and a Frequency - Forty Years of Forces Broadcasting*. This covers all the theatres of war, and includes eleven pages on Radio SEAC. It describes the early days of forces broadcasting from Delhi, when some talented and enthusiastic people established a service which was limited by the amount of time they could borrow on the transmitters of All-India Radio. The book mentions the installation of Radio SEAC's Marconi 100 kW transmitter, and the huge increase in coverage that resulted. It says something about how the station came to be based in Colombo, rather than Delhi. The delay in the completion of the project was also mentioned. However, as with all the other British Forces Broadcasting stations she covered so well, her account is mainly concerned with programme production, and how it became a training ground for radio presenters and personalities who have entertained us so often and so well in the ensuing fifty years. It seemed there was probably a story still to be told about the difficulties involved in shipping a very large transmitter from Chelmsford to Ceylon and installing it, and the erection of six aerial towers about 300 feet high.

The library of the National Army Museum also had a copy of Mountbatten's huge report to the Combined Chiefs of Staff, in about 1952. Annexure 8, under a heading 'Broadcasting', includes 47 words on the station as it was when using a 7.5 kW transmitter, and a further 117 words, in a second paragraph about the decision to install a 100 kW transmitter for Radio SEAC, and the subsequent delays. Annexure 8 has only slightly more under the heading 'Publications', which covers the SEAC newspaper and two magazines.

It was obviously worth looking at the official biography of Mountbatten by Philip Ziegler. This includes everything one might wish to know about his family background, his time in the navy, and the events leading up to his appointment as Supreme Allied Commander

South East Asia. Even before leaving for the Far East, Mountbatten had arranged for the setting up of the forces daily newspaper. This was an important initiative in the task of improving the morale of the troops, and merited a mention in the biography. However, it was a relatively minor undertaking in comparison with setting up a forces broadcasting station, so I was greatly surprised to find no mention of Radio SEAC in the book. There had to be a reason for the omission, and it made me even more interested in finding out more about how the station came to be set up.

I had no idea where to look next until a television documentary pointed the way forward. It was about someone who was determined to investigate some sort of cover-up in the RAF. It showed them visiting the Public Record Office (PRO) and browsing through numerous files. Until then I had not appreciated that the PRO might have the sort of information I wanted. On my first visit it was impossible to know where to start, but thanks to the courtesy and helpfulness of the staff there, I was quickly able to find the files I needed.

There was plenty in War Office files about the setting up of forces broadcasting generally, and Radio SEAC in particular. I was soon scribbling pencil notes in an exercise book, because pens are not allowed, and I had no laptop computer. At some stage it occurred to me that the station must have cost a great deal of money, so I wanted to know who might have sanctioned the expenditure. Knowing nothing about government finances I decided to start at the top and looked at the prime minister's files. This proved to be a very lucky choice because it opened up the whole question of welfare provision for the troops, and Churchill's initiative in sending Lord Munster on a fact-finding tour of the Far East to find out what deficiencies needed to be addressed. The cost of setting up Radio SEAC, and more particularly the 100 kW Marconi transmitter, were sanctioned at War Cabinet level with Churchill's backing.

The PRO is now the National Archives. Its importance in providing information for this book will be evident from the numerous pages having one or more footnotes in the form WO 203 5207. (WO = War Office, and PREM = Prime Minister).

The installation of the big transmitter made Radio SEAC unique among forces broadcasting stations. A transmitter of this power usually became available only as a result of allied troops occupying territory in which a suitable existing transmitter was located. There were signals and letters, mostly between London and SEAC, in which the plans for the 100 kW transmitter were finalized. More material dealt with the difficulties and frustrations in trying to get a huge transmitter, and its associated equipment, from England to Sri Lanka.

All this persuaded me that I could now piece together a story which would be of great interest to me, and hopefully to the few old colleagues I was in touch with who had worked on the transmitters. I also wished to deal with the roles played by the senior serving officers and politicians.

A first draft of the story was circulated to those directly involved. Important additions have been made based on material from Paul Sollom about the aerials, and about maintenance problems which arose after most of us had left for home. There was also information about the transition period between our leaving and the handing over to Radio Ceylon. So this volume attempts to bring together the recollections of my colleagues, and information from the files of the National Archives and several books.

My old colleagues and I have sometimes wondered whether it was all worthwhile. Apparently the studios received a lot of mail, so there were probably many more listeners than we might have supposed. Undoubtedly the shortage of suitable radio receivers greatly reduced the numbers able to listen to the station in 1945, when it was on relatively low transmission power, pending the installation of the 100 kW Marconi transmitter. More and better receivers became available at about the same time.

The war was over before these improvements were made, but many men were left to endure long drawn out boredom while waiting for their turn to be sent home. Some have said how this was made less tedious by the availability of entertainment from Radio SEAC, tailored to the tastes of the forces audience.

I noticed that, in a prologue to Alan Grace's book *This is the British Forces Network*, Alexander McKee is quoted as having made the comment on the role of a radio announcer that 'there is nothing miraculous or exceptional in knowing that his voice is coming out of the radio. The wonder lies in the fantastic machinery and the engineers who make it possible'.

I hope I have been able to say something worthwhile about that wonder.

Acknowledgements

This book would not have been written without the encouragement of my old colleagues from Radio SEAC transmitters.

Peter Burland was the prime source of information about the Hora Hena receiving station, where he spent the second half of his time in Ceylon. He also provided some of the photographs reproduced in this volume, and has been a strong supporter of the idea of writing something about our experiences. Through him, the extent of our relationship with the high speed wireless unit was brought to my attention, and I was most fortunate in being able to contact Harry Moore, Jack Nield, Ken Hall and Norman Shires. They helped in various ways with the story, and Norman provided details of the station's first aerial array, which at one time seemed likely to remain a mystery. He made a detailed drawing which was the basis of an illustration herein.

A first draft of the book was completed many years ago, but the task of completing the slender volume has taken so long that several people who made important contributions have passed away while the work has continued. Sadly, Andy Whetstone died before even the first draft was complete, so he never saw the way his photographs had been used. He had been keen to help, and his special contribution was that he went from the transmitting station to work in the studios in Colombo. His sudden death during Christmas 1996, whilst still working as a freelance recording engineer, came as a great shock. He and I met for lunch in a West End pub a month or two before his death, and he produced a large plastic bag full of small photographs, which he gave me to use as I wished. Many of the photographs in this volume were produced from those prints. A number of them were pictures which several of us had in our collections, but it was often convenient to use Andy's copies, not least because they had never been stuck in an album. Unfortunately nobody had any of the original negatives. A few of the pictures were used in an article I wrote for *Short Wave Magazine*. These are annotated to indicate that permission has been obtained from the publishers for their use in this volume.

Harold Priestley supplied the very important copy of the *SEAC Forces' Radio Times* for May 1947 which contained an article by Bernard Blakemore on the technical aspects of the station. He was Chief Engineer for most of our time there. This has been invaluable in so many ways; not least to correct errors which would have arisen from reliance on my unreliable memory. Harold contributed his own story, and has been a source of information and encouragement. It was his idea to submit an article to *Practical Wireless*, after speaking to the editor at a local radio society meeting. This was passed on to, and published by, the *Short Wave Magazine*, as mentioned above. Through his amateur radio contacts, he got in touch with Paul Sollom, who had been an army captain on the station, and went on to become the Chief Engineer. August 2003 was a terrible month, Harold and Paul died within the space of a week.

Paul joined the unit a few months before some of us left, and stayed for much longer than any of us. He remained for some time after the station was handed over to its new administration, and became a civilian employee. His contribution to this volume has been invaluable in providing information about the station after Radio SEAC closed down. This included details of how he dealt with equipment failures caused by the climate which, without air conditioning, can be very unkind to electronic devices. His special interest in aerial design proved to be most valuable when coping with new demands on the station, and he provided an account of how he dealt with various technical problems. Fortunately he was a keen photographer with a good camera, and had kept a considerable number of negatives, several of which have been added to the collection of prints we already had. Unfortunately, delays in the completion of the book, including the addition of much information supplied in writing by Paul, meant that the meeting I had hoped to have with him never took place.

The first draft had been amended and extended, and the work of finalising the project was in hand, when Peter Burland phoned to say he had seen a TV documentary with a brief appearance and mention of a Bernard Blakemore. The programme was about restoring three sites of historical interest, one of which was the pioneering radar site at Bawdsey. In response to a letter, Mary Wain, one of the organisers of the Bawdsey Radar Group, very kindly phoned to say that their Bernard Blakemore was the Radio SEAC man we wished to contact, and put us in touch by phone. He showed great interest in what was being attempted, and he knew the man who could provide an eye witness account of the building of the station, including the assembly of the 100 kW transmitter, and its associated equipment.

Bill Reis, who had been an AQMS in the REME at the time, has kindly provided an invaluable briefing on the huge undertaking, and details of many of the people involved. Until that became available, the relevant text relied on War Office reports, and minutes of meetings at SEAC headquarters. He also provided some unique photographs, including several taken during a visit to the station by Admiral Mountbatten. Bernard Blakemore supplied photographs taken at the studios in Colombo, amongst others. His visit to the BFBS station on Gibraltar enabled us to draw comparisons between our experiences and the very different way in which forces broadcasting operates today.

As a result of a letter I wrote to the Lloyds Bank pensioners' magazine I was fortunate in contacting a fellow pensioner, Colin Martin, who provided two copies of the *SEAC Forces' Radio Times*, one of which is reproduced at the end of this volume. Yet another Lloyds pensioner, Tony Martin, provided the story of listening to the station in India, on a receiver constructed by someone in their RAF unit.

From the outset, Doreen Taylor's book *A Microphone and a Frequency*, with its 11 pages about Radio SEAC, has been invaluable. I found a copy in the library of the Army Museum, and this led me to contact Alan Grace, whose books have been informative and most enjoyable. He very kindly sent me CDs with recordings of several broadcasts. The earliest of these was in the Home Service of the BBC on 6 November 1964, and was called *Battledress Broadcasting*. It celebrated the 21st anniversary of the start of forces broadcasting in North Africa in 1944. Earl Mountbatten's voice is heard expressing his belief in the value of forces broadcasting generally, and of Radio SEAC in particular. The BBC and the Mountbatten Estate have kindly given permission for the text of his contribution to the programme to be included in this volume.

Patrick Morley's book *This is the American Forces Network* has been useful in providing insights into the sometimes difficult relationship between the BBC and AFN.

I have been able to draw on this when considering the BBC's approach to British Forces Broadcasting generally, and Radio SEAC in particular. I was also greatly appreciative of his encouragement. The staff of the Public Record Office (now National Archives) were particularly helpful in initially pointing me in the right direction, and generally assisting me during subsequent visits.

On the Short Waves 1923-45, by Jerry Berg, includes a piece about Radio SEAC and its American listeners. He showed great interest in a draft of this book, and has been most encouraging. His extensive internet archive of material related to short wave radio is a wonderful resource (ontheshortwaves.com). He kindly accepted a copy of extracts, on tape, of a few minutes of a Radio SEAC broadcast. This has been on the website for many years.

Another notable internet contact was with David Ricquish and the Radio Heritage Collection in New Zealand. He put me in touch with Dr Adrian M. Paterson, DX Editor, Wavescan, of Adventist World Radio. The latter had visited the transmitting station, and AWR used the services of the Sri Lanka Broadcasting Corporation for about thirty five years.

Finally, I have to thank my wife Bea for her support, and for allowing me to indulge my fantasy of being an author. This has caused me to disappear for long sessions on the word processor, when I could have been doing something more sociable.

Abbreviations

AC	Alternating current
AFN	American Forces Network
AFRS	Armed Forces Radio Service
AGC	Automatic gain control
A-I R	All-India Radio
AF	Audio frequency
AM	Amplitude modulation
ATS	Auxiliary Territorial Service
AVC	Automatic volume control
AW	Army welfare
AWR	Adventist World Radio
BBC	British Broadcasting Corporation
CBI	China, Burma, India theatre
CRT	Cathode ray tube
DAWS	Director, Army Welfare Service
DJ	Disc jockey
DX	Long distance radio communication
EHT	Extra high tension
ENSA	Entertainments National Service Association
FM	Frequency modulation
GEC	General Electric Company
GHQ	General headquarters
GI	American army soldier
HSR	High speed relay
HMV	His Master's Voice
I & CA	Information and Civil Affairs
ITMA	It's that man again
IST	Indian standard time
kV	Kilovolt
kW	Kilowatt
LCC	London County Council
LCD	Liquid crystal display
LF	Low frequency
Mfd	Microfarad
NCO	Non-commissioned officer
OR	Other ranks
M of I	Ministry of information

NAAFI	Navy Army and Air Force Institutes
PM	Prime Minister
PREM	Premier (Prime Minister)
PRO	Public Records Office (now National Archives)
RCA	Radio Corporation of America
RE	Royal Engineers
REME	Royal Electrical and Mechanical Engineers
RF	Radio frequency
RN	Royal Navy
SAC	Supreme Allied Commander
SLBC	Sri Lanka Broadcasting Corporation
TV	Television
SWB	Short Wave Broadcasting
UG	Underground (cables in particular)
WD	War Department
WO	War Office

1

Short Wave Broadcasting

In the spring of 1923, Guglielmo Marconi sat at his desk on his yacht *Elettra*, just south of Spain, and wrote a letter about the reception of a short wave signal from Poldhu, in Cornwall. This was one of many tests carried out to determine how useful short waves might be for long range communication. He was puzzled, as were many other radio experimenters. The problem was that radio signals, like other electromagnetic waves, normally travel in straight lines, so he could not understand how they could have reached him when the mountains of Spain were in the way.

In the early 1920s, there was increasing evidence of radio communication taking place over long distances. How this could happen was a mystery. The most likely explanation seemed to be that there might be a layer of gases, many miles above the earth, that had the capacity to reflect the signal back to earth. However, practical tests had made it clear that the effect was very variable, and dependant on unknown factors.

Amateur radio enthusiasts were not waiting for the physicists to come up with an explanation. They carried on with their hobby of talking to other amateurs in as many places and circumstances as they could. They had originally been given permission to use wavelengths lower than 100 metres because it had been thought these would be unsuitable for long distance communication. It was not long before the unexpected started to happen. There were instances of signals travelling thousands of miles. One of the most successful amateurs was E. J. Simmonds, G2OD, of Gerrards Cross, who had a two way contact with Canada in December 1923, and whose transmission on 16 October 1924 was picked up in New Zealand. So the Atlantic was bridged on short wave for the first time in 1923, and in October 1924 messages were successfully exchanged between a radio amateur in London and one in New Zealand.

Developments in the second half of the 1920s were given a firm foundation when the existence of the ionosphere was established by Appleton in 1924. An accurate assessment of its height, was made in 1925 by Briet and Tuve in the USA. They did this by sending a radio signal pulse vertically from a transmitter, and obtaining an echo on a nearby receiver. The signal and the echo were each displayed as blips on a cathode ray tube similar to that used later in radar, and in television until the 'flat screen' arrived. The distance between the two blips represented the distance from which the signal had been reflected, thus enabling the height of the reflective layer to be determined. Such experiments were repeated in all sorts of circumstances, and it became apparent that there was not just one reflecting layer but several, and they had different properties.

It is convenient to think of the radio signals being reflected, but in fact they are refracted, and their path bent so that they head back towards the earth. Radiation from the sun, particularly ultra violet, causes the layers of gas to become ionised. In this condition, radio signals of a suitable frequency are likely to be sufficiently refracted to be returned to earth.

It had been assumed that wavebands below 100 metres would not be suitable for long distance communication. The mistake was easily made. Much radio experimentation had taken the form of tests over various distances between transmitter and receiver to see how the range could be improved. As the receiver was moved further away, the signal gradually became weaker until it could no longer be detected. It was assumed that was the end of the matter. One might increase the power of the transmitter, or improve the aerial systems and the sensitivity of the receiver, but really long range communication would never be achieved.

Eventually, as we have seen, experimenters reported that they had received signals from a thousand or more miles away. The error in thinking that short waves were not suitable for long distances had been caused by what became known as the skip distance. This is the gap between where the ground wave ceases to be receivable, and the area much further away where it starts to become possible to receive the sky wave coming back from the layers of ionised gas.

A diagram, Figure 1.1, adapted from one in the *BBC Engineering Handbook (1942)*, illustrates this point.

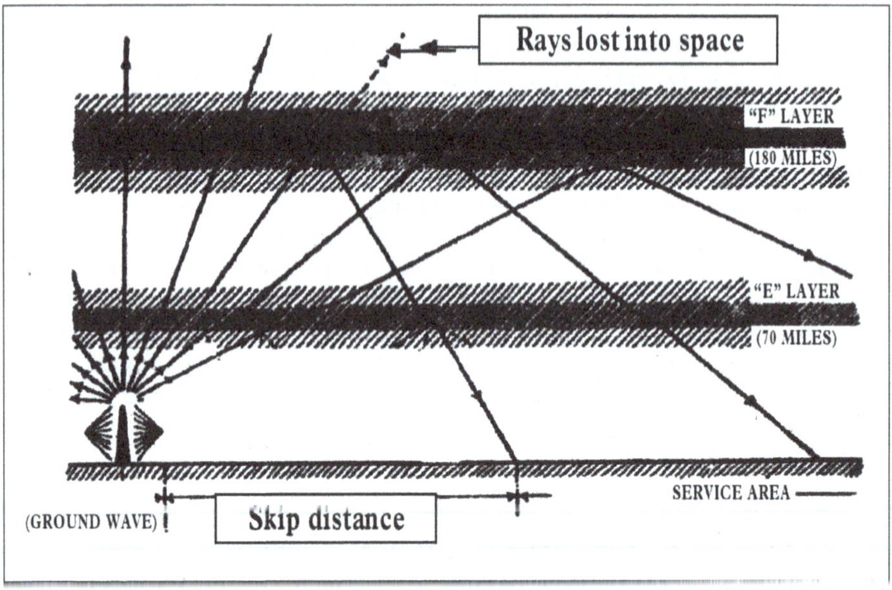

Figure 1.1 Short wave radio propagation.

Starting from the left hand side where the transmitting aerial is shown, there is a short distance covered by ground wave, which although used in special circumstances, such as the WWII army transceivers on which we were trained, the principal use of short wave is by means of sky wave, which is where the skip distance applies. It arises because signals sent up at an angle, as shown, may skip over several hundred miles of the earth's surface before reaching ground level again, and becoming receivable once more. The diagram also illustrates the fact that, subject to other variable conditions, signals sent up at very high angles may simply pass through the ionised layers and be lost in space. Two such layers are shown,

E and F, the positions of which had been established experimentally, as described above. In a 1944 publication there was a rather a rather tentative reference to a D layer, which could not be located by those methods. When its height and characteristics were established some years later, it showed that the layer seriously attenuated short wave signals passing through it when it was strongly ionised. However, higher frequencies were less attenuated, which is why long distance communication is often possible on such frequencies in daylight hours.

So when Radio SEAC (South East Asia Command) went on the air there was still a lot to learn about the ionosphere. Research continued in the second half of the century, and it is now much better understood. There are two F layers, F1 and F2, for example, but that information does not affect the general picture being attempted here. Nor did the absence of such details seriously affect the increasing use of short wave by amateurs and professionals, because a huge body of knowledge had been accumulated on the basis of experience. By 1945, the BBC's Overseas Service had, for some time, been well placed to decide what frequency to use over any particular path, depending on time of day/night, season, state of the sunspot cycle, and so on. Such information was available to Radio SEAC, of course. Although it is not intended to go into the subject in any depth here, it is worth mentioning the main factors affecting short wave broadcasting, and considering the uncertainties which are always present, and the unfortunate effects which can be minimised but not eliminated altogether.

One of the earliest features to be noted was that long distance communication seemed to be achieved more easily during the hours of darkness. This applied even to the medium waveband, where ordinary listeners in Britain sometimes experienced interference from continental radio stations after dark. As mentioned above, the D layer is ionised by radiation from the sun during the daytime. This greatly reduces the strength of radio signals passing through it on the way up to higher layers which, in suitable circumstances, will refract the signal back to earth. After sunset the ionisation starts to diminish and the absorption of the signal in the lower layer is greatly reduced, allowing it to pass through to higher layers where it may be refracted back to earth.

The idea, fostered by experimental transmissions, that long distance communication was better after dark was true only for the wavelengths commonly used at the time. Some of Marconi's early experiments used a wavelength of about 100 metres. Later, when communication was attempted with much shorter wavelengths, such as 20 metres, these were less attenuated by the D layer and could be refracted back to earth by higher layers if other conditions were suitable. If the wavelength used was much shorter still, the signals passed through not only the D layer but the higher layers as well, and were lost in space.

The practical result of some of these effects can be observed by tuning a receiver through the short wave bands, starting with 16 metres and on through the 19, 25, 31, 41, and 49 metre bands. Many stations will be received on the shorter wavelengths during the day, but fewer on the longer wavelengths. The situation will be reversed after dark. Anyone who has listened to the BBC World Service on short wave will probably be familiar with the announcement that listeners should retune to another band. This, again, is to ensure that, as far as practicable, the most suitable frequency is always used. The variations between light and dark, are affected by the seasons because there is less daylight in winter, and so less ionising radiation from the sun. Obviously the converse applies in the summer. Similarly the variation is greater in areas further from the equator. The variations day/night, winter/summer, and distance from the equator form a predictable ongoing pattern, year after year. However all such predictions need to take account of sunspots.

Galileo developed a greatly improved telescope in 1610, and, in the following year, records started to be kept of sunspot activity. Early in the nineteenth century Hendrich Schwabe, a German pharmacist and amateur astronomer, started counting the sunspots he saw, day by day, year after year, and in 1843 published his findings. He concluded that they varied between minimum and maximum numbers of spots in a cycle lasting about eleven years. The keeping of such records has continued.

If Herr Schwabe had been able to look up 'sunspot' on Wikipedia he would have been as surprised as I was to find that the earliest records go back to 364 BC, and that by 28 BC Chinese astronomers were regularly recording sunspot observations in official imperial records. Hopefully the description of how short wave radio signals may be received hundreds or thousands of miles away will provide sufficient explanation of how short wave broadcasting stations like Radio SEAC provide their listeners with reasonably good reception. At the time of writing more detailed information can be found on Wikipedia, under 'Radio Propagation'.

The use of the word 'cycle' denotes a certain regularity, but every cycle is different in detail. Activity was at a low level in 1900, after which the peaks of the cycles stated to increase. When Radio SEAC went on the air in 1945, sunspot activity was moving towards a maximum, so a frequency in the 19 metre band was used very effectively. The high point of the cycle was reached at about the time ownership of the transmitters passed to Radio Ceylon.

It has been mentioned that one of the factors that determines whether the signal is refracted is the frequency of the signal. An important factor, therefore is the maximum usable frequency. So this must not be exceeded. On the other hand, experience has shown that the best frequency to use is the highest available, which is less than the maximum usable. The concept of the maximum usable frequency was mentioned by S/Ldr Bernard Blakemore (Radio SEAC's Chief Engineer) in an article in the *SEAC Forces Radio Times* in 1947. Since he wrote this when the sunspot cycle was approaching its peak, this limiting frequency was very high; so high, in fact, that it was greatly in excess of 21 megahertz, which was the highest frequency on which the main transmitter could operate. Ordinary receivers available to forces personnel could not receive transmissions higher than about 18 megahertz. Communication receivers would typically go up to 30 MHz.

At low points in the sunspot cycle the choice of waveband is restricted because the maximum usable frequency is much lower. This never applied during Radio SEAC's brief existence. Unfortunately these broad principles are subject to much detailed variation. Account needs to be taken of the differences existing geographically. While in equatorial regions, the greater exposure to the sun causes higher ionisation.

It has been mentioned that there are several layers of ionised gas in the ionosphere. The height of the layer causing the signal to be sent back to earth varies, but for present purposes may be considered to be around 200 miles. This is much lower than would be ideal for long distance communication, because the curvature of the earth (and hence the layers of ionised gasses above it) will be a limiting factor in the distance the signal can be sent. Most of Radio SEAC's aerial arrays were designed to direct most of the signal at an angle of about fifteen degrees above the horizon, to give a long throw. This would have greatly restricted the potential of the short waves were it not for the fact that when the refracted signal reaches the surface of the earth again it is reflected back to the ionosphere for a second hop, as shown in Figure 1.2.

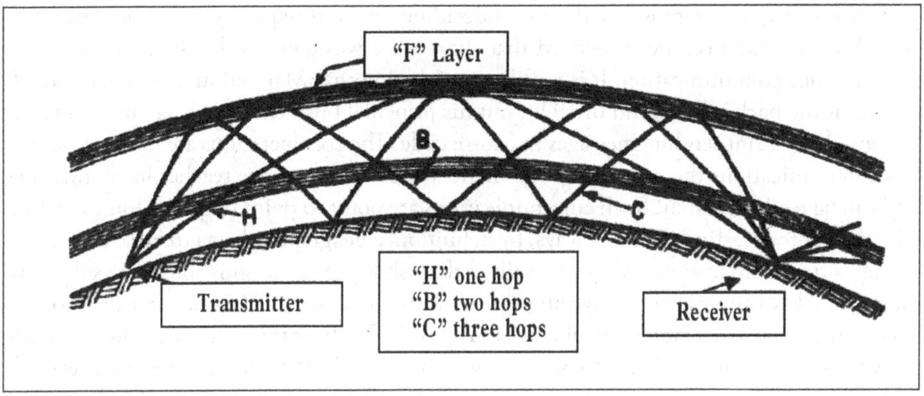

Figure 1.2 Propagation involving more than one hop.

A BBC World Service transmission from the UK intended for India would probably use three such hops. So far so good, but each time the signal goes back to the ionosphere it is attenuated by the D layer, and the ionisation of the higher layers needs to be high enough to lead to the required refraction. The further the signal goes from the transmitter the less likely it is that ideal conditions will be obtained over the whole path. Decisions about the choice of frequency often have to involve some compromise to allow for the differing conditions associated with each hop. In the extreme case of transmissions to the Antipodes the difficulties cannot always be overcome.

Radio researchers eventually rationalised this complex mix of factors involved in making use of the ionosphere. Tables were compiled which gave predictions of the best choice of frequency for any given set of circumstances. These take account of the sort of variables already mentioned, such as the path between transmitter and receiver, time of day/night, season of the year, and the state of the eleven year sunspot cycle. In recent years, computer programs have been developed for the same purpose. They are particularly useful because the number of variables involved made charts and tables rather complicated.

When Radio SEAC's main transmitter first went on the air there was a break in the transmission so that the 11.77 MHz frequency could be brought into use, instead of 15.12, during the evening. This was presumably because it was thought the reduction in ionisation after the sun had set would have reduced the maximum usable frequency. A year or so later, when the predicted maximum useable frequency had gone even higher, following the sunspot cycle, this change was discontinued.

This is not quite the end of the matter, because the table, or computer programme, that indicates what frequency should be used does not provide a firm prediction of something that will definitely be so. Ionisation depends on activity on the surface of the sun, and that activity is subject to variations well outside the predicted most likely situation. The predictions hold good most of the time, but nobody knows when the abnormal will occur; how serious it will be, or how long it will last.

Paradoxically, what can be a problem for professional broadcasters, and communications engineers, provides interest and sometimes excitement for radio amateurs. They suddenly find that a band becomes active which would not normally provide good communication at that time, and they rush to make contact with others to celebrate and record the unusual event. They obviously share the professionals' unhappiness when conditions are unexpectedly poor, or completely impossible.

Years before such sophisticated ways of deciding the best frequency to use became available, Marconi had become convinced that short wave was going to be the best choice for long distance communication. It is worth remembering that Marconi may have had broadcasting at the back of his mind in 1924, but his principal business interest lay in communications. This meant sending messages in Morse code. The considerations are rather different. For communications the only thing that matters is that the message reaches its destination, and can be read accurately. Such communications are point to point (e.g. London to Delhi), whereas in broadcasting there is always, by definition, a geographical area to be covered. This has important implications. Marconi realised that short wave transmissions were subject to fading, and his answer lay in using sufficient transmitter power, and beamed transmission. In other words, the aerial system would, as far as possible, deliver the message to the one place for which it was intended, and nowhere else. This would make the transmitter effectively more powerful, and the stronger resultant signal would make the extent of fading more acceptable. Short wave aerial systems do not provide as narrow a beam as that suggested, but are a great improvement over omni-directional systems.

In broadcasting, it is not sufficient that the signal should be just readable. Even when listening to a news bulletin or a talk, the listener will hope to enjoy good quality reception. If music is to be enjoyed, a higher standard still is called for. So the problem of fading becomes much more important.

With increasing knowledge of how to make the best use of short wave transmissions, the BBC started experiments in 1927 which were to lead to the start of the Empire Service in 1932. While the BBC was conducting a course of long distance test transmissions, and Marconi was more than ever confident about the future of short wave, others were pointing out the problems yet to be resolved. The most commonly encountered difficulty was fading, which could be fast or slow, and could sometimes result in the sounds in the programme being distorted. Static, causing sounds like cracks and bangs, also made the programme less enjoyable. None of these things could be eliminated, so efforts had to be directed to improving receivers and increasing the power of transmitters. As the millennium approached, transmitter power had reached such a level that fading ceased to be a problem. It is still occurring, of course, but the extent of the variations in signal strength can be reduced by the operation of AVC (automatic volume control) in the circuits of receivers. Many broadcasting stations do not have such high-powered transmitters, so their listeners still need good receivers to minimise the effects of fading.

So short wave transmitters became more powerful in themselves, and effectively more powerful still by using beamed transmission, as Marconi had suggested. The object was to direct a strong signal to where it was needed, and as little energy as possible elsewhere. They included narrow beams for very long distances and broader ones where the service area was nearer. Listeners with first class receivers enjoyed good listening even though well outside the intended service area. It came as a surprise to learn of listeners enjoying the station's programmes in Australia, when using aerials not intended for that area. There were aerials for that country, but used only for special programmes.

Why is it so important to get a strong signal to the receiver at the other end? Surely the receiver could be made more sensitive by adding more and more stages of amplification? The answer to that lies in a simple comparison called the signal to noise ratio, which should be as high as possible. When it is, the radio programme the listener wants to hear will be much louder than any electrical noise being experienced at the same time. This noise is of two main types; that being picked up by the aerial, and noise being generated within the receiver itself. Both types of noise are liable to be amplified by the receiver, along with the signal one wants to hear.

If the signal is weak the noise level may well be unacceptable. Even if the best transmission techniques were adopted, receivers needed to be improved to make the best use of the signal available. Radio engineers had been busy during World War One and after it, in improving the technology in various ways. Sometimes the ideas came before the devices that would make them practicable. For example, Armstrong invented the superheterodyne (superhet) receiver in 1920, but it was not possible to take full advantage of the principle until better radio components, particularly valves, had been developed. Radio receivers consist of a number of stages between the aerial (input) and the loudspeaker (output). Each stage consists of a valve or transistor and other components associated with it. Each stage has a function; amplification at radio frequencies; conversion of the radio signal to an audio signal, or audio amplification. In the 1920s a receiver might consist of just those three stages. A better receiver might have had additional audio stages. Such receivers were called straight sets, to distinguish them from the superhet receivers which became almost universal in the 1930s. The superhet was greatly superior, and is still in use today, for television and radio sets.

In the 1930s, radio salesman left customers in no doubt that the superhet was what they should have. In most such sets the aerial fed directly into the frequency changer stage, where the frequency selected by the tuning components (picking out the required station) was changed to one frequency called the intermediate frequency (IF). Most sets had one IF amplification stage, followed by the stage that produced the audio signal from the IF signal. This was then amplified, as in a straight set, and fed to the loudspeaker.

An IF of about 460 kHz has commonly been used, but other frequencies are used, and there are even high performance short wave receivers which change the frequency twice and so have two or more IF stages, but these are mainly for professionals or enthusiasts. Several benefits of the superhet derive from the IF stages, since input to each of these stages, and output from it, involves the use of two tuned circuits (four in all). This results in good selectivity, so signals close to the frequency one wants to hear are rejected. Such signals are called adjacent channel interference. This is particularly important on the short wave bands. If the receiver has a second IF stage, the extra tuned circuits improve selectivity still further, and the additional gain (amplification) makes the AVC more effective.

Automatic volume control has been mentioned, but it was only with the arrival of the superhet that AVC became really useful. When a receiver with AVC receives a strong signal, the efficiency of its RF and/or IF stages are reduced. If the signal starts to fade, that efficiency is increased proportionally. This is a useful refinement in medium wave sets, but is particularly effective in offsetting the fading that so often occurs on short wave. It is more effective with better sets because they provide more amplification of the signal, so the AVC has a bigger margin in which to operate.

As already mentioned, the signal strength may be improved by the use, at the transmitting station, of an aerial system which concentrates the radiation into a beam. There is also scope for this approach at the receiving end. If it is a professional receiving station, or an amateur enthusiast, the use of an efficient aerial may be assumed. Directional aerials are used in suitable situations. Only in exceptional circumstances was Radio SEAC's receiving station required to pick up anything other than the BBC from London, so directional aerials were always used. A technique known as diversity reception was also used, which will be described in greater detail later in the book. The objects, as always, were to improve the signal/noise ratio and minimise the effects of fading.

In the 1920s, ordinary listeners were obliged to use a reasonably good aerial to get decent reception, but, as the performance of domestic receivers improved, the tendency was for the aerial to be a piece of wire from the back of the set up to the picture rail. This was usually adequate for reception of local medium wave stations, but it was advisable to have a better aerial if more distant stations were to be received. For short wave reception a good aerial is the first step towards a good signal in the receiver, thus helping the AVC to reduce any fading. Some of Radio SEAC's listeners might have had better reception with a good, well sited aerial.

Early in the 1920s, the broadcasting industry in the USA realised that there were programmes on short wave that the ordinary listener might wish to hear. Some medium wave broadcasting stations started to relay particular programmes from short wave stations for their listeners, as part of their programme schedule. Their reasoning was that such listeners were best served by radio stations picking up the short wave transmissions (using their excellent aerials and receivers) and re-broadcasting them for their listeners on medium wave. The quality of reception was expected to be considerably better than that the listeners could enjoy from a short wave set of their own (assuming they had one, which was not very likely at that time). Many listeners were still using crystal sets. In England, a small start was made in about 1923, when a commercial radio station in Manchester included relays from America in their scheduled broadcasts. This was, of course, before the BBC's monopoly made this impossible.

'Relay' is mentioned here, because this approach became fundamental to the way the Armed Forces Radio Service (AFRS) delivered programmes to its listeners in the American armed forces. When setting up the service they had looked at short wave, and continued to use it in some situations, but their standard approach was to broadcast to the troops on medium wave, even on remote islands in the Pacific. However such items as baseball commentaries were picked up from USA on short wave, and included in the forces station's regular medium wave broadcasts.

One reason offered for the avoidance of short wave by AFRS was that tuning could be described as fiddly. Tuning in medium wave stations on domestic sets was easy, with attractive looking illuminated tuning dials. The tuning system (a vital component of which was a piece of thin cord) was fine for medium wave but less satisfactory for short wave use, where the stations were closely packed together. The position of individual stations was clearly shown on the medium wave tuning scale. On short wave, a number of station names might be listed as being in, say, the 19 metre band, but you had to tune through that band to find the station you wanted among a dozen or more others. These tuning arrangements could have been improved, but not cheaply. Set manufacturers were aware that they needed to include a short wave band because it was a selling feature, but most listeners rarely used it. When producing communications receivers (mainly for professionals and keen radio amateurs) they used properly engineered tuning drives and dials, which overcame the problem.

For many 'ex-pats', short wave radio was the only way to hear radio broadcasts from the home country. The BBC's Overseas Service used short wave effectively to deliver such entertainment and information. No doubt many of them invested in much higher quality receivers than the four valve 'welfare' sets originally issued to the forces. They will then have had mostly good, but by no means perfect, reception, but less than perfect reception is better than no radio from London at all. The internet has no doubt provided the ultimate answer for many people, and can be expected to provide more and better services in the future.

This chapter has provided a historical perspective for the rest of this volume. As young men aged about 20, we had never known a world without radio, so had no concept of how new radio was. When Radio SEAC started, the BBC's Empire service had been on the air for only thirteen years. The decision that forces broadcasting in the Far East should be delivered by one station on short wave is central to this narrative. The BBC was probably the most influential of the parties involved in taking the decision, so the next chapter is concerned with the early history of the BBC, its place at the centre of the British Empire as it then was, and its relationship with forces broadcasting.

Over a number of years, the public has become used to the idea of there being women in all three services, so the reference above to men aged about 20 might have caused the reader to wonder why the work of the women in our midst had been overlooked. There were no women at the transmitting station. The studios were another matter, of course, since one of the pleasures for our listeners was to hear the voices of female programme presenters.

2

The BBC and Forces Broadcasting

At the start of the war, and for many years after it, the BBC had a monopoly of broadcasting in the UK. There is, perhaps, a need for a pause at this point, to allow time for the reader to adjust to this idea. Switch on one's FM stereo radio in the twenty first century and the stations are crammed in from one end of the allocated band to the other. The BBC's contribution, although hugely important and influential, is now a small proportion in terms of the number of stations.

During the 1930s, most people in Britain had bought radio sets, and listening to the radio usually meant listening to one of the BBC's stations. However, there was competition from commercial stations Radio Luxembourg and Radio Normandie. They broadcast, legitimately, from outside the UK, but had enough listeners to make them commercially viable. I recall listening to those stations, particularly on a Sunday, because I wanted something a bit livelier than the music the BBC considered suitable for that day.

The man behind these programmes was Capt. Leonard F. Plugge MP, who was involved in the formation, in 1930, of the International Broadcasting Company. This organisation purchased air time on various continental stations, including those mentioned above. In his entry in *Who's Who* he claims to have been responsible for the first broadcasts to the British Expeditionary Force in France. His record is an amazing catalogue of technical and organising activity. In this volume, programmes intended for the forces produced by the BBC or any commercial organisation are not considered to be forces broadcasting. That phrase is used when referring to broadcasting produced by the forces for the forces.

By 1939 the BBC had become a highly professional organisation for delivering entertainment, news, and information to virtually everyone in the United Kingdom. It was also broadcasting to much of the rest of the world, having started its Empire Service in 1932, after several years of experimental transmissions. A BBC publication described how it began:

> Four people, led by Sir John Reith, had gone together into studio 3B. They were about to open the new Empire Service.
>
> The other three were Mr. J. H. Whitley, Chairman of the Board of Governors and former speaker of the House of Commons; Mr. Noel Ashbridge, Controller of Engineering; Mr. C. G. Graves, the first Director of the Empire Service. The studio red light winked at them twice and went on. Mr. Whitley stepped to the microphone and the very first words of the

> Empire Service were on the air. Off they went from the mists of London, in the winter, to the sunshine of Australia and New Zealand.
>
> The actual ceremony was modest. The mood was almost that of an experiment; and those taking part felt a little as if they were signalling in the middle of Dartmoor on a black night with a box of matches. A minute programme allowance of ten pounds a week had been arranged; so that if nothing happened at least they would not go on wasting matches.
>
> Six days later it was known throughout every part of the Empire that there had arrived a new instrument of almost unimaginable power; an instrument which, it was felt, could give a new expression to the intangible yet vital sense of the Empire as a whole.[1]

On Xmas Day 1932 King George V included the following in his broadcast:

> 'I speak now from my home and from my heart to you all, to men and women so cut off by the snows and the deserts, or the seas, that only the voices out of the air can reach them'.[2]

Hitler became Chancellor of Germany a month later, and soon began re-arming. Dr Goebels ensured that his propaganda machine would have a powerful means of spreading its message.

The BBC publication noted that:

> By 1936, in time for the Olympic Games in Berlin, eight 50 kilowatt transmitters had been installed at Zeeson. These outstripped ours in power for some time to come, and by now Hitler was talking in English to our own Empire.[3]

Some readers may share my ignorance in never having heard of Zeeson. Most of the dust-cover of a book called *The Cat's Whisker* is a photograph of the Murphy AD 94 receiver, in a smart black plastic cabinet.[4] This was one of the few new receivers to go on the British market during the war, and the tuning scale listed about half a dozen station names above each short wave band. Zeeson was included in the lists for the 16, 19, 25, 31, and 49 metre bands.

The BBC continued to extend the breadth and range of its programmes, and the technical competence to deliver them throughout the world. The broadcasts on short wave were beamed to the part of the world for which the programme was intended, as described in the previous chapter.

By the time the BBC was broadcasting Mr Chamberlain's announcement of the start of the war, the Corporation was well placed to play its part in maintaining morale on the home front, and providing listeners everywhere with the news, as seen from London. The service was much respected, and was a lifeline for untold numbers of people.

The BBC's audience included armed forces personnel of course, most of whom remained in this country in the early months of the war, so the question of who should provide their entertainment hardly arose. When the army expeditionary force went to France, they were

1 T. O. Beachcroft, *Calling All Nations*, London, BBC, circa 1943, p. 3.
2 Ibid., p. 4.
3 Ibid., p. 11.
4 Jonathon Hill, *The Cat's Whisker, 50 years of wireless design*, London, Oresko Books, 1978.

outside the range of BBC medium wave transmitters for a few months, but may have heard the commercial broadcasts directed to them, as mentioned previously. The terrible events of 1940 saw many of them back again in the UK. The BBC started a Forces Programme that was intended to provide suitable programmes for a new kind of audience. They were in an army camp, listening to a communal radio in the NAAFI canteen. I enjoyed listening to the programme before I was called up in August 1944, but it was criticised quite severely in some quarters, as we shall see later.

By no means all armed forces personnel were within range of BBC transmissions. There were garrisons scattered round the world, and there was the navy. When the Japanese attacked the USA by sinking a substantial part of the American fleet in Pearl Harbour, they spread the war to the other side of the globe. British armed forces had to attempt to defend remote parts of the Empire, and suffered serious setbacks as the Japanese extended their presence in Asia. India came under threat.

The Burma campaigns found the British Army fighting in dreadful conditions against a formidable enemy, with very little chance of enjoying any radio entertainment from home. With good reason the phrase 'the forgotten army' began to be used. For a long time, welfare amenities were very inadequate, as we shall see later.

In that respect, things were better around the Mediterranean, where forces broadcasting, on a small scale, had begun as early as 1941. In the same year, Frank Muir made his early attempts at script writing on a forces station in Iceland.

A War Office committee was formed, which met for the first time on 4 September 1942. It was accepted that liaison with the BBC would be essential, and the aim of the committee was to improve broadcasting for the forces. This included making suggestions to the BBC about how the Forces Programme might be improved.

It was intended that the next committee meeting would be held in five weeks, but it actually took place on 17 November. The War Office AW2(b) representative reported they had been able to exert some influence on the content of the BBC's Forces Programme. It seems they were being careful not to upset the BBC. A sub-committee was proposed which would hold weekly meetings with BBC representatives. It was recommended there should be fewer War Office than BBC representatives, partly so that the latter might not feel themselves to be under any pressure.

Major Eric Maschwitz, a well known composer, and very experienced in light entertainment, had produced a report for consideration by the committee. In his view:

> He felt there was too little fighting spirit and fighting tempo, and did not seem to have a picture of the average listener, and could not decide whether he was a foolless dolt with no time or inclination to think, or a rather uncertain intellectual with infinite time and leisure on his hands.[5]

He went on to compare the programmes unfavourably with German broadcasts for their forces. For Maschwitz, perhaps the ultimate accolade was that they gave the impression of being produced by the forces for the forces. He also commented, mostly favourably, on the equivalent Russian programme.

The shortage of receivers was still very serious and was to remain so for a very long time. Maschwitz made the comparison with the Americans who aimed to have one receiver for every fifty men. He went on to mention that:

5 WO 163 200.

> They, the Americans take broadcasting very seriously as an auxiliary military weapon. With the aid of the BBC they were arranging to set up short wave Camp Transmitters in this country and broadcast to their own troops.[6]

At the third meeting of the committee, on 27 January 1943, it was said that the Secretary of State had approved a joint planning committee with the War Office and the BBC. It was to provide a regular focus for the discussion of ideas and the working out of plans to fulfil the Army Council Directive to the Army Broadcasting Committee. It was appreciated, even at this very early stage, that there was going to be difficulty in providing an adequate number of wireless receivers for the services.

The fourth meeting on 29 March 1943, was mainly concerned with various initiatives to improve the supply of receivers. It took place during a period of several months when American forces broadcasting representatives were negotiating with the BBC with a view to providing a broadcasting service for American servicemen in Britain. A directive had been issued from General Eisenhower's headquarters that there was a requirement to:

> Supply American military personnel in Europe with a radio programming service for the information, education and entertainment of such personnel. The service was to be as much a duplication of American broadcasting at home as it was possible to achieve overseas.[7]

It had already been well, and perhaps painfully, established that the BBC's Forces Programme was never going to match the terms of the directive. When the GIs started to listen to it they were less than impressed. It was said they wanted the kind of rapid fire frenetic-paced entertainment they had grown up with. Apparently they had difficulty understanding the language as spoken on the BBC programmes. Quite apart from the shortage of baseball match commentaries, the music was pretty third rate compared to Tommy Dorsey, Harry James and Glenn Miller, and the humour of *ITMA* was very different from that of Bob Hope or Jack Benny.

The problem was that the BBC's charter provided that the BBC was to be the only broadcaster in Britain. It was not going to compromise that situation without a struggle, and a struggle there certainly was. It has been described elsewhere in fascinating detail,[8] so this account will merely record the outcome. Suffice it to say that the GIs got their own radio programmes, with considerable co-operation from the BBC, and the BBC was able to comfort itself with the thought that the power of the American Forces Network transmitters in the UK was to be limited to 50 watts. At one time there were more than sixty of them, mostly serving areas where large numbers of American troops were stationed. Broadcasts in London were not allowed. The programmes had to be sent by land-line to clubs, canteens, and so on.

So although the BBC lost the battle, they had some success in what might be seen as a damage limitation exercise. They were right, though, in their apprehension about the extent to which civilian listeners might listen to the American programmes and make unfavourable comparisons with the BBC's output. The five wavelengths used were probably passed on among civilian listeners by word of mouth. Many probably assumed the programmes were coming from London (which in a sense they were, because that was where the studio centre

6 Ibid.

7 Trent Christman, *Brass Button Broadcasters*, Paduka, Kentucky, Turner Publishing, 1992, p. 40.

8 Patrick Morley, "*This is the American Forces Network*", Westport, Praeger, 2001, (most of the book).

was). Quite often though, the transmission they were receiving was from just a few miles down the road. After more than half a century, there are still British listeners who remember with great pleasure listening in the late afternoon to programmes such as *Strictly off the Record* and *Downbeat*, and in the evening to *Supper Club* and other programmes.

As it happens, it was not at all unusual for the AFRS to use low-powered medium wave transmitters, although in many places they were rather more than 50 watts. Their global policy was to deliver programmes locally on medium wave. Where immediacy was required, such as baseball commentaries, they were received on short wave by the station, and relayed as part of its programme schedule. This applied even in South East Asia and the Pacific area, where many a small island had its own station. The studio centre might well be a leaky tent, until they could arrange something better. Locally produced programmes included record programmes from their own DJs. The GIs lacked for nothing in terms of quality as a result of this policy, because of the excellent pre-recorded programmes, on newly developed disks.

Many of these programmes of variety, comedy, and musical offerings, were of the highest quality, using some of the world's greatest artists; many of whom were based in Hollywood. No commercial organisation could have afforded the artists' fees in some of these star-studded shows. The artists gave their services free, and seem to have been virtually queuing up to do it. With these gems in the programme schedule, it was less important that announcing and disc jockey standards may sometimes have been less than professional. Forces broadcasting was about the forces providing its personnel with the entertainment they wanted, rather than something someone else thought they ought to have.

This American policy had inevitably been worked out from first principles. The great majority of radio broadcasting was commercial, so there was no obvious way of co-opting this diverse market. As a result, when the question arose as to how forces broadcasting was to be provided, the answer was to appoint someone with the right qualities and experience to set it up from scratch. This process was not without pitfalls and hang-ups, but once the decision had been made to set up a forces broadcasting organisation, the process was driven forward by people of talent, ability and initiative.

The situation in Britain was entirely different. It was inevitable, and obviously desirable, that the BBC should be closely involved. So the series of committee meetings was probably predictable, but progress might have seemed slow to anyone who believed in the importance of forces broadcasting in maintaining morale.

The fifth meeting of the committee on 12 July 1943 was, like the fourth meeting, mainly concerned with the supply of receivers. The same subject was reviewed at the sixth meeting on 30 September 1943. There was also mention of the availability of recording equipment in the Middle East and India, and the intention was to have similar provision in all other commands. They were to promote the use of the machines for recording programmes of local interest.

There was a gap of almost six months between that meeting and the seventh held on 9 March 1944. Forces broadcasting started officially during that gap, with the opening of a station in North Africa on 1 January 1944. At the seventh meeting, the Director of Army Welfare Services proposed that:

> The BBC should be deemed to be the principal purveyor of broadcasting overseas, and the transmitters available to the Army should be used for re-transmission or to supplement the BBC, should the occasion arise.

The committee turned the wording around, presumably to make it sound more acceptable at first glance. The committee:

> Agreed that the policy should be to provide broadcasting for British troops by means of transmitters under Army control wherever they could not be served by the BBC or local broadcasting stations, and that the War Office Army broadcasting organisation should be developed to this end.

It was also agreed, in principal, that:

> Army broadcasting stations should be set up overseas, subject to the command being able to justify its demand for such a section, and able to fund the necessary personnel from within its ceiling.[9]

There was to be some flexibility allowed in the funding requirement, in that swaps of people with no broadcasting skills might be made for expert broadcast technicians.

So, after a period of about eighteen months, during which six committee meetings had been held, the committee was so enthusiastic about forces broadcasting that each command had to ask for it, and justify why it wanted it! The contrast between that and the directive from Eisenhower's headquarters could hardly be more stark.

The Director of Army Welfare Services (DAWS), when considering the need for army transmissions, mentioned that Delhi was all right – there was a transmitter there. At that stage SEAC had been in existence for only a few months so DAWS had probably not given much thought to anywhere further east than Delhi. He was replaced at about the same time Lord Munster departed for India, and the latter was being sent only because the government were reasonably sure he would find that welfare provision in the Far East, including broadcasting for the forces, left a lot to be desired.

Another six months went by before the eighth committee meeting on the 13 September 1945. This supplied some evidence that more thought had finally been given to the Far East, when the adjutant general observed that the necessity for a powerful transmitter in the Far East had become more urgent owing to the fact that we would have forces in Hong Kong, Malaysia etc.

A further comment in the minutes casts the gravest doubt on the sort of expert advice supplied to the committee. There had been a comment that it had not been thought practical to pick up BBC relays through the day, but that these had turned out to be excellent. Anything less would have been amazing, in view of the high quality reception equipment being used. Anything less than excellent would have meant that civilian listeners to the BBC with just good quality receivers would have had poor reception.

Long before such considerations arose, and with bombs falling on London, the BBC had been starting to formulate its role in the post-war world. The BBC publication mentioned previously looked to the future after the war:

> In peacetime the range of Empire broadcasting will grow. Throughout the Empire we need more knowledge of each other: knowledge not so much of

9 WO 163 200.

> laws and statutes, but lively personal knowledge which can come through the human contacts of broadcasting. The past ten years have seen the Empire achieve a new sense of its own identity. One plan is that there should be an Empire Service continuously on the air, with material contributed regularly by every part of the Empire. In every part of the Empire you could always find the Empire programme and it would always be the mouthpiece of the Empire.[10]

The message was very clear. The BBC would be continuing, indefinitely, to extend its beneficent influence on the world. New technical equipment was going to extend the reach of BBC short wave transmissions, and improve the quality of reception for many overseas listeners. However, the BBC engineers were well aware that there were technical reasons why transmissions to the other side of the globe would not reliably provide reception of acceptable quality.

Long distance short wave transmission is effected as described, in general terms, in the previous chapter. The choice of frequency for any given broadcast has to be made in the light of the time of day and season of the year, amongst other factors. This is fine when considering a path of two or three thousand miles between transmitter and receiver. With longer distances the choice of frequency becomes increasingly difficult.

A BBC technical manual went to the nub of the difficulty:

> The selection of wavelength for the longest distances is complicated, for if the first reflection takes place at midday in midsummer, the last will take place at midnight in winter, and the wave chosen must be short enough to avoid excessive absorption at the first hop, yet long enough to secure reflection at the last hop. In practice this is not always possible, and short wave transmission to the antipodes without intermediate relay cannot generally be assured throughout the twenty-four hours, even if wavelength and direction are selected to secure the most favourable propagation conditions.[11]

The condition to note is 'without intermediate relay'. It seems unlikely that the broad outlines of the BBC's plans for the future of Empire broadcasting would have changed much between 1942 and November 1944, when BBC representatives were party to discussions with the War Office on the best way of implementing the War Cabinet's decision to provide additional transmitters to improve the reach of forces broadcasts. The alternatives were seen to be numerous low-powered medium wave stations, or one powerful short wave station, probably in India. Needless to say, the choice was a difficult one, and it was sensible to take account of short term and long term considerations. Whichever choice was made, the need for a huge increase in the number of suitable radio receivers was crucial to the overall success of the enterprise.

The short term view, as of November 1944, needed to take account of the fact that the end of the war, in Europe at least, was hopefully not too far off. This would be expected to release fighting personnel and equipment to join those engaged in defeating the Japanese.

The people taking the decision had no knowledge of the atomic bomb, so it was reasonable to assume that the war in the Far East would be long and hard and would be fought over a vast area of the globe. At the same time it would take a considerable time to plan and

10 Beachcroft, *Calling All Nations,* p. 22.

11 BBC, *Engineering Division Training Manual,* London, BBC, 1942, p. 168.

build a large transmitting station, thousands of miles away from the factories making the equipment. In the event, it took much longer than expected.

The advantage of the numerous low-powered medium wave stations would have been that each of these could have been provided relatively easily. It could have been rolled out, a phrase much heard at the time of writing. This would have had the advantage that a few stations could have been set up in selected areas quite quickly, so that at least some troops started to benefit from the service without too much delay. Others could anticipate their turn would come. There would have been no need to provide receivers capable of receiving short wave reasonably well.

The disadvantages, as seen by BBC representatives, seem to have been that there would have had to be a large number of studio centres, which would clearly be expensive to build and staff, and such talent as was available would have been more thinly spread.

The long term view may have appeared to be more clear cut. A large short wave transmitter sited in India or Ceylon would be an asset for the future, since it would not only cover the immediate need for forces broadcasts, it would also fit in well with the BBC's view of its post-war role, as set out earlier in this chapter. The station would be ideal for relaying BBC programmes to the Far East and Australia, for technical reasons already mentioned.

In the European theatre, in Italy, and later in France and Germany, it was reasonable to provide forces broadcasting from several large lorries, deployed just behind the advancing troops. The nature of much of the fighting in the Far East, and the huge spread of the theatres of war, suggest that possibilities for this approach would have been limited for SEAC.

This overview of the BBC's role would not be complete without mentioning the role played by BBC staff in the story of British Forces Broadcasting. Other writers have recognised fully the part they played, particularly on the programme side, and as studio technicians. It is therefore necessary only to mention that two of the eleven Royal Signals men who I went with to Radio SEAC were BBC men. Geoff Shaw started on the transmitters, but was fairly soon moved to the studios in Colombo. He returned to the BBC after demobilisation, and his name appeared later on the credits of TV productions. Pat Guare joined us later, I believe, and I remember seeing him working with Bernard Blakemore (then the chief engineer) making some adjustment to the aerial feeders. Blakemore flew to Ceylon on 9 July 1946, and was the first BBC man to be seconded to forces broadcasting, as I learnt fifty years later from public records. Craftsman Hobbs (REME) remained at the transmitting station, and used his knowledge and experience to good effect. However, the man selected to set up and run the station was Lt. Col. Benjamin McNabb, whose background, before the war, was with the International Broadcasting Company, mentioned early in this chapter.

The BBC was conscious that Radio SEAC was likely to establish its own programme style and mixture. In an early planning document it appears the BBC assumed Radio SEAC would devote a higher proportion of its output to BBC relays, (as opposed to locally produced programmes) than proved to be the case. I believe this may have applied also in other commands. In a broad mix of entertainment, Radio SEAC featured American big band records, as well as British dance music and some jazz. Lovers of classical music were not forgotten. My lifelong preference for jazz began in Radio SEAC's transmitter hall. The cultural divide was brought home to me when I arrived back in England to find that not only were some foods still rationed, but that jazz on the BBC was restricted to half an hour a week.

3

Admiral Mountbatten (SACSEA)

On 7 December 1941, Japanese aircraft attacked the United States fleet in Pearl Harbour. America had been supplying aid of various sorts to the allies, but had stopped short of joining the war, because isolationist elements could argue that it was none of their business. With US battleships on the bed of the Pacific, President Roosevelt had little difficulty in persuading Americans that they were now involved.

From Britain's point of view there was a huge benefit in having the USA as an active ally, but it turned a European war into a world war, and there was an obvious threat to the British Empire east of Suez. This threat was to become reality all too soon. British rule had been maintained with an amazingly small military presence, and, whilst this seemed to work in practice, Japanese spies in the Far East were well aware of the true situation, and their masters were able to plan accordingly. Their plans were helped by errors in the assessment of the Japanese military capability, and the proficiency of the Japanese army, by some of those who should have been better informed.

The shock of the Fall of Singapore was followed by a demoralising retreat across the whole of Burma. As far as the native population were concerned, the majority of local opinion wished to see the end of British rule, and activists were working hard to that end. However for most Burmese, the arrival of the Japanese was seen as one imperialist power being replaced by another, and their incentive to fight the Japanese was diminished accordingly.

China had been at war with Japan for several years already, which meant that the principal countries opposing Japan were China, the United States, Britain and the Dutch. The need to provide some co-ordination was obvious. To unite the French and British against Germany was difficult enough, to do the same with China, USA, Britain and the Dutch was virtually impossible. Nevertheless the impossible had to be attempted.

The American-British-Dutch-Australian Command (ABDACOM) was established by the combined Chiefs of Staff in Washington on 30 December 1941 and Archibald Wavell was appointed as commander. Wavell arrived and took over on 5 January 1942, setting up his HQ in Java. The command included Burma, Malaya, the Philippines, the Dutch East Indies and the approaches to northern Australia.

However, it proved not to be a satisfactory solution, and at the Quebec Conference in August 1943, after the most terrible reverses, Churchill and Roosevelt agreed that a new approach was needed. It was decided to set up a South East Asia Command, initially to be located in Delhi, although separate from India Command. The new Supreme Commander had to be able to assume overall command of land, sea and air forces, but needed diplomacy of a high order. He had to be a great leader of men, capable of turning round a very serious problem of morale and fighting spirit.

Leo Amery, Secretary of State for India, was strongly in favour of having a supreme commander, and suggested Mountbatten for the appointment. Initially, Churchill did not accept the suggestion, and a number of candidates were put forward, and rejected by either the British or Americans or both. After much discussion Mountbatten was selected for the huge task. In spite of his usual self-confidence even he was somewhat overawed at the scale of the responsibilities he was to undertake.

Amery was a friend of Churchill's at school, and his influence in the setting up of Radio SEAC was not unlike his foresight in the matter of Mountbatten's appointment. When questions arose about the adequacy of welfare facilities in the Far East he persuaded Churchill to a course of action which led eventually to the installation of Radio SEAC's big transmitter.

Mountbatten's appointment was not likely to receive universal approval. Promoting someone over the heads of others almost always provokes some adverse reaction. Some of those who were unhappy went on to accept that the appointment had some merit. His immediate deputy 'Vinegar' Stilwell hated the British, never mind the British Royal Family, so it was not an easy working relationship. I believe it was an American who thought that SEAC probably stood for 'Save England's Asian Colonies'.

Later, when Mountbatten decided to move his headquarters to Ceylon it was not accepted as a good idea by some senior commanders. Nevertheless, on 15 April 1944 SEAC headquarters began the move to Kandy, and went by air, and in four special trains. With his headquarters in Ceylon, it was going to be difficult, when the time came, to persuade Mountbatten that Radio SEAC should be anywhere else. He kept a close watch on the development of the station, and the installation of the Marconi 100 kW transmitter. When he felt his intervention was necessary, he lost no time in seeking assistance from those in the highest places. He was well placed to do this because, as the saying has it, he knew everybody. His interventions tended to be effected in the Mountbatten style, and it is worth considering what this was, and how it came about.

Mountbatten's start in life was unique, as was his career. He was born in a house in the grounds of Windsor Castle, the great grandson of Queen Victoria. The British Empire was at its most powerful, and he was destined to join the Royal Navy which ruled the waves. In that service he acquired outstanding competence as a radio technician, a specialist qualification which might be surprising to those more familiar with his activities in high office, both military and civil. He seems to have been what has sometimes been called a late-developer and did not make any great mark at school.

That he was destined to be a naval officer was not in doubt. After initial preparation at Osborne, he moved on to the Royal Naval College at Dartmouth in January 1915. At the end of his time there he was desperately keen to go to sea, but this ambition was temporarily frustrated when he was sent to the Keyham Naval College. His earlier undistinguished performance was left behind when he came out at the top, and he seems to have liked the idea of this, and decided always to be best at everything from then on.

He was the best again on the Higher Wireless Course at Greenwich in 1925, and subsequently became an assistant to the Fleet Wireless Officer. The year 1929 found him back in Portsmouth, after much sea-going, as a lieutenant commander in charge of wireless instruction. He proved to be an exceptionally good lecturer. He reformed the courses, devised clearer circuit diagrams of the various items of equipment, and rationalised the documentation. One particular handbook was a monument to his efforts. It brought together information about every type of wireless set used in the navy.

> In August 1931 Mountbatten was back in the Mediterranean as Fleet Wireless Officer, either aboard the Fleet flagship or, when in harbour, at the Commander-in-Chief's headquarters in Malta, the Castille. He was already celebrated within the signals world; with this appointment he established himself as a leading contender for the biggest jobs the Navy had to offer.[1]

It is evident from a book (associated with a television series in the 1960s),[2] that Mountbatten found his position as Fleet Wireless Operator very much to his liking. He was in charge of radio communications for the whole fleet (about 70 ships). It provides an early example of his concern for the wellbeing of those under his command. The wireless operators were responsible to him but were providing a service for the officer in charge of the ship. Wireless was still very new and mysterious for most people, and Mountbatten sensed that the operators were lonely and had no contact with him. It was impracticable to keep in touch with many of them by personal visits, so he made himself known by using the Morse code to send messages to them.

Twelve years later, when appointed Supreme Allied Commander, Mountbatten was to apply these methods which became a hallmark of his style of leadership. He paid great attention to detailed personal information about people under his command, and succeeded in creating a sense of belonging to something worthwhile. Above all he imposed his personality by making numerous appearances before the troops.

In 1964 Mountbatten contributed to a radio programme which celebrated the 21st anniversary of the start of British Forces Broadcasting, and wrote the foreword to a book by Gale Pedrick which is a brief history of the enterprise. The second paragraph of the foreword was substantially the same as part of his contribution to the radio programme which was broadcast on the BBC Home Service on 6 November 1964. He recalled how in 1932 he had been faced with a special task:

> One day the Commander-in-Chief sent for me and told me to arrange for the Fleet in Malta to receive what was to be the first broadcast of a reigning monarch – the Christmas Message of King George V. Of course, in those days there was no Forces Broadcasting Service and the only thing we could do, and which we did, was to build special radio receivers and low powered transmitters which, together with aerial arrays sited on a high point on land, enabled us to receive the King's voice from London and re-transmit the Message on local frequencies that could be received by all ships of the Fleet. We provided the first naval loudspeakers to all ships, as well as to Army and RAF units. Thus it was that the Forces heard the King's voice for the first time through a special one day's Forces Broadcasting Service overseas.[3]

The reason why they had to build special transmitters and receivers is thought to be because the navy was equipped to communicate using telegraphy rather than telephony.

The previous reference to the Morse code reminds us that for most people in the early 1930s, broadcasting was a wonderful new kind of entertainment, in which speech and music was delivered by telephony. For those concerned with communications, such as that

1 Philip Ziegler, *Mountbatten — The Official Biography*, London, Collins, 1985, p. 82.
2 John Terraine, *The Life and Times of Lord Mountbatten*, London, Hutchinson, 1968.
3 Gale Pedrick, *Battledress Broadcasters, A History of the British Forces Broadcasting Service*, London, British Forces Broadcasting Service, 1964, foreword.

between ships, telegraphy was still in general use. Messages were sent using the Morse code, so the radio transmitter had only to be able to switch rapidly between being on or off. For telephony, a continuous signal has to be modulated.

From 1900 to 1963 the company which manufactured Radio SEAC's big transmitter was called Marconi's Wireless Telegraph Co. Ltd. This arose from the company's concentration, in its early days, on communications rather than broadcasting. Mountbatten would have been very familiar with their transmitters on ships. The high speed wireless unit, which was adjacent to Radio SEAC's transmitting site, had a number of similar transmitters. Marconi produced modulators as an optional extra which could be added to some of their transmitters for users who required a telephony capability.

Following a remarkable peacetime career, Mountbatten distinguished himself in action when war finally came. His exploits were so exciting that Noel Coward starred in the film *In Which We Serve*, which was based on some of the events involving Mountbatten's ship, HMS *Kelly*. This side of his activities, and his work in Combined Operations, and in preparations for D-Day, have been well covered in many publications, and need not to be repeated here.

The official autobiography contains, as one would expect, a full appreciation of Mountbatten the man, the leader, the statesman, and all the rest. Many other books contain references to various aspects of his character, and much will obviously depend on the angle from which it was written. Flags and other emblems were important to him, and he was happy to design them himself, as in the case of the SEAC image of the phoenix arising from the ashes.

This was all part of the image. He and Field Marshal Montgomery, and perhaps the American Douglas MacArthur, may be seen in retrospect as a new breed of senior commander, with a charisma that the popular press recognised as something its readers would appreciate. They went, perhaps, a small way towards today's concept of celebrity. Field Marshals Auchinleck, Wavell, and Alexander were of the old school. Mountbatten had an ability to make contact with ordinary soldiers, sailors and airmen.

When Mountbatten was appointed, Churchill saw his merits, including those just mentioned. However, it seems he was concerned that Mountbatten might attract too much attention to his command, and its activities. This might distract the attention of the public from the first priority, which was to win the war in Europe. He therefore made arrangements to keep Mountbatten in check.

Charles Eade was the editor of the *Sunday Dispatch*, and was given leave by the paper's owners to become Mountbatten's press adviser. He was briefed by Churchill, whose directive, as described in a report written in 1946 by Eade, was apparently not very clear, and certainly very surprising in some respects. He recalled that Churchill said something like:

> It is your duty to guard M's rear. No general can fight a war if he is looking over his shoulder to see who is stabbing him in the back. The PM also told me that in his view it was undesirable for M to make statements to the press, or to hold any press conferences, and he gave me the impression that it would be undesirable to over-publicise the S.E.Asia campaign, or exaggerate its importance to the overall picture of the war.

Eade seems to have felt that, when he left England on 11 November 1943, the nature of the job was still rather vague, but he later summarized the objects of the exercise as follows:

> The real justification and reason for the existence of Public Relations was not merely to provide newspapers with good reading, but to make the army

> feel proud and confident in its strength. Relations' letters, from UK to the troops, following newspaper and radio publicity in UK, was the way this was accomplished.

In a letter dated 17 February 1944 to Mrs Hill (Churchill's personal private secretary) Eade referred to:

> My main task of keeping the admiral's mind free from press worries, which I think I am doing without his knowing too much about my 'protection'. So far he has not given a single press conference or interview and I hope things stay that way.[4]

The purposes Eade was to serve, and his involvement in the early days of forces broadcasting from Delhi, were described by Mountbatten as follows:

> Before leaving London I had done my best to arrange that adequate publicity should be given to the command in the press at home, for this would react on the troops by way of their families. The Prime Minister had obtained from Lord Rothermere the loan for six months of the services of Mr. Charles Eade, Editor - Sunday Dispatch as my Press Adviser, so that adequate publicity might be given to the forces in South East Asia in the press at home.[5]

It is interesting to contrast Mountbatten's view that Eade was there to ensure there was adequate publicity with Churchill's intention of trying to avoid too much.

A few other features of Mountbatten's character should be mentioned here, insofar as they seem to be in evidence in various parts of this story. He was certainly an inventor; or to be really unkind, and perhaps unfair, a gadget contriver. As we have seen, he was heavily involved in the technology of his younger days, in a professional way. It was also a hobby. He was always looking for more efficient ways of doing things.

He was said to have invented the use of the zip fastener for men's trousers. A seriously useful development, and we all know what a zip is. Other items have been mentioned such as a wireless telegraphy history card, a valve buzzer circuit, and a wireless tuning calculator. Without more information we shall never find out exactly what function these items performed, but they were clearly something to do with radio communications.

As might be expected, with a royal background and a very rich wife, he was at ease with luxury. Mountbatten encountered what must have been a delightful conjunction of luxury and radio technology when he visited the Nawab of Rampur on 26 February 1944, where he was shown fabulous jewels in a splendid palace.

> We then went to the Nawab's private palace and were shown his collection of 250 radio sets. Not only has he a standing order for the latest types of sets to be sent to him but he has a private workshop where he assembles radio-gramophones, etc. On the top of the palace there are some thirty

4 WO 203 4869.

5 Earl Mountbatten, *Report to the Combined Chiefs of Staff by the Supreme Allied Commander South East Asia 1943-45*, HMSO, 1951, Introduction.

> aerial arrays and down below there is an aerial exchange so that suitable aerials can be plugged into any of the sets.[6]

It has been said that one of the less praiseworthy aspects of Mountbatten's character was to claim the credit for something which might more appropriately have been given elsewhere. On a related point, his official biographer found him sometimes guilty of giving an account of how he would have liked things to have happened, rather than what actually occurred. Many of us will own up to sharing this trait to some degree.

Reference has been made above to the foreword he wrote for a book on forces broadcasting, and the fact that he used identical words in an associated radio programme. This applied also to the following extract:

> When I went out in 1943 to South-East Asia as the Supreme Allied Commander, I asked for a powerful Broadcast Transmitter to reach all the one and a third million men in the Command, scattered over thousands of miles. I got it eventually, and called it Radio S.E.A.C. It was erected in Ceylon and proved a great success in India, Burma, and later Malaya, and all other Far-Eastern countries in which we had forces.

So Mountbatten's words were not untrue, but anyone hearing them might reasonably assume there was a connection between the request and its being met. In the light of the later events this seems very unlikely.

When he found, late in 1944, that, following a War Cabinet decision to implement many recommendations of the Munster Report, agreement had been reached on the provision of a very large transmitter, he moved quickly and effectively to ensure that it was installed in Ceylon, under his command, rather than in Delhi, India Command, where a sizeable forces broadcasting organisation was already in existence, and in much need of additional transmitting facilities.

In the foreword, and the radio programme, he also said:

> I have been personally interested in the idea of broadcasting to the forces for a long time. This dates back, in fact, to 1932, when I was the Fleet Wireless Officer of the Mediterranean fleet.

This is a reference to the relay of the King's Christmas broadcast, mentioned earlier in this chapter. Although a worthwhile exercise, it hardly qualified as forces broadcasting as we understood it in WWII. Nevertheless, there is no reason to doubt that this started his interest in broadcasting to the forces. He also expressed his continuing belief in the importance of forces broadcasting:

> I am convinced that this is right; not only because broadcasting is an integral part of life today, and therefore has a rightful place in the Services, but especially because broadcasting to the Forces has an essential part to play in maintaining morale - a factor vital to the fighting fitness of the Serviceman.[7]

However, what will also become clear is how much Mountbatten's greatest strengths, enthusiasm and determination, contributed to the long and difficult task of installing the

---

6 Philip Ziegler (Editor), *Personal Diary of Admiral The Lord Louis Supreme Allied Commander, South-East Asia, 1943-1946*, London, Collins, 1988, p.73.

7 Pedrick, *Battledress Broadcasters*, foreword.

Marconi 100 kW transmitter which was to turn Radio SEAC into a world class broadcasting organisation. The project had much of the Mountbatten style about it, in that it was a bold, ambitious undertaking costing a lot of money. People who went to the SEAC headquarters in Kandy sometimes remarked on the expense involved in the whole enterprise. Even Churchill was said to have been concerned about the number of staff. However, I have to declare a personal interest here. The large staff almost certainly included a generous number of typists and record keepers. As one would expect from his background, Mountbatten had a keen sense of history, and made sure that the records of SEAC were comprehensive. This undoubtedly helped me, fifty years later, to find information which might well have been lost or destroyed under a different commander.

With Mountbatten's staff and information in mind, it is worth introducing here a senior figure who will be mentioned later on many occasions. When assembling his senior staff in October 1943, he asked recently-retired Air Marshal Sir Philip Joubert de la Ferté, former Inspector General of the RAF, to become a deputy chief of staff, with particular responsibility for communications and civil affairs. Joubert accepted the job, but with some reservations. He was doubtful because Mountbatten had previously served under him, and he thought the role reversal might be difficult. He was also uneasy because he was not clear what the job was to entail.

The setting up of a section of his staff to cover civil affairs may be seen as a far-sighted attempt by Mountbatten to prepare for the huge task that would arise when the Japanese left the various countries they had occupied. Before that, the job was to involve communication with the forces under his command, and with the public back home. There was also the less publicised task of supervising any propaganda work that was undertaken.

In Joubert's experience, these were functions with which the military had not usually been much concerned. Although the details were vague, he understood the general idea. When, years later, he reflected on the way it had turned out, his conclusion was that it was a most interesting and valuable conception which had only just failed to be a resounding success.[8]

Joubert was born in Calcutta and his father was a doctor and surgeon in the Indian Medical Service, by looking briefly at his extraordinary career one may begin to understand why he was chosen. His first qualification was availability. He had just retired from a distinguished career in the RAF. This had started in the days of the Royal Flying Corps, which he joined early in WWI, having qualified as a pilot before the war. He served in France, Italy the Middle East and India. The RAF was established, as such, in 1918.

In the inter war years he rose through the ranks, and became involved in planning the war which was to come. As he reached the higher levels of command, he attended inter-governmental meetings, between England and France, and so acquired some insight into European politics. This background may have been in Mountbatten's mind when considering the civil affairs aspect.

In the late thirties he was concerned with bringing the RAF up to date, and in the application of radar for the Home Chain of radar stations. When he later became chief of Coastal Command, he found himself at the centre of the crucial war against the U-boats. A vital part of this work was concerned with getting improved radar sets designed, produced, and installed in RAF aircraft. Before the war he went out to the Far East to look at the state of the RAF, which was far from good. He was able to get some Beaufighters shipped out to replace antiquated aircraft.

8 Sir Philip Joubert de la Ferté, *The Fated Sky*, London, White Line, 1977, pp. 243-4.

All this may go some way to explaining Mountbatten's choice. Perhaps one further consideration may have been in mind when considering the communications brief. He was an experienced communicator. At around the time of the Blitz on London, he was called on to broadcast on the BBC to give listeners a further insight into the course of the war. He seems to have been reasonably fearless when flying aircraft, but was absolutely terrified when he faced the microphone for the first time. He must have done well because he gave a good many talks, and got to know Ed Murray, the distinguished American whose broadcasts from the blitzed city became famous. Murray persuaded him to broadcast to the USA, which he did for a time.

Two faults, if they may be so called, led to his falling out with Mountbatten when the civil affairs part of his activities was in full swing. The first was that he was not just old, but one of the old school, in the company of Churchill and others. For all Mountbatten's sense of history and tradition, he was a realist who knew the world had to develop. The second a serious difference arose over the future of the Burmese National Army, which at one stage had supported the Japanese. It was time for Joubert to continue his long delayed retirement.

The experience of difficulties in setting up Radio SEAC may have had unpleasant similarities with Joubert's time in Coastal Command, when he was desperately trying to get new and better radar sets for his aircraft. In SEAC he was trying to get delivery of a radio transmitter, and frustrated at being unable to do much about it. He headed the Information and Civil Affairs Committee, extracts from the minutes of that committee appear in later chapters. Radio SEAC was usually on the agenda. He was also involved with a committee on forces radio in India, which is mentioned later. So when technical radio matters arose, both Mountbatten and Joubert had specialised knowledge. They must also have been well aware that the radio industry in Britain was very fully stretched in meeting demands for communication sets of every kind, and a wide range of radar items. When putting forward requests for more welfare radio sets for the troops, there was little chance of getting any priority over the production of operational equipment.

Lieutenant Colonel Noonan, Director Service Relations (SEAC), appears several times in the story, including the occasion when he was due to make representations to Ernest Bevin, Foreign Secretary, in London.

Most great men seem to have both very enthusiastic supporters and people who detest them. One characteristic Mountbatten had in abundance was enthusiasm, and some officers serving with him in the Mediterranean are said to have felt he took this quality much too far. His appearance was always immaculate, and this is said to have been a morale booster for the troops he visited. He liked to live in some style, but his biographer finds the criticism of the life-style at the Kandy headquarters as overstated. He drew the conclusion that if there is a morale-boosting need of the greatest importance, and you decide that Mountbatten is the best person for the job, you have to be prepared to pay the price.

Mountbatten's tremendous determination was a major factor in his success. If he thought a decision was sufficiently important he would invoke the help of very senior people when unable to get his way over something he considered vitally important. We shall find an example of this where he appealed to Churchill for assistance, and another where, (probably with justification, and certainly in desperation) he asked Wavell, then Viceroy of India, to assist in the allocation of frequencies for Radio SEAC's use.

In later years he took pleasure in remembering the success of his initiative in arranging for the setting up of a forces newspaper even before he arrived in India to take up the command. The excellent idea was relatively easy to realise, and something he could be proud of. The Radio SEAC enterprise was hardly an unqualified success, for reasons which are set out in detail in this volume. Delays in implementation, and the serious shortage of receivers, meant that it could never be the resounding success he must have wished it would be.

Not long after leaving SEAC, the Prime Minister, Clement Attlee, asked him to undertake the extremely difficult task of arranging the transition to an independent India. As the last Viceroy, he was unable to avoid the partition of that country, in spite of long and difficult negotiations. As I travelled across India on my way to Ceylon, early in 1946, there were crowds on some stations calling out 'Pakistan Zindabad'. It was the call for an independent Pakistan. Subsequent very high level appointments can hardly have matched the awesome responsibility of being India's last Viceroy.

Having reached the highest rank in the navy (Admiral of the Fleet), and having held the position Chief of the Defence Staff, Earl Mountbatten of Burma eventually enjoyed a well-earned retirement. He was killed by an IRA bomb while on a family yacht holiday in Ireland.

4

Early Welfare and Radio Organisation

Mountbatten landed in India, to take up his command, on 6 October 1943. The official date of his appointment was in the following month. He knew that a high priority had to be given to improving morale, and had already arranged for the production of a forces newspaper to assist in that process. His personal visits to many forces units were to be a way of impressing his personality and outlook on many who felt they were in 'the forgotten army'. Good welfare provision could also contribute to the improvement of morale, but, although he knew morale was low, he was not aware of how bad the welfare situation was. He was very soon making the most exhaustive and detailed enquiries.

At his instigation, the first meeting of the SEAC Welfare Committee was on 9 December, just two months after he had arrived. Its brief was Mountbatten's personal minute P17 (or P18). Unfortunately, neither was found in the file in the National Archives, although the contents sheet of the file lists, as the first item, 'Supreme Commander's Personal Minute'.

It is possible to get some idea of the contents from the powerful introduction to the meeting, which made it clear that Mountbatten attached very great importance to the proper co-ordination of welfare matters. He called for monthly reports on the subject.[1]

The minutes identify finance as a huge problem. Britain had been engaged in an extremely expensive war since 1939, and it would not be surprising to find that, in some quarters, good welfare facilities were seen as something of a luxury. Where British forces found themselves coming into contact with American troops the difference in provision was painfully apparent.

The meeting considered the various kinds of amenity. The provision of books and games was said to be satisfactory, whereas the availability of films was extremely unsatisfactory. This would have caught Mountbatten's eye, because he was a cinema enthusiast. To this day, visitors to his home, Broadlands, pass through what was his private cinema. Guests were often entertained with a film. He was not a highbrow, in films or anything else, but enjoyed unpretentious entertainment. He knew people in the film industry and had, for example, taken part in a home movie with Charlie Chaplin.

Judging from the minutes, the first welfare meeting must have been long and exhausting. After an extremely wide-ranging review, item ninety one of the minutes is about broadcasting. The Chairman, Brigadier E. N. Clarke mentioned that a committee was being formed to consider all aspects of broadcasting, and that the constitution of that committee was to be decided shortly. Some members of the Welfare Committee would be invited to become members of the new committee.

1 WO 203 3217.

It would be wrong to assume from all this committee work that Mountbatten was content to see people sitting around in committees and writing memos to one another. He had made it clear that informal and direct communication was far quicker and more desirable than working through official channels.

This quickly led to some officers realising they had better brief themselves better in future. Shortly after that committee meeting, on 30 December, a lieutenant colonel in SEAC HQ, wrote to Lt. Col. A. R. Wakeham of GHQ (India), (both were in Delhi, at that time). In this he asked about the 'Cert Club of Lahore', a forces social club, and mentioned that there were probably many self-supporting organisations of this type in India. He requested a list because:

> I am so sorry to trouble you but I am getting an increasing number of minor enquiries on welfare matters. As you know, our Supreme Commander takes a very active interest in Welfare, and I would like to be in a position to answer at least some of the enquiries I get without having to worry you on every minor point.[2]

The second meeting of the welfare committee followed soon after, on 10 January 1944. Item seven covered welfare in hospitals and mentioned that:

> Hospitals in the Arakan and Chittagong area are not well supplied with amenities and Red Cross supplies. Wiring and loudspeakers for connecting up the wards with a centrally controlled radio would be very welcome.

Item twelve dealt with a familiar theme:

> It is reported that the Fourteenth Army are extremely short of battery radio sets and spare batteries for existing sets. Both are on order. Can anything be done to expedite?[3]

The same item in the minutes went on to report a shortage of gramophones, musical instruments, books and periodicals. We shall see, later, that these shortages were still in evidence when Lord Munster made his inspection in the autumn of the same year.

It was at about this time that Eade was shocked to find that in southern Arakan the British troops were being entertained by the Japanese radio from Saigon. The shortage of radio batteries may have been no bad thing. At least it stopped some of the Fourteenth Army being entertained by the Japanese.

The file contains a great deal about the need to improve both the supply of films, and the availability of projection equipment. Mountbatten decided that the shortage of films should be drawn to the attention of those at the top. A 'secret' message went from his HQ to the Secretary of State for India on 5 March 1944:

> Supply of entertainment films for British Services use most unsatisfactory. Supreme Commander SEAC and C in C India request Jarrett should obtain an agreement with American and English film companies for free showing their films on services controlled equipment to all services this theatre of war. Small number of prints, mostly 35 mm., some 16 mm. required until

2 WO 203 3218.
3 WO 203 3217.

> more equipment is available. Prints must be delivered to and under the control of services organisations here, and not through local trade channels.[4]

This message may have helped to improve our lives. Two years later we were in Ceylon, and there were two cinema shows on occasional offer; the conventional cinema at RAF Negombo, and an open air 16mm projector at a nearby naval station.

So Mountbatten intervened decisively to improve the supply of films. Meanwhile his newspaper was already being published daily. The following is Mountbatten's own account of this enterprise:

> Before leaving London I had done my best to arrange that adequate publicity should be given to the Command in the press at home for this would react on the troops by way of their families. The Prime Minister had obtained from Lord Rothermere the loan for six months of the services of Mr. Charles Eade (Editor - *Sunday Dispatch*) as my Press Adviser so that adequate publicity might be given to the forces in South East Asia in the press at home. I obtained from the War Office, whilst still in London, the services of 2nd Lt., later Lieut. Colonel Frank Owen (former editor *Evening Standard*) whom I had instructed to organise in Calcutta the production of an inter-service daily newspaper *SEAC* for distribution to the forward areas to keep the men in touch with news from Home. So that they should think of *SEAC* as being their own paper, and not as being imposed on them, the forces were to be encouraged to send in criticisms, and to use its correspondence columns as a forum for the free expression of opinion. Since in civilian life they had been among the readers of a great variety of papers, I laid down that *SEAC* must embody as many features, and of a great a variety as the layout permitted.[5]

It is interesting that his recollection is that he had instructed Owen to organise *in Calcutta* the production of the paper. Eade, in his report, claims he was responsible for the preliminary organisation of the SEAC newspaper, and the decision to have it produced by the *Calcutta Statesman*. Eade's story is that Owen had ordered some special machinery so that the paper could be printed in an aircraft, and that he [Eade] had realised this would all take too long and so arranged for the *Calcutta Statesman* to do the printing.[6]

Joubert makes no reference to any involvement by Eade. He recalled that Owen had ingratiated himself, very early on, with Ian Stephens, the editor of the *Calcutta Statesman*, and had arranged to use part of his offices, and more importantly, his printing presses, free.[7]

There may have been some professional jealousy between Eade and Owen – both Fleet Street editors. Much more serious was the fact that the Secretary of State for War objected to the appointment of Frank Owen, and Mountbatten was obliged to involve Churchill to get his way.[8] This is one instance where Mountbatten felt something was sufficiently important to appeal to the highest authorities.

---

4 WO 203 3218.

5 Mountbatten, *Report to the Combined Chiefs of Staff*, Introduction.

6 WO 203 4869.

7 Joubert de la Ferté, *The Fated Sky*, p. 245.

8 Ziegler, *Mountbatten — The Official Biography*, p. 256.

An entry in Mountbatten's diary for 17 January 1944 indicates that Owen lost no time in launching his newspaper:

> I found the first three editions of our new daily paper *SEAC* (pronounced See-Ack) on my return [to his HQ]. Frank Owen has done a magnificent job. General Giffard, who is down on the Burma front, tells me the soldiers are absolutely delighted with it. Considering he has only got one Marine Subaltern, two ORs from the Army and two ORs from the Air Force and a naval telegraphist to help him, and produces seven days a week, it really is a wonderful show.[9]

Much later, at the twenty sixth I & CA meeting on 24 April 1946 (when SEAC was being wound down, prior to its termination) a draft of that part of the Supreme Allied Commander's dispatches dealing with Public Relations had been considered. Mountbatten's pride in the newspaper was undiminished, and he was not happy with the draft:

> The SAC said this draft did not stress clearly enough that *SEAC* was the first inter-services paper to be introduced during the war, and that the magazine *Phoenix* was the first Allied magazine to be introduced. He wished details of the original proportions of the original staff of *SEAC* to be shown. He also considered the RAF and RN Public Relations sections had been lightly passed over.[10]

It is thought that this strong emphasis on inter-services projects may provide the reason why the Radio SEAC transmitting station, originally staffed by the army, had personnel drafted in from the RAF and the Navy, not long after we arrived there.

So the newspaper was in being in January 1944, and film supplies were being chased at a very high level in early March. Now we come to broadcasting. As already mentioned, this had been raised in the first welfare committee meeting, when it was noted that a committee was being set up. At about this time Eade had come back to New Delhi from southern Arakan, and found a meeting in progress, with Joubert in charge, discussing the future of radio services to the troops in SEAC. Eade told Joubert that the Fourteenth Army in the Arakan were listening to Japanese radio.

At a further meeting it was decided to form an Inter-Services Radio Committee with Eade as chairman and representatives of the three services, Indian Army, American forces in China/Burma, Indian M of I, and US Office of War Information.

Eade wrote in his report:

> There was at that time a small radio section run by the welfare department of India Command. It was under the direction of Major Frost. It was decided to absorb this section into a radio division which was being organised by the Inter-Services Radio Committee. I applied, in the name of the Committee, for special facilities from All-India Radio, and also for the allotment of time on the air. We were also given the temporary use of a transmitter which had been obtained for the Far Eastern service of the M. of I., and which suited our purpose by being beamed to the 14th Army areas. We secured, from the American forces, an experienced radio announcer, Ensign Henry. The

9 Ziegler, *Personal Diary of Admiral The Lord Loius Mountbatten*, pp. 57-8.

10 WO 203 4869

> RAF provided us with a radio producer named Froshaug and these men, together with Major Frost's staff, were the original team which launched Radio SEAC.[11]

Information later in Eade's report was less than helpful, as were the last few words quoted above, presumably because he was writing from memory. It is difficult to understand his comment about the people he regarded as the original team which launched Radio SEAC. He later wrote that the first programme went out in February 1944, whereas in actual fact it was in January. He claimed that the quality of reception, even in the earliest days, was always of a very high order. It is not known where that fine reception could be enjoyed. It was certainly not Burma.

However this is a generous tribute to Major Frost, from a man who seems to have been inclined to save all the credit for himself. In the diary note which follows, Mountbatten is in no doubt that Eade should have the credit, with the overall credit going to Mountbatten himself for having given Eade the initial directive. It seems doubtful if either of them could claim much credit, and it is better to rely on Eade's own tribute to Major Frost.

In March 1944 Mountbatten was driving in a jungle area when he suffered an accident which involved potentially serious damage to an eye. Both eyes had to be bandaged. He wrote in his diary:

> The US Army Signal Corps very kindly provided a radio set so that I could listen to the Anglo-American All Forces programme which Mr Eade got going at my request so as to give our troops in Burma something to listen to besides the enemy propaganda from Saigon. Although it is only an hour a day (1830 to 1930) it is really excellent and tremendously popular and a much-needed innovation. We must try and extend the hours as soon as we can.[12]

The evidence suggests that not all commanders were as enlightened as Mountbatten in the degree of priority felt to be justified for welfare expenditure. From the start, he had set up a welfare framework to ensure that, at least, there was good information about shortcomings in provision. This will have been useful when resources became available. Where only a relatively small expenditure was needed, as in the setting up of the forces newspaper, this was done very quickly. Useful improvements were also made in the supply of films, but the shortage of projection equipment took longer to remedy.

In his book, Joubert dealt at some length with his time in New Delhi, and recalled Mountbatten's efforts to get more films and entertainment for the forces. He did not mention the early broadcasts from Delhi. This is even more remarkable when he devoted more than half a page to the assistance he gave to an American officer, Capt. Lee Black. He had been given the responsibility of setting up AFRS stations in the China, India and Burma theatre. In a situation rather reminiscent of the difficulties AFN had in setting up broadcasting stations in England, he had met with probably bureaucratic objections to the setting up a number of low-powered transportable stations. This was the standard AFRS method, which they adopted in the Pacific, and elsewhere. He had to face a delay of about a month, but Joubert managed to contact someone with the authority to have the regulations set aside.[13]

11 Ibid.

12 Ziegler, *Personal Diary of Admiral The Lord Loius Mountbatten*, p. 80.

13 Joubert de la Ferté, *The Fated Sky.*

The first of the American AFRS stations was set up in New Delhi, with a 50 watt transmitter and a staff of four. Other stations were to follow in Karachi, Agra, Calcutta, Lalmahirat, Bangalore, Gaya, Tezzaon, Jorhat, Misamari, Kandy, Ledo, Chabua, Shinybwiyang, Myitkina, and Bhamo.[14]

Attempts to increase the supply of radio receivers were only marginally successful. Assembling people to produce programmes was relatively easy, but providing suitable transmitters adequately to cover the huge area involved was another matter. It seemed unlikely the large sum of money needed would become available. In the next chapter we shall see how the purse strings came to be loosened during what proved to be the last few months of the war.

14 Trent Christman, *Brass Button Broadcasters*, pp. 47-8.

5

Lord Munster's Report

Sunday Pictorial readers who picked up their favourite newspaper from the front door mat on the morning of 6 August 1944 were in for a disquieting read when they reached page 6, particularly if they had a loved one, or relative, serving in the Far East. The introduction to a piece by a Capt. F. J. Bellenger MP provided a good summary:

> OUR MAN IN INDIA - An alarming report.
>
> The revelations of the appalling conditions of the British Army in India made by Captain Bellenger on this page today must arouse the indignant anger of the people at home who should be satisfied with nothing short of a full-scale enquiry. In Normandy and Italy the army has a modern, well-staffed and highly efficient medical service. It is admirably fed, leisure is made pleasant, and invigorating. Conditions are far different in the Far East. There, when the peril from tropical disease is at least as great as the peril from Japanese bullets, the medical service is starved of personnel and out of date in its equipment, with a result of avoidable death and a vast amount of unnecessary suffering. The soldier has nothing to read but dirty antiquated magazines, nothing is done for his entertainment. On leave he is fleeced by native profiteers and snubbed by his high and mighty fellow countrymen and countrywomen.

There was more, and the article itself went into considerable detail. There was much about the shortage of beer, and mention of the unfamiliar and unpalatable cigarettes. The following extract is not typical, but chosen for its relevance:

> As for radio sets they are practically non-existent. Mr.Amery (Secretary of State for India) admitted as much. He said 8,000 sets are on order, and he hoped they would be got out as soon as they could be manufactured. Why this delay when for some time past large British armies have been garrisoning India?

The *Sunday Pictorial* article met with some scepticism in high places, but when Amery asked Auchinleck he said it would not be easy to refute some of the accusations. Amery thought the best course would be for the Earl of Munster (Under-Secretary of State for India and Burma) to go and establish the facts, and report back to the government. He sought Churchill's approval, whose response included a very typical phrase:

> I do not think Munster roaming about the dreary splendours of New Delhi is going to effect very much. The thing is to have a programme and give the orders.

On this point, Amery's reply:

> It is not a question of his roaming about New Delhi, but of visiting canteens, leave camps, etc., on the spot, and giving me an intelligent observer's view of what the men most need. It would certainly be a great help to me to have the advantage of his independent judgment, and not to have to rely on information through the ordinary hierarchical channels.[1]

Agreement was reached, and Munster went out early in October 1944. Amery was right. In a letter sent with the report, Lord Munster said he had visited 82 clubs/canteens, 12 leave centres, 9 transit camps, 34 hospitals, 28 units, and other places. The details of one of these visits are in a press release, dated 22 October 1944, included with SEAC HQ papers:

> In a basha in the Arakan jungle for three hours, officers and men of the Fourteenth Army told the Earl of Munster what Arakan troops think about Army Welfare in India. Lord Munster listened carefully to the views of 5 officers, 3 NCOs and 2 privates who had come straight from foxholes in forward jungle positions to represent the feelings of forward fighting troops. At the outset he told them not to mince matters, and encouraged them to speak frankly on any subject relating to welfare and amenities. They did so. Among subjects discussed were repatriation, pay, leave centres, and entertainment. The meeting came at the end of a busy day for Lord Munster. He arrived at a forward airfield at 9 a.m., and spent the morning touring an RAF camp. In the afternoon he inspected 4 hospitals and a rest camp. At the rest camp he chatted with BO's who had just returned from leave. At an RAF mess where he lunched, Lord Munster tasted his first soya link and thought the sausages must get a bit tiresome after a time.

In view of the thorough way Lord Munster approached his task it seems rather churlish to point out the top-heavy representation of the troops implicit in the selection of 5 officers 3 NCO's and 2 privates.

There seems to have been a disagreement between Joubert and Mountbatten on the publicity to be given to the Munster tour. If Joubert committed his views to paper they have not been found, but the following was Mountbatten's response, dated 23 October 1944:

> Publicity - Lord Munster's visit
>
> I am afraid that for once I find myself in disagreement with your views on Lord Munster's visit. I must explain that the PM [Churchill] told me in Cairo that he was personally backing the visit, and had instructed him to send him regular reports on what action was immediately required. It does seem as though something really is going to happen as a result of his visit.
>
> Another advantage from giving a certain amount of publicity ... is that it publicly places the burden of responsibility for providing addition amenities

1 PREM4 13/2, part2.

> fairly and squarely in Whitehall. I feel that this is the right place for it to rest since neither SEAC, nor GHQ (India), can do much more than we are doing without help from Whitehall.
>
> Finally, the greater the publicity for Lord Munster's activities, the more vital it is, for his reputation, and incidentally that of the government at home, that immediate action should be taken. It is not we but the home government who have elected to give this publicity, in order to meet the growing criticism in the press at home. This publicity will recoil on their own heads unless they implement his proposals, and I am therefore in favour of letting the policy they have started pursue its course.[2]

The point made that neither SEAC nor GHQ (India) could do much more without help from Whitehall perfectly summarised the whole welfare situation. The help needed eventually came in many forms, including live entertainment, more beer, better cigarettes, cinema equipment, and the Marconi 100 kW transmitter. An account has already been given of the way Mountbatten, and those in his command and in India Command, had attempted to improve the welfare situation within weeks of his arrival. The shortages of resources had been a continual brake on their ability to get things done.

As we have seen, when Auchinleck was asked by Amery about welfare, he made no attempt to whitewash the situation, and this honesty no doubt played a part in persuading Amery that he should send Lord Munster. It was certainly a sensitive subject. In a personal letter to Mountbatten dated 10 October, Auchinleck complained about an article in the 5 October issue of the *SEAC* newspaper, entitled 'What is wrong with welfare?' He felt many of the proposals were quite impracticable, and raised false hopes in the minds of the troops. He added:

> The most unfortunate part of the article lies in the implication it contains of an unwillingness on the part of India [Command] to provide what the troops in your command may reasonably expect. These lightly veiled attacks cannot fail to discredit service in India and to create ill feeling between our two commands. As you are aware, we have been working all out to overcome the disabilities which confront us, and I am definitely of the opinion that these ill advised articles are having a bad effect on the discipline and morale of the army in India.

Mountbatten replied at once, but, according to Joubert, he refused to admit there was a campaign against GHQ. The Supremo pointed out that credit was given to India for what it had done, and although some of the suggestions may not have been realistic in the predictable future, the bulk of them were reasonable and capable of achievement. Nevertheless, Joubert told the *SEAC* newspaper editor, Frank Owen, that his staff should avoid controversial matters for the time being.

It is not known who wrote paragraph 7 of the SEAC HQ War Diary for 14 October 1944, but it illustrates the strength of feeling, at high level. This was two weeks before a top-level meeting on the subject, at which Lord Munster was present. As always, the shortage of wireless sets was mentioned:

---

2 WO 172 1733.

> AMENITIES - I don't know whether the Supreme Commander is likely to discuss this important subject, but if it crops up we should like to make it abundantly clear to representatives from UK that there may be considerable difficulty keeping morale high in this theater [sic] after the war in Europe is over.
>
> Increased pay will of course help, but this is only one item. SAC has already cabled giving an outline of what is necessary - live entertainment, cinemas, home newspapers, faster and cheaper mail, duty free prices in canteens, etc. We must also be given high priority on all amenity items, e.g. projectors, films, wireless sets etc., batteries and gramophones NOW, if necessary at the expense of other theaters.
>
> The fact that we are getting visits from Munster and Jardine shows that some interest is being taken, but amenities are more acceptable than visitors, and we want action and no arguments about expense, which is negligible compared with the cost of the war as a whole, and would pay the highest dividends.[3]

It seems unlikely that the author of this forceful memorandum would have been impressed with the details of Munster's background.

> MUNSTER, 5th Earl of/ Geoffrey William Hugh Fitzclarence
>
> Born 17/2/1906. Educated Charterhouse. A Lord in Waiting 1932-38.
>
> Member of the LCC for North Paddington 1931-37.
>
> Paymaster General 1938/9.
>
> Under-Secretary of State for War Feb-Sept. 1939.
>
> Parliamentary Under Secretary of State for India and Burma 1943-44.
>
> Home Office 1944-45.
>
> Captain in the Grenadier Guards. Member of the Turf and Carlton Clubs.[4]

Nevertheless, this typical pillar of the establishment, right down to the name Fitzclarence, did a thorough job, and produced a comprehensive report which formed the basis for government action.

By the 30 October, Munster must have heard from hundreds of people at all levels. On that day, at 17.30, he joined Mountbatten in his room at headquarters for a meeting to discuss 'Welfare in SEAC'.

Those present were listed in the Minutes as:

> The Lord Louis Mountbatten
>
> Rt. Hon. The Earl of Munster (Under-Secretary of State for India)
>
> Maj. Gen. Sir Colin Jardine (Inspector General Overseas Welfare)
>
> Air Comm. S. Graham (Director RAF Welfare, Air Ministry)

3 WO 172 1732.

4 *Who's Who* (1950).

Brig. G. Portman (GHQ India)
C. J. D. Wakeley Esq. (Govt of India - Defence Department)
Lt. Gen. Sir Henry Pownall COS
Air Marshal Sir Guy Garrod (Air Command SEA)
Commodore D. de Pass R.N. (Eastern Fleet)
Maj. Gen. R. F. S. Denning (DPAO)
Maj. Gen. G.E. Wilman-Lushington (ACOS)
Brig. G .A. Clarke (DAC)
Col. A. B. Phillpotts (11 Army Group)
Gp. Capt. E. L. Tomkinson (Air Command SEA)
Lt .Col. T. G. Morton (AAG(A))

The minutes record that Mountbatten opened the meeting by putting Lord Munster's visit in context, and explained that India and SEA Commands had to be considered together for welfare purposes. The treatment was broadly equal, but there was slightly better treatment of some aspects in Operational Areas, where, for example there was a slightly higher ration of cigarettes. He explained that Joubert was in London, and hoped that Munster would discuss any problems with him on returning to the UK. A list of points for discussion had been circulated and the meeting worked through the list.

Item two of the minutes was about publicity and Mountbatten spoke of his disagreement with Joubert, mentioned above. Munster suggested senior officers returning home should address MP's informally. The object would be to let them know more about the situation in the Far East. Mountbatten said the Viceroy (of India) had suggested newspaper proprietors should come out and see the conditions for themselves. It would also help greatly if newspapers would send out some of their best reporters to Burma.

Item three was about the indoctrination of personnel coming to SEAC. Ever the film enthusiast, Mountbatten pressed for a film to be made for the purpose – the Americans had one. Others said pamphlets were being prepared.

Under amenities in general, at item four, the construction of leave facilities was discussed, and it was said there was no labour available, which brought the suggestion that German prisoners of war should be shipped in to do the construction work. ATS women should be brought in to run them. Mountbatten wanted SEAC and India to have priority over Europe for welfare facilities, because the forces in Europe enjoyed the huge advantage of being able to go home on leave, or if sick.

The shortage of film projectors was mentioned, and Munster said that 150 per month were being produced in the UK, and only twenty four had gone to India and SEAC in the last five months. Item five was about finance. Item six was about equipment, and covered radio sets and gramophones. Mountbatten asked Munster if he could enquire whether HMV could be persuaded to re-open their Calcutta factory.

As for radio, it is worth quoting the minutes in full:

> The SAC (Mountbatten) pointed out the anomalous position existing whereby arrangements for the transmission of considerably increased broadcast programmes from the Radio Stations in SEAC and India had been completed, but there were not enough radio sets with which all troops could

> listen to those programmes. It was stated that a proportion of a consignment of 3000 sets made in US had already been shipped. It was agreed that many more sets would be required.[5]

This paragraph repeated what most people knew already, but it is revealing when taken in context with other information. The SEAC War Diary for 11 October 1944, at item nine, records that:

> BROADCASTING - Our 7.5 kW short wave station has now been established at Colombo, and is on test. We hope very soon to start a 4 hour daily programme. This will be arranged to operate at different hours to the 4 hour daily programme already broadcast by All-India Radio, so that troops will be able to listen to several programmes during 8 hours of the day. Arrangements are already being made for the establishment of a medium wave transmitter at Colombo, which will broadcast the same programmes as the short wave station, and will be designed to cover Ceylon.
>
> The position with receivers is however bad, and unless we receive a considerable number shortly we shall merely be broadcasting to troops who have no receivers with which to listen.[6]

The 7.5 kW short wave transmitter was presumably the one mentioned by Bernard Blakemore when he wrote in an article in 1946 that Radio SEAC first came on the air as experimental station ZOJ in October 1944, for only a few hours each day on a borrowed transmitter and from borrowed studio space.

So 'the transmission of considerably increased broadcast programmes' spoken of by Mountbatten at the meeting, was his description of these two, four hours a day services provided by India and SEAC. The SEAC service had only recently started, and was still on an experimental basis. It is clear that Mountbatten felt nothing further could usefully be done about programmes or transmitters until the shortage of sets had been remedied. There was much sense in this view. When we come to the Munster Report, later in this chapter, we shall find that although he, too, said how essential it was to have many more radio receivers, he also recommended more programmes, and more transmitters. The latter recommendation led to the purchase of the Marconi 100 kW.

It is important to consider where the idea for more programmes and transmitters came from. It seems likely that Munster was well briefed by Brian Cave-Brown-Cave, who was in charge of the well established broadcasting unit in Delhi. There is nothing to suggest that any account was taken of Mountbatten's request in October 1943 for a powerful transmitter. However, as we shall see in the next chapter, once the proposal for a big transmitter had been agreed in discussions in London, he was very quick to press for it to be sited in Ceylon rather than Delhi. The remainder of the minutes of the meeting on 30 October, dealt with mainly predictable matters, but a few points of general interest emerged. More live entertainment was called for, and the representative from the Eastern Fleet wanted to see more newspapers from the UK.

This was a meeting of very senior men, and it was not too long before they started to think about women. Mountbatten pointed out how good women in the forces were for

5 WO 172 1734.
6 WO 172 1732.

morale. In the next item, fourteen, he said that in two weeks, 700 nurses had volunteered for service in SEAC. It had taken eight months before even 250 had been allowed to travel to SEAC. He urged Munster to get more sent out.

There were said to problems with the postal services, with travel, and that the men needed to be better informed about repatriation arrangements. Mountbatten asked Munster to try to get the woefully small beer ration increased.

Fortunately Munster had already spoken to numerous people at all levels, as we have seen. There is evidence of one item where the very senior people at the meeting seem to have been out of touch with the latest position. The unsatisfactory situation with some canteens was mentioned, and the solution suggested was to get NAAFI to venture east of Suez. A confidential intelligence briefing at around this time referred to the demand for NAAFI as seeming to be a thing of the past. Things had been improved without them.

A confidential briefing, dated 31 October 1944, the day after the meeting, was headed:

> Report on the Morale of British, Indian and Colonial Troops of Allied Land Forces South East Asia Area, for the months Aug/Sept/Oct 1944. This report is based on the monthly security intelligence reports of units, and on field censorship intercepts.

As we shall see, the report mentioned the well known welfare deficiencies, but it also gave a very frank account of how the troops were feeling about everything. Confidence and fighting spirit were said to be at a very high level, but the forgotten army tag still rankled:

> They feel that the complete lack of interest exhibited by the British press and radio, and apparent refusal of the government to make any great effort to improve the soldiers' conditions of life in what is a manifestly unpleasant theatre of war shows a real lack of gratitude for a difficult job well done.

It was recognised that some action was being taken, with improvements in pay and repatriation. The report continued:

> The increased interest in welfare attested by the visit of the Earl of Munster shows that the government is taking positive steps to improve the lot of the soldiers in this theatre. However:-
>
> ...such action may have come too late to repair the harm already done. The BOR [British other rank] cannot fail to notice that increased attention has at last been paid to him at a time when the war in Europe shows signs of coming to an end, and when it is very much in the government's own interest to take special notice of the Far Eastern theatre of war. He appreciates the change, but he is still suspicious, and remains unimpressed with the government's good intentions.

The three month period covered by the report seems to have seen great improvements in the availability of films. Supplies of reading matter were good. However, item twenty three of the report confirmed other available evidence about the shortage of radio sets:

> The acute shortage of wireless sets is perhaps the greatest of all the units' welfare complaints, and in this sphere there has been no progress in the

> last three months. Not enough comments on the BBC's General Forces programme have been received to justify any assessment of its popularity.[7]

The Munster Report said that this programme was only received on the best sets. Some people, of course, needed the best for their work. Jack Nield, who worked on several high speed wireless installations apart from Ekala, recalled having a Marconi CR 100 communications receiver tuned to the BBC's General Forces Programme all the time they were on duty in Batavia.

There were good comments about food, and the gradual elimination of soya links was said to be much appreciated, but units complained that they are still being issued to them. This is no doubt why at least one unit had made sure Munster had to eat some.

Munster was under instructions to feed information back to Churchill without waiting to complete his tour or write his report. The government was therefore able to start to consider, and even to act on, some of the recommendations which Munster was going to make. This was some weeks before Churchill told the Commons about the report, and made copies available to MPs. Churchill, ever the consummate politician, followed the tradition of releasing unpleasant information at a time when MP's minds were occupied with the good news of Christmas.

On 20 December 1944, Churchill told the House there was been concern about the welfare of the armed forces in the Far East,[8] and that the Parliamentary Under-Secretary of State for the Home Department [Lord Munster] had made a tour of the India and the Burma front in order to assess, at first hand, the improvements needed. His report, as a White Paper, was made available to MPs that evening. The PM went on to comment on some of the items in the report, and said:

> Measures are in hand to accelerate the provision of cinema apparatus and wireless equipment, most of which I should mention can only be obtained from the USA.

Later he said:

> I have also ....appointed Lieut. General King to be my personal representative in the India and South East Asia Commands for welfare matters. It will be General King's duty to ascertain how matters are progressing, and to report to me on difficulties which may arise, and on the assistance which may be required from this country.[9]

The delay in bringing the report to the attention of the House allowed Churchill to refer to measures in hand. This demonstrated that action was being taken as a matter of urgency, which may have alleviated MP's anxieties when they came to read the report, and realise how serious the welfare deficiencies were. The urgent action had been made possible by Churchill's insistence that Munster should send initial findings immediately. The contents of two telegrams have been seen by the author which were sent even before the high-powered meeting with Mountbatten mentioned earlier in this chapter.[10]

---

7 WO 172 1734.

8 HC Deb 20 December 1944, vol 406, cc1786-93.

9 White Paper Cmd 6578, IOR/L/PO/4/24; PREM4 13/2, part 1.

10 Unfortunately it has not been found possible to repeat the computer search, possibly because of a major re-organisation of Churchill's papers that took place in 2010.

The first was sent on 19 October 1944, and recommended sending Auxiliary Territorial Service members to India to 'meet lack of white women'! The shock caused by reading these words is a reminder, perhaps, of the great changes in society over the last fifty years. Other recommendations were more predictable, and included more cinema projectors, more beer, and the suggestion that air letter cards from India to the UK should be carried free. The second telegram, sent on the 28 October, included his impression (from his tour of the Fourteenth Army) that morale was excellent. However, Munster felt that a personal statement from Churchill on repatriation prospects would be useful. He also reported on a shortage of refrigerators and fans in hospitals, and the poor conditions on leave trains.

A report in November 1944 noted that Ducker and Cave-Brown-Cave had arrived in the UK, and discussions had taken place with a view to opening a broadcasting service to cover both commands, India and SEAC.

The new appointment of General King was not the only change that had been made. The Director of Army Welfare Services had been replaced by Major General J. M. L. Grover MC on 2 October 1944. This was at around the time Munster flew off to India. It may be that the government had become convinced, even before his departure, that there had been serious negligence in the failure of welfare provision generally, and had decided to act accordingly.

The report mentioned many factors, and difficulties over pay, for instance, bulk at least as large as the shortage of wireless sets. Production of beer in India had been increased, but was not adequate to supply the current ration of three bottles per man per month.

He reported on experiments in the production of beer, or what was described as a beery beverage that could be made in the forward areas. A form of portable brewery had been evolved and was under test. Nobody reading the report could complain seriously of any sort of whitewash. General King was not going to be short of work if he carried out his progress-chasing remit in all the aspects listed below. This was a summary of the Munster recommendations:

1. Continuous publicity at home through the medium of press and wireless.
2. Information and instruction should be given to British troops before their departure from England, and on the voyage to India.
3. Reinforcement camp at Deolali to be maintained at a high standard.
4. All possible measures to be taken to improve cleanliness of trains.
5. Improvement of the conditions at transit camps.
6. Erection of additional Leave Camps to be expedited.
7. Increase in the staff of SSAFA. (Soldiers Sailors and Airmen's Families Association).
8. All Indian Section of the Free Legal Aid organisation in London to be established.
9. Projected re-organisation of canteen services.
10. Beer shortage to be met by importation.
11. EFM Telegrams to be speeded up.
12. Additional ENSA parties to be provided.
13. Importation of more bands and musical instruments.
14. Supply of cinema projectors to be greatly increased.
15. Special transmitters for broadcasts to the troops to be installed, and more receiving sets to be imported.

16. Additional personnel required for philanthropic and voluntary bodies.
17. Importation of electrical plant and fittings, and fly-proof netting.
18. More trained British cooks to be supplied to hospitals.
19. Many more doctors, trained nurses and VAD's to be sent out from the UK.

Item fifteen, above, is a summary of paragraphs 53-55 of the report. The following is the complete text of those paragraphs:

> Wireless and broadcasting.
>
> 53. Good broadcast programmes are of great importance as entertainment and as a means of sustaining morale. Four programmes are available for troops in India:-
>
> 1. The General Forces Programme of the BBC I am informed that this cannot be heard everywhere, except on the best sets.
> 2. The ordinary programme of All-India Radio. This contains only a small proportion of items designed for European tastes, and while it meets the needs of Indian troops it is not listened to by British troops.
> 3. A special Forces programme arranged by GHQ (India) and radiated by All-India Radio, who are however only able, owing to their many commitments, to allot 30 hours of airtime a week to this service.
> 4. In some centres, programmes radiated by small low power stations put up by the Americans to serve their own troops.
>
> 54. In my opinion, the programmes available are not sufficient to meet requirements. For the reasons given above, the BBC and A-IR broadcasts do not provide adequate programmes throughout the hours that troops want to listen. The position can only be improved by the provision of more programmes, produced and radiated in India, especially for British troops. If, as I believe the A-IR transmitters cannot be made available to a much greater extent than they are at present, additional transmitters, reserved exclusively for broadcasts to the troops would be required, and if they can be provided within a reasonable time I would recommend their installation.
>
> 55. The best programmes will however be wasted unless receiving sets are available in sufficient numbers. There is at present a very great shortage. They are not procurable in India, and it is urgently necessary that large numbers of sets be imported at the earliest moment.[11]

It is worth noting that Munster's recommendation about additional transmitters applied only if they could be provided in reasonable time. The 7.5 kW transmitter was operating from Radio SEAC, Colombo, in April, under four months after the report was published. However, this service seems to have been always intended to be a development of the experimental start already mentioned in this chapter. The Munster recommendation may have given impetus to the wish to set up a regular service.

11 WO 165 111.

As far as the main transmitter was concerned, the original target date for the Marconi 100 kW was July/August 1945, and this would probably have been considered reasonable too, although the unexpectedly early end to the war meant that all plans had to be seen in the light of that event. The transmitter finally went on the air officially on 8 May 1946, almost certainly later than Munster would have considered reasonable. There were still plenty of troops to be entertained, and most of them were itching to get back home. It is known that many of them were glad to have some radio entertainment to while away the time. They would have been surprised to know that Capt. Plugge, MP had brought the shortage of sets to the prime minister's attention in the House of Commons on 21 February 1945:

> Is my Rt. Hon. Friend aware of the great lack of radio receiving sets in the South East Asia Command, and will he take steps to send 10,000 sets out immediately for the troops there?

Plugge was supported by Mr Henderson Stewart who asked:

> Will my Rt. Hon. Friend consider evidence which I will submit to him in this matter?

Mr Churchill replied:

> Certainly I will consider any evidence. I received a report from my officer General King two or three days ago and I have carefully selected the points which seem to require attention, and I have sent them to the various ministries concerned. I hope in the near future to receive the replies, and to have action taken accordingly.[12]

Even he was not in a position to send 10,000 sets to SEAC immediately, but improvements were made in their availability. Paragraph fifty four of the Munster Report, which is quoted in full above, provides the clearest possible argument in favour of supplying additional transmitters for forces broadcasting. Members of the War Cabinet were faced with a very wide range of recommendations for welfare improvements elsewhere in the report, and it is not surprising they accepted Munster's recommendation of additional transmitters amongst all the other items. This followed directly from the decision by Churchill and Leo Amery to send Munster to the Far East to make recommendations for what he judged to be appropriate welfare improvements, and Mountbatten's reasons for supporting the idea of Munster's survey are mentioned earlier in this chapter.

However, in 1964 he wrote a greatly simplified version of how he came to acquire the 100 kW transmitter. This was included in his foreword to a book celebrating the 21st anniversary of British Forces Broadcasting. His voice was heard, using the same words, in an associated BBC radio programme. This was preceded by his account of his involvement, while in Malta, in the relay of the first Christmas message by a reigning monarch, King George V:

> When I went out in 1943 to South-East Asia as Supreme Allied Commander, I asked for a powerful Broadcast Transmitter to reach all the one and a third million men in the Command scattered over thousands of miles. I got it eventually and called it Radio S.E.A.C. It was erected in Ceylon and proved

12 HC Deb 21 February 1945 vol 408 cc794-5.

> a great success in India, Burma, and later Malaya, and all other Far Eastern countries in which we had forces.[13]

There is no reason to doubt that he made the request, and it is known that he wrote to the Director General of the BBC in October 1943. Unfortunately, it has not been possible to obtain of copy of the letter, or of any reply which would have been just as interesting. His use of the word 'it' is problematic because it implies that the transmitter he acquired in 1945 was a belated response to his request, rather than the implementation of a Munster recommendation.

He rightly claimed that he decided the station should be called Radio S.E.A.C. and he designed the phoenix emblem for S.E.A.C. with it arising from the ashes. However, his paragraph has a surprising error because it reads as though the big transmitter was called Radio S.E.A.C., whereas that name was, of course, applicable to the whole organisation, including the studios, record presenters and engineers and the whole transmitting station which included several other transmitters.

He called it Radio S.E.A.C., but in general usage the name became Radio SEAC, and is so described in this volume, except where quoting from another source.

13 Pedrick, *Battledress Broadcasters*, foreword.

6

Planning the Station

The Munster Report said that additional transmitters reserved exclusively for broadcasts to the troops would be required. This suggests that more than one was envisaged, but beyond that Munster left it for the experts to decide how many and of what type.

A message about the requirements went from the Director of Signals at the War Office to the Chief Signals Officer (SACSEA) on 7 November 1944, about six weeks before Parliament was told about the Munster report. Clearly the matter was being dealt with very urgently:

> I have been approached by Director Army Welfare Services recently on question of Army Entertainment Broadcasting for troops in Far East. The technical aspect will inevitably fall to Signals, and I have agreed that we shall be responsible for erection, technical management and maintenance of any such broadcast equipment. In recent meetings in this country at which reps from BBC and MOI [Ministry of Information] were present it has been suggested that from technical and personnel points of view the most economical solution to the problem would be to install one 100 kW short wave transmitter in Ceylon. This would provide coverage for all troops with minimum technical and programme staff, and as such is preferable to the alternative solution of a number of 1 kW medium wave semi-mobile stations. There is a possibility of obtaining either a United States GEC 100 kW or a British Marconi 100 kW short wave transmitter. The Marconi set is said to be more reliable and since British is of course preferable.
>
> I have asked DAWS to obtain the necessary financial sanction for the complete station, inclusive [of] generators and aerial gear. Estimate approximately £100,000 total.
>
> Before I can take definite procurement action may I have your views on the plan and comments on the following. I regret they cannot be more specific at present.
>
> 1. Estimated Signals technical personnel required for installation and technical operation and maintenance is 2 officers and 50 other ranks.
> 2. I will select specialists required.
> 3. Is there a suitable site and building for such a station in Ceylon? Transmitter building must be two storied.
> 4. What RE Works assistance in building plumbing ventilation power engineering would be forthcoming to assist signals in installation?

5. Target date for the transmitter to be on the air would be July or August 1945. The Marconi set would probably be available for shipment February 1945.
6. We would ship complete with generators for 24 hours service and aerial and studio gear. Political aspects of this project being taken up separately by Ministries concerned with C in C and Government of Ceylon.[1]

It seems to have been assumed that the station would be in Ceylon. Munster had recommended 'more programmes, produced and radiated in India'. In a message dated 14 December, reproduced later in this chapter, the question 'Delhi or Colombo?' appears to be a very live issue.

The meeting between representatives of the War Office, BBC, and Ministry of Information was dealt with previously. In the decision to be taken, the BBC was not only a very interested party, but the only one which could speak with authority on broadcast radio engineering. As mentioned there, the choice was between a number of low-powered medium wave stations, or a single high-powered short wave station. The latter was chosen for the reasons given.

The cost estimate of £100,000 was a suspiciously round figure, which suggests 'back of an envelope' costing. It proved to be a serious under-estimate.

Progress in implementing the accepted Munster recommendations was monitored by the War Cabinet. The first of a series of meetings on the subject of 'Morale and Welfare in the Far East' took place on 3 November 1944. A report to the prime minister had been prepared by the service ministers and the Secretary of State for India on the measures recommended for the improvement of the morale of the men serving in the Far East Theatre.

A number of subjects were discussed, including doctors and nurses, air transport and mails, accommodation and amenities in leave centres and static camps, and, last but not least, beer. The report called for the support of the prime minister in the following terms:

> Steady progress has been made ... but we feel that ... nothing short of a whole-hearted drive, with your full backing, will serve to produce appreciable results in time to be of value.

The report provided a list of subjects needing attention, which included cinema and wireless, in general terms. A comprehensive schedule was drawn up, which had columns with these headings:

1. The recommendation from the Munster report.
2. The government department primarily responsible.
3. The action proceeding.
4. Remarks.

For broadcasting, item seventeen, the data under those headings was:

1. Special transmitters for broadcasts to Service Men to be installed, and more receiving sets to be imported.
2. War Office / Ministry of Supply.
3. Action: One 100kW transmitter and one 7.5 kW transmitter have been obtained by the War Office, and are being shipped to Ceylon. Installation

1 WO 203 5207.

> should be completed by the autumn of 1945, and good coverage of India/SEAC and the Pacific will be afforded. BBC programmes will be relayed. Until then, All-India Radio will continue to broadcast to the troops for part of each day, and India's budget for this purpose has been approved.
>
> Production prospects for wireless receiving sets are at present rather better than at one time seemed possible. India's requirements in mains and battery sets are being finally ascertained and in the meantime some procurement action has been taken. It is hoped that full procurement action will be taken in the next 2 or 3 weeks.[2]

The person responsible for drafting this note seems to have been ready to gild the lily by reporting future events in the present tense, in particular that the transmitters were being shipped to Ceylon. As we shall see, the next report, about a month later, says the Marconi transmitter should have left by mid-March. The hope for the supply of receivers also proved to be unrealistic. The statement that All-India Radio will continue to broadcast to the troops was untrue. It was an India Command Forces Broadcasting unit that was broadcasting to the troops, using air time on an All-India Radio transmitter. This is an important distinction.

The unqualified mention of Ceylon is interesting, because the message quoted below, sent about a month later, is all about deciding whether the station should be in Delhi or Ceylon. This message, dated 14 December 1944, was from the War Office to C in C India (copy to SACSEA):

> Subject : Provision of Entertainment Broadcasting service to cover:-
>
> A. Forces under SEAC including reinforcements being held in India Command.
> B. British troops in India Command.
>
> 1. Detailed discussions have been taking place with Admiralty, Air Ministry, India and Colonial Offices, MOI and BBC, attended by CAVE-BROWN-CAVE, representative of India Command, and DUCKER representative of SEAC, during which considerable progress has been made.
>
> 2. Unanimous agreement has been reached on the following points:-
> A. Necessity of erecting special transmitters to broadcast exclusively a full entertainment service for the forces.
> B. A single service radiated from the station comprising 1 x 100KW transmitter for long distance coverage and one 7.5 kW transmitter for inner coverage will put down an adequate short wave signal throughout both commands. From this station coverage is also ensured as operations move eastwards.
> C. Broadcasting to be run on an inter-service basis and controlled by a joint command board.

2 CAB 78 – 27.

D. Programme content to be made up of 60% BBC replays, and 40% local option. Joint recommendation is now required from you as to location of the station at either (i) Ceylon or (ii) Delhi.

3. This has already been fully considered by the parties referred to in First and the following arguments advanced.

4. In favour of Ceylon:-

A. SACSEA [Mountbatten] has stated his personal wish to provide a broadcasting service for the forces under Command SEAC over which he can exercise direct control through his HQ and make personal broadcasts.

B. BBC and MOI advise Ceylon will give coverage at slightly greater signal strength over the whole area for the following reasons:-

  i. To obtain full coverage of both commands from Ceylon it is not necessary to make use of the back-beam as it would be in the case of Delhi. Therefore a directional as opposed to an Omni-Directional aerial system would be employed with the result that there is less dispersal of signal strength.
  ii. Ceylon is approximately equal distant from the outer perimeter of the area to be covered and the most distant point of SEAC is some 1000 miles further from Delhi than Ceylon. This will affect both the signal strength and the selection of frequencies.

C. One 7.5 kW transmitter has already been installed in Ceylon and is putting out a limited service.

D. Admiralty stress that Ceylon transmitter will provide best service for the Pacific fleet.

5. In favour of Delhi:-

A. Existence of an AW staff including broadcasting at Delhi under GHQ, India. This is at present responsible for the distribution of all welfare amenities for both commands and is already putting out a forces service over transmitters made available by All-India Radio.

B. SEAC's requirements can be met equally well and more appropriately from Delhi than from Ceylon.

C. Office and studio accommodation available at Delhi.

6. Weight of opinion here as at present advised is definitely in favour of Ceylon. Particular emphasis here on the technical reasons given in 4 (B) and on need for maintaining close liaison with the other Services, especially the Navy.

7. Early settlement of the question most desirable. Suggest useful to bring ROWLANDS into discussions. Grateful therefore if you will consider jointly, and signal me your joint recommendations through him.

8. As 100KW transmitter available shipment ex U Kingdom February, it is important decision should be reached earliest so that preliminary work can be started without delay. Target date for beginning of service August.

9. If recommendation in favour of Ceylon essential for SACSEA

A. To advise C in C Ceylon and Governor Ceylon in confidence of project soonest. Meantime Colonial Office will be giving a brief intimation of project to C in C.

B. To confirm that signals personnel amounting to two officers and fifty other ranks can be found within existing SEAC ceiling to operate and maintain the transmitters.

10. If recommendation in favour of Delhi, please state whether as an alternative to technical responsibility for transmitters being undertaken by Army personnel. All-India Radio could provide necessary power supply from existing resources and undertake their erection operation and maintenance and which alternative you recommend.[3]

The object of the message was clearly to persuade Auchinleck that Ceylon was the better option because the experts said so. In effect, Auchinleck was being strongly advised to dissociate himself from the views put forward by Cave-Brown-Cave, his representative in the discussions.

There are a number of points that can be made about the arguments advanced in favour of Ceylon. As stated in the message, India Command was represented by Cave-Brown-Cave who had been a pre-war BBC drama producer. He had conducted successful negotiations with All-India Radio, which had resulted in their generously providing additional air time, making four hours daily altogether, for forces broadcasting from Delhi. (Charles Eade claimed the credit for arranging – with his committee – the original one hour, from February 1944). So Cave was an experienced broadcasting man, but possibly not qualified technically, and this discussion was supposed to be about choosing the best technical solution to the problem of delivering short wave transmissions over a defined wide area. In fact, Mountbatten's preference for Ceylon (on non-technical grounds) was probably the deciding factor. The very first argument in favour of Ceylon is hardly an argument at all; it boils down to the fact that Mountbatten wanted control. Admittedly, he represented the main body of potential listeners to the station, but the audience was also to include British troops in India Command and naval personnel in the Pacific Fleet.

Two items are particularly worthy of note. Item four (A) about his control, concludes with the words 'and make personal broadcasts'. This is rather ironic, because:

> In May 1944 the Chiefs of Staff ruled out the possibility of broadcasts to the troops by the Supreme Commander on Forces Radio. Churchill came to the rescue and argued that 'in the special circumstances which prevailed in the SEAC', occasional broadcasts could be permitted provided that the text was cleared in London first.[4]

Evidence that the Chiefs of Staff took their censorship duties seriously, is provided by the following which are Mountbatten's accounts of visits to two studios on 15 February and 22 February 1945:

3 WO 203 5207.

4 Philip Ziegler, *Mountbatten — The Official Biography*, p. 256.

> At 22.00 I went to Radio SEAC studios to make a recording for a broadcast to the troops on the occasion of the fall of Mandalay, in case by any chance it fell unexpectedly in my absence! I also sent a telegram to the Chiefs of Staff saying what I proposed to broadcast.
>
> At 12.15 I made a new record at the All-India Radio studio of my Mandalay broadcast, as the Chiefs of Staff wanted some of the wording altered.[5]

So much for item four (A) as far as his wish to make personal broadcasts was concerned.

Item four (D) argues for Colombo because the Admiralty is said to have emphasised that the Ceylon transmitter would provide the best service for the Pacific Fleet. This is particularly rich. The main beam from the 100 kW was aimed at roughly the centre of the area to be serviced, and, as this was a wide area, the beam width was seventy degrees, centred on thirty six degrees east of north. To reach the main Pacific area a signal had to be sent almost due east. This was done later, using an additional 7.5 kW transmitter with a suitably beamed aerial. So the original proposal being made (100 kW and 7.5 kW) did not, in the event, cover the Admiralty's requirement.

Use of a cheap globe may provide food for thought for anyone keen enough to want to examine the Delhi option further. If the seventy degree wide beam just mentioned had been in Delhi but directed roughly south-eastwards, a remarkable coverage would have resulted. It would have serviced almost all of Burma, Singapore, Malaysia and Borneo. It would still have been necessary to provide separately for India, as was done anyway. Looking further out it would have provided excellent coverage of Australia, instead of the USA. Although it is nice to think that quite a few people in USA enjoyed Radio SEAC, surely, with the Empire in mind, it would have been preferable to have had the long range bonus of Australia, rather than USA. The beam as installed was designed to cover Japan, to provide, presumably, for the probability of our troops having to invade it (in support of US forces, of course). However, by the time the 100 kW went on the air it had been known for eight months this was not going to happen.

Paragraph ten is a strange mixture of options, which need not concern us. However, it does raise the interesting point as to whether there would have been sufficient power available locally in Delhi. If the answer had been yes, which seems possible, it would have been an argument in favour of Delhi, because it would not have been necessary to build a powerhouse. In paragraph four (C) there is a reference to a 7.5 kW transmitter putting out a limited service. This was no doubt the experimental station using the ZOJ call sign mentioned by Bernard Blakemore.

Earlier in this chapter there is an extract from the first report to the War Cabinet on the progress made with implementing Munster's recommendations. Just over a month later, the section of the next report covering radio read:

> Various components of the 100 kW are being collected at Woolwich for shipment. Marconi's are taking down the main transmitter and crating it for tropical shipment, and it should have left UK by mid-March. The necessary building work may not be ready by the time it arrives. One of the two 7.5 kW transmitters already in Ceylon will be allocated to broadcasting for the forces. Scale of receiver requirement agreed.[6]

The earliest detailed technical information found is in a message sent on 11 January 1945 from the War Office to Ceylon Army Command, and passed by them to SACSEA. It is not

5 Ziegler, *Personal Diary of Admiral The Lord Louis Mountbatten*, pp. 180 & 188.

6 CAB 78 – 27.

reproduced here because it requires a considerable amount of explanation and comment on the differences between what was stipulated and what, in the event, actually happened.

The argument over 'Delhi or Colombo' had obviously been settled, and Ceylon Army Command was given the responsibility for building the transmitter hall, the power house, and installing the equipment. This also included the high quality telephone lines linking the studios, the transmitter site, and the receiving station.

The transmitters required were the Marconi 100 kW and one or two 7.5 kW transmitters. The big set was to be shipped in about six weeks. Negotiations were in hand to obtain a Marconi 7.5 kW SWB 11 transmitter with a modulator. The set provided in the event was an RCA transmitter with the same power output. Marconi's telegraphy background was apparent in that the SWB 11 was essentially a telegraphy set, but it could also be supplied with a modulator included. This turned it into a set suitable for speech and music, as required for broadcasting. The RCA model was used in the Middle East and elsewhere for forces broadcasting or propaganda.

Six aerial towers, 325 feet high, were to be dismantled in the UK and shipped soon. These would support the aerial arrays. The message stated that an aerial array for the 100 kW transmitter was going to cover an arc from Karachi to Singapore. It must have been realised later that such a broad beam would not be feasible, and the western side of India could not be covered by the beam centred on Burma and Japan. The beam for use by the 7.5 kW set covering southern India was not very efficient, and was replaced several years later. Not all the towers were 325 feet high.

What is particularly striking is the absence of any mention of the majority of the aerial arrays actually provided, which were for use in transmissions to the UK or Australia. The beam was reversible, which made it possible to possible to broadcast to either direction. The 'Blighty beam' was used by Radio SEAC for its Sunday night transmissions. At some stage the BBC must have intervened, or the people designing the aerials must have referred to the BBC. It seems clear that the additional arrays were installed in anticipation of the station being taken over as a relay station by the BBC.

The message gave details of the power house which was to provide the power for the transmitters. It said that three 308 kW Bayliss and Morcom diesel alternators were being diverted by engineers to Ceylon. For some reason this did not happen. The marine diesels installed were by Mirlees.

The message detailed the power requirements of the various transmitters. All required three phase four wire, (i.e. three live plus one neutral.)

For the Marconi 100 kW transmitter there were to be:

One feed at 60,000 volts, 400 kW, for the high voltage supply.

One feed at 400 volts, 120 kW, for its ancillary equipment.

An estimate of the load for the 100 kW set was 320 kW average on broadcast service, 455 kW peak modulated.

For the RCA ET4750 7.5 kW transmitters there were to be three feeds at 400 volts, 32 kW.

The message also envisaged the use of a small generator for emergency lighting.[7]

If it were decided to move three SWB 11 telegraphy transmitters from the Army Chain station there was to be provision for further 400 volt feeds with a total load of 60 kW. This never happened, and it is not known why it was considered. The Army Chain transmitting

7 WO 203 5207.

station occupied a huge area not far from the broadcasting station, and provided international communications using high speed telegraphy. Much of it was secret and encoded. There is more about this station shortly.

The message stated that technical equipment for the studios and the receiving station was being obtained and would be shipped concurrently with the transmitter. This was written before the difficulties and delays arose in obtaining various kinds of equipment.

The message made it clear that it dealt only with the transmitting station, and that others would deal with the studios. This applied also to the receiving station which would be equipped with high quality receivers to provide for relays of BBC programmes. This was dealt with by housing the Radio SEAC receiving station within the high speed wireless receiving station. The studios were set up in Colombo in an existing building which required a considerable amount of conversion.

No such easy options were available for the transmitting station. The message stated that the big Marconi set needed a floor space of approximately one hundred by fifty feet, and required under-floor space of at least three feet. Outline plans were in hand and being sent out through engineer channels.

So plans for the building were in hand, but where to site it was to be a matter for the officer who needed to be appointed to be in charge. The message suggested that this might be a BBC or Marconi engineer in uniform. This did not happen, but a very senior Marconi man, not in uniform, with an assistant, supervised the installation and testing of the transmitter. BBC representatives arrived on the station much later.

An approximate establishment for the station was to be one major, two captains and forty four other ranks. Approval for this was being sought urgently in January 1945, so it would have been intended to cover the task of building the station. Many more people were needed to run it. The major proved to be Major Nutt, who is on Mountbatten's left in a photograph of the Supremo's visit. Some of the work, including the erection of the aerial towers, was undertaken by locally employed civilians, working under army supervision.

The message concluded by mentioning that the prime minister was personally interested in the project, and that it was hoped the station could be on the air in August.[8] In the event there was still a great deal to be done. A copy of the message went to the Signal Officer in Chief for action. It was at about this time we were starting our Royal Signals Radio Mechanics courses, at Catterick and elsewhere.

Files in the National Archives mention that a suitable site needed to be found. However, no record was found of the process of finding the eventual site, or of the fact that a site had been found. If there were documents it may be that the proximity of the high speed wireless station resulted in the papers remaining secret. A friend who served in that unit provided a copy of a press release by Reuters in December 1945 which described a visit to their establishment, and gave a brief account of the great importance of what they did. Essentially, they were part of the Army Chain which provided communication between the various headquarters in places such as Kandy, Delhi, and Singapore, and with the War Office in London.

The technical background to this was that short wave radio, using directional aerials, enabled Morse code messages to be sent reliably across thousands of miles. It so happened that the rhombic aerials, which were considered to be the most suitable for various reasons, had a layout that took up a great deal of space on the ground. They were used for both transmitting and receiving. As a result, the receiving station site occupied about 700 acres and the

8 Ibid.

transmitting station about 500 acres. The Reuters report described the areas as having been carved out of the jungle. Needless to say a major clearance had also been needed for Radio SEAC's transmitting station and its aerials, although these were of a completely different design. The expression 'high speed wireless' referred to that fact that hand operated Morse keys were supplemented with equipment that enabled the message (encrypted when necessary), to be put on paper tape. The tape was fed into a machine which provided the input to the transmitter at high speed, thus enabling each link to carry much more traffic than would otherwise have been the case. As the Reuters report made clear, traffic was very heavy at times, and speed and accuracy were of the highest importance. This was explained in more detail in a book published in 2003 which includes histories of units of the Royal Corps of Signals.[9] The command structure changed from time to time, and the unit's name was also subject to several changes. For present purposes 'Ceylon high speed wireless Company' seems as good as any. As we shall see in the next chapter, Radio SEAC's first transmitter (an RCA 7.5 kW set) was installed in the high speed wireless transmitter hall at Ekala which housed Marconi 10 kW sets. Their receivers were at Hora Hena, about twelve miles away.

It is standard practice to have receiving stations several miles away from the transmitters because the powerful signals from the transmitters are liable to break through the tuning circuits in the receivers, and interfere with the signal the receiver is tuned to.

The Reuters piece described the living conditions for the men working on the station, which, as might be expected, were not unlike those we enjoyed, although flower beds were mentioned, and I do not recall any such amenities on our site.

9 Cliff Lord and Graham Watson, *The Royal Corps of Signals, Unit Histories of the Corps (1920-2001) and its Antecedents,* Helion and Company Limited, Solihull, 2003.

7

Building the Station

As mentioned previously, the War Cabinet regularly reviewed the progress being made in the implementation of Munster's welfare proposals. Broadcasting was just one item in a long schedule which included shortages of doctors and nurses, entertainment and beer.[1]

The welfare branch of the War Office had overall control of forces broadcasting, and the transmitters at Ekala were, from the outset, described as an Army Welfare Broadcasting Station. That branch of the War Office therefore compiled monthly reports about forces broadcasting stations, particularly those in the Middle East and SEAC.[2] Further down the chain of command, SACSEA had a welfare committee, but the committee which monitored progress with Radio SEAC was the I & CA Committee (Information and Civil Affairs). This was Joubert's territory, but Mountbatten usually attended the meetings, and occasionally issued directives on matters which arose. Planning of the station continued during January 1945. As it was obvious it would be many months before the installation of the 100 kW could be completed, it was decided that a lower-powered service should be provided as soon as possible.

On 20 January, a message from the War Office to SACSEA sought confirmation that 'one or two existing transmitters (Colombo and ex-Bombay) will be devoted entirely to forces broadcasting, thus forming half of proposed new station.'[3] A strange idea of a half, but let us not quibble. A report, dated 8 February, said that the 7.5 kW set had arrived in Ceylon from Bombay.[4] The reason why they wanted confirmation that it would be for forces broadcasting *only* was probably because Joubert might have wanted to use it for another of his responsibilities, the Psychological Warfare Division which later became the Political Warfare Division. After the Japanese surrender, one of its functions was stated to be the provision or control of the supply of news to the Japanese before their return to Japan, with a view to their indoctrination.[5]

The War Office message went on to indicate that the 100 kW transmitter and other stores would be ready for dispatch monthly as from February. The Ceylon authorities were consulted about the installation of a large broadcasting station on their territory, but no record has been found of their response.

Although fuller details will be given at a later point, this may be a suitable point at which to say something about the size and general nature of the three types of transmitter used, which

1 CAB 78 – 27.
2 WO 165 111.
3 WO 203 5207.
4 WO 203 4410.
5 Ibid.

could reasonably be identified as small, medium, and large. In this context the RCA 1.5 kW set would be small, and is similar in size and shape to a good-sized bedroom wardrobe. It was complete in its grey box, and just needed to be plugged into the power supply, connected to an aerial system, and supplied with programme input. Unfortunately there is no photograph of it.

The medium transmitter (of which ultimately there were several) was an RCA 7.5 kW set. As may be seen in Figure 7.1, it occupied the space of a modest suburban sitting room, and consisted of several panels to which most of the components were attached. This assembly was bolted together, but some other large components were fixed to the concrete floor. You could walk into the area, although there was an interlock so that the current was switched off if the door was opened. It had a contemporary art deco front, and so looked more stylish than the 100 kW, but it should be noted that our 100 kW set was said to be a utility version. In our installation the sides of the RCA sets were a sort of wire cage, but it seems likely there would usually have been walls or substantial partitions. It could not be plugged into the power in the usual way because it required a three phase power supply, but apart from this all it needed was an aerial, and programme input. So this transmitter was fairly easy to take apart and put together (given the right skills) and it could probably have been carried to a new location in an ordinary removal van. Norman Shires recalled that the instructions for assembly were very good.

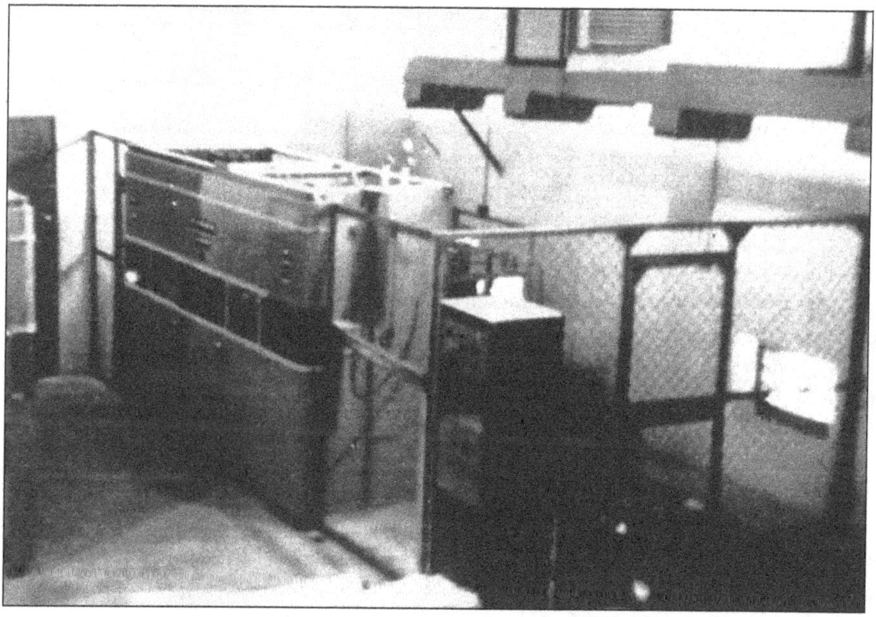

Figure 7.1 The first RCA 7.5 kW transmitter. (C)

In terms of power output, the medium set was five times as big as the small one, but the large transmitter was thirteen times as powerful as the medium one, and the task of transporting and installing it was of a completely different order. Its several power requirements included an 11,000 volts DC supply which was provided through a mercury arc rectifier, which occupied about the same amount of space as the whole of the medium sized transmitter. So when speaking of the 100 kW transmitter one might be talking about the radio part, made by Marconi, or the whole assembly including water pumps, rotary converter, mercury arc rectifier and so on. The distinction was very significant when reading a report that the transmitter had been crated up and shipped by Marconi. That was very good news, but not so good when one realized later that essential items such as the mercury arc rectifier were not included, and were to come from a different manufacturer. It was months before it arrived, with a second one as back-up.

In view of developments over the last half century, it is worth putting the 'large' category into perspective. 100 kW was about as large as short wave transmitters came in 1945, although there were exceptions, no doubt. One is tempted to add 'very large' and 'absolutely huge' to the choice now available to broadcasting stations. A few hundred kilowatts is no longer exceptional, and any broadcasting station absolutely determined to make its voice heard would probably do well to think about a megawatt or so. Although important improvements in efficiency in converting 50 Hz power to radio frequency power have been made, such users need to be prepared for very large electricity bills. Better still, they could have an oil well at their disposal, and it may not be entirely co-incidental that some of the states with these transmitters are oil producers.

The reality in 1945 was that it had been decided to open the station using the first RCA 7.5 kW transmitter. The minutes of the I & CA meeting of 7 February 1945 included the following:

> Col. Ducker reported that the 7.5 kW transmitter would probably be in operation before April 1st, and that considerable assistance had been given by the US Signal Battalion in its installation. The equipment to be supplied from the US Armed Forces Radio was now available, under the stipulation by General Wheeler that the station would be separate and distinct. It was now hoped the 100 watt [sic] transmitter would be in operation shortly after September.

The only comment that can be made about General Wheeler's proviso is that it seems to have been completely ignored. Perhaps the Supremo used his well-known charm to talk him out of it. On 6 February 1945, a message was sent by the War Office to SACSEA giving approval for the project to proceed. The second point read:

> A representative of Marconi's accompanied by a signals officer [will be] visiting you shortly as WD consultant. After consultation with Marconi representative you should submit full details and conditions necessary for completion for agreement to be made by War Office with Marconi.

There were other minor points. The Marconi man was Mr Caspard, and he had Major Nutt, (Royal Signals) with him. Army troop movements went through C in C Delhi, so a message was sent there by the War Office on 22 February, copied to SACSEA, which read:

> Unit allotted to operate 100 kW Army Welfare Station is AW Broadcasting Unit sailing KMF 41.

After other details it continued:

> Recce party consisting of OC SEC and Marconi engineer proceeding by air to Ceylon, ETD 23 February.[6]

Hopes were high, to judge by a report dated 8 February, which expected that the main transmitter would have left by mid-March. Its arrival in Ceylon was expected to synchronise

6 WO 203 5297.

with the completion of the necessary building works there. Sadly, it did not work out quite like that.

Later in the month, a message went to SACSEA which included the directive that construction was to be as economical as possible consistent with the requirements of an efficient broadcasting service. The earlier War Office hope that Marconi's would erect the aerial towers was dashed, but the WD consultant was said to be prepared to supervise the erection of the steel towers.[7] In the event Marconi's representatives did supervise.

Neither tower nor mast gives the right impression to someone who has not seen these structures at close quarters. The impression, from a distance, is of something quite slender, as shown in Figure 7.2, but Figure 7.3 is a close shot which shows what massive structures they were. Erecting anything 300 feet high seems likely to require considerable expertise. It may be wondered why the towers had to be so high. This is because they had to support the complex aerial arrays that had to be high because the station's audience was many hundreds of miles away.

Figure 7.2 The transmitter hall and two aerial towers. (C)

It will be remembered that the BBC was involved in the initial discussions about the station, and the decision to use a 100 kW short wave transmitter. Obviously the BBC had a legitimate interest in the activities of the station, insofar as it was directing programmes to the same parts of the world, albeit aimed at different audiences. From time to time, then, the Corporation tried to ensure it had some influence in the overall direction Radio SEAC was taking, and in its ultimate destiny. In late February 1945, the BBC indicated a wish to send a liaison officer, but a message went from SACSEA to the War Office turning down the idea. A few days later it was learnt that the BBC had agreed that the liaison representative was not necessary until the 100 kW came into operation.[8] From then on, of course, Radio SEAC was going to be providing many of its listeners with a stronger and more reliable signal than the BBC could.

7 Ibid.
8 Ibid.

Figure 7.3 The lower part of an aerial tower. (C)

On 19 March a message (from SACSEA to the War Office) mentioned that the Marconi engineer, Mr Caspard, and Major Nutt had returned to the UK after their reconnaissance.[9] Apparently, they had looked at the studios and did not like what they saw. It is true that the studios were rather primitive at that stage, but it is difficult to say whether that need have worried the engineers. If the audio signal quality from the studio was not good it would obviously have affected the quality of the signal being transmitted. The fact that one studio was probably still in the state of being a converted wash room need not, of itself, have had a detrimental effect on the quality of the output. An ordinary domestic room can be turned into a satisfactory studio, by using old carpets, blankets and sacking, to deaden the acoustic.

The response to their concern was to say, in effect, that it would have to do in the circumstances. In the War Office files there is a report during April 1945 that the 100 kW was ex-Marconi works. This meant, of course, that everything Marconi were supplying had left them.

Regular reports to the War Cabinet on the implementation of improvements to welfare provision continued, and one dated 24 April 1945 noted that about a third of the 100 kW had left England, and that building in Ceylon had started on 7 April. It was estimated four to five months would be needed to complete the building and that it would then take three months or more to install the transmitter. There was therefore no hope that it could be operational before December. Representatives of Royal Signals and the contractors had flown to Ceylon to expedite, but it was unlikely that would improve on the December target date. However the 7.5 kW transmitter had started a service from 15 April 1945.[10] (Actually ten days later).

This very concise report contained the bare facts which are all that is needed to explain why installing the 100 kW transmitter was such a big undertaking. The possible misunderstanding of what might be meant by the 100 kW transmitter has already been mentioned. This chapter is mainly concerned with the difficulties in arranging for the delivery of so many large pieces of equipment from several manufacturers to a site thousands of miles away.

A message from C in C India to DSR SACSEA, on 15 April said that the Secretary of State for India had informed them that the 100 kW transmitter would not be available to

9 Ibid.
10 CAB 78 – 27.

operate before 1 December 1945. It went on to suggest that All-India Radio should be asked to give extra time. Cave would be visiting Ceylon about the end of April.[11]

Having lost the argument about the location of Radio SEAC, Cave, and the others who had started the broadcasts from Delhi, may not have been too saddened to hear that the project was subject to embarrassing delays. It seems likely they would have been happier to see a steady development of the service they had started in India. Further embarrassment came with the announcement in the *SEAC* newspaper of the opening of the station, which was said to be for SEAC. This wrong impression had to be corrected at the earliest opportunity. Radio SEAC was intended to serve India as well as SEAC, a sensitive point with India Command, as mentioned earlier. Probably by chance, the eighth I & CA meeting was on 25 April 1945, and the minutes include the following:

> It was reported that Radio SEAC would be going on the air that evening. In connection with this Sir Philip pointed out that the Prime Minister had mentioned in a recent address in parliament that the high-powered station for Radio SEAC was now well under way. The fact was that there had been several delays in constructing this high-powered station, and on the present form, the Engineer-in-Chief did not expect that the project would be completed earlier than 1 December.
>
> The impression of the Prime Minister and other authorities in London would have to be corrected. When it was discovered that the information might have been obtained from General King, the Supreme Allied Commander said that a letter should be prepared to the former immediately.[12]

In fact the panic was not necessary because the Cabinet Office knew there was no chance that the big transmitter would be operational before 1 December 1945.

General King had been sent to the Far East by Churchill to ensure that those Munster recommendations which had been approved were carried out with a minimum of delay. At one stage King had suggested the job was finished, and he would like to come home. Churchill told him he should carry on with it.

It was mentioned earlier in this chapter, that, to avoid the long delay in waiting for the 100 kW set to be operational, it had been decided, by February 1945, that Radio SEAC would open a regular service in April, using a 7.5 kW transmitter. This raised the question as to where the transmitter was installed, because construction of the Radio SEAC transmitter hall had not begun. High speed wireless colleagues have confirmed it was in their transmitter hall when the station began official testing, and then went on the air.

The high speed wireless transmission site (about 500 acres) was next to the Radio SEAC site. Nevertheless the men on the former site were close enough to receive Radio SEAC by clipping a pair of headphones to the wires holding up the mosquito nets over their beds.

Norman Shires had very good reason to remember this first 7.5 kW transmitter. He was doing assembly work, inside it, with his back against the six thousand volt line, when somebody switched it on. The electric shock put him in an RAF hospital for three weeks. Norman remembers the person concerned as a second lieutenant who had been a dentist in civilian life, but he did not recall his name. On return from hospital, Norman was posted to 32 M Section, which was en route to Singapore, and believes this was done to avoid the need for a court of enquiry.

11 WO 203 5207
12 Ibid.

Norman was present, of course, when the US Signals personnel were providing what was described earlier as considerable assistance. He remembers twelve sergeants who had been sent there to be instructed on the British method of erecting three-section tubular aerial masts. Not much benefit seems to have been derived, on either side, but Norman's unit was able to draw a spirit ration for 12 sergeants. They did not know what they were entitled to, so they received less attractive drinks, while Norman's friends were able to enjoy an occasional Gordon's gin, or a decent scotch. Quite apart from this, he found the Americans to be a hell of a crew who brought a welcome change to their quiet life among the cinnamon shrubs and coconut trees. He had no recollection of their having given any assistance with the installation of the transmitter.

Obviously the intention was to use it throughout the initial period of testing, and on the day the station opened officially. Nothing in the SACSEA documentation suggests this is not what happened. However, the War Office report for April 1945 indicated that on the evening of 24 April the transmitter went out of action due to the breakdown of the modulation transformer and spare.[13] In view of the advance publicity given, the service opened on 25 April using another transmitter.

Our very limited knowledge of the high speed wireless equipment suggested that one of their Marconi sets would have been about the same power, but they did not have amplitude modulation, (an optional extra for these telegraphy sets). It seems most likely that the transmitter used was a BC610 running about 500 watts. Apparently there were two or three of these sets there at the time, and Norman remembers there had been some impromptu (and probably unauthorised) use of these while the 7.5 kW RCA set was being installed. Obviously this was a rather poor substitute for 7.5 kW, which in itself was a temporary solution while the 100 kW was awaited. The BC610 did not have to plug the gap for too long, however. The War Office report for May said reception of the 7.5 kW set was excellent in Burma and Rangoon.[14]

A message from Mountbatten was broadcast to mark the formal opening of Radio SEAC. The text of this has not been found, but in the message from him, broadcast when the 100 kW started transmitting normal programmes on 8 May 1946, he referred back to what he had said. It seems likely he recorded his opening remarks for the 7.5 kW service on the 29 March 1945. His diary at around this time records the numerous celebrations and other meetings he was attending, and he described one in Colombo on that date as follows:

> At 13.30 I went to Queen's House where I got involved with a colossal lunch party which the Governor and Lady Moore were giving for all the Red Cross and St. John lady workers in Colombo. However, I was able to slip out before the end of lunch as I had to go and make a record at the Colombo Broadcasting Station after which Nick collected me again as we went to visit HMS *Mayina*, the Naval Transit Camp.[15]

Nick was rather more than a chauffeur, and better known as Rear Admiral Nicholson, Flag Officer, Ceylon. Although this was nearly a month before Radio SEAC opened officially, it was probably sensible to take advantage of an occasion when it was planned for Mountbatten to be in Colombo, because he was continually traveling huge distances throughout

13 WO 165 111

14 Ibid.

15 Ziegler, *Personal Diary of Admiral The Lord Louis Mountbatten*, p. 197.

the vast area under his command attending meetings and parades. His heavy responsibilities were not only military but political as well.

After a brief glimpse of high society it is necessary to return to the problems faced by those were trying to build a radio station. When it was found that the aerial towers needed to complete the station did not start to arrive until the summer of 1945, it raised the question of what sort of aerial was used when the station opened, and for months afterwards. Height is very important to provide an efficient beamed array for broadcasting. Norman was able to provide the answer. The best available masts were one hundred feet high, and four of these were used, in a square, to support a dipole and reflector. Somebody in the Radio SEAC group had the idea of suspending the active elements in such a way that the direction of transmission could be varied, within limits. The idea was to follow the movement of troops down through Burma.

Use was made of the ability to change the direction of the transmissions. The Japanese surrendered to the American General MacArthur in Tokyo on 2 September, 1945. A ceremony marking the surrender of Japanese forces to South East Asia Command took place in Singapore on 12 September. A report with that date stated that beaming of the 7.5 kW set had been changed to give good coverage to Singapore. It added that unfortunately this meant that listeners in certain parts of India would now be dependent on All-India Radio until the 100 kW became operational.[16] No doubt this was intended to refer to the forces broadcasts from Delhi which had to use air time on an All-India Radio transmitter.

On 18 September 1945, a message was sent asking for the following to be inserted without delay in the Singapore edition of the newspaper:

> Radio SEAC, one of the most powerful forces radio stations in the world, has begun beaming its programmes to Singapore and the occupational areas in South East Asia. War prisoners in Malaya, Thailand, and Sumatra can now while away the hours before repatriation with Jack Benny, Bob Hope, Tommy Handley, Dinah Shore, and a host of other top-line British and American radio stars.

The message went on to say that transmission was on 19 metres from 11.30 am to 1 pm, and 2.30 to 7 pm, and from 7.30 to 10 pm, (Indian Standard Time) on 25 metres. The programme could also be heard in Burma, Ceylon (on 88.3 m), India, and in certain parts of Australia.[17]

It must have reached Australia by some quirk of radio propagation. The reference to its being one of the most powerful forces radio stations in the world was wrong, and would continue to be so for the next seven months, until the 100 kW transmitter went into service.

The following reception reports confirmed that some people, over a wide area were getting good reception, but such information is almost useless unless details of the receivers used are included. It is more than likely the following results would not have been the same if welfare sets had been used. As senior officers were involved it is not unreasonable to suggest that high quality communications receivers were used. The report, in September 1945, signed by someone on behalf of the Chief Signals Officer, mentioned a new aerial directed to Malaya:

16 WO 163 260.

17 WO 203 5207.

> Singapore - Received over the period 11.00 to 22.00 hours. Reception perfect on both frequencies.
>
> Kuala Lumpur - First reports indicate reception first class. Further reports awaited.
>
> Rangoon - 19m. reception good. 25m. reception good, but atmospheric interference and interference from All-India Radio were observed.[18]

Having established where the first transmitter was, and what aerial was used, there remained the mystery of how the programmes got from the studios to the transmitter. The lines linking the studios in Colombo with Ekala and on to Hora Hena were not completed until November 1945. Norman pointed out there were already lines between Hora Hena and Ekala (the receiving and transmitting sites of their unit), and these were also able to carry the relay of the BBC programmes from Hora Hena to Ekala. He had been briefed by a Royal Engineers NCO about the general scope of the arrangements for Radio SEAC. The use of the lines just mentioned was part of that brief, from which Norman gathered that control of programme content was to be at Hora Hena (the receiving station).

We know, of course, that work was in progress completing the studios in Turret Road, Colombo, and that people were devising and writing radio programmes there from late 1944 onwards. The only reason why programmes did not go from Colombo to Ekala, assuming they did not, would have been the absence of suitable lines.

It is worth looking at the programme content as set out in a War Office report in June 1945:

British recorded material, from the Overseas Recording Broadcasting Service	30%
American Armed Forces Radio Service Recordings	30%
BBC Relays	20%
Local production, (mainly DJ type programmes)	20%[19]

This mix changed later, but on the face of it, at that stage, only about 20% of the programmes needed even the most rudimentary studio. So a very basic studio could have been set up at Hora Hena, to which a handful of people could have gone each day from Colombo (in army transport). The studio would have needed a turntable, sound mixer and a microphone. A suitable turntable would also have been needed to play some of the special discs. This equipment could have been installed in a vehicle such as the van which was fitted out as an outside broadcast unit at some stage.

Less likely, perhaps, is the possibility that a radio link was used. Hora Hena was only about thirty miles from Colombo on a coastal plain. There were existing lines between Hora Hena and Ekala, used by the high speed wireless unit, so there would have been no difficulty as far as that connection was concerned.

At the ninth I & CA meeting on 23 May 1945, as we were nearing the end of our Radio Mechanics' courses, it was said that the 100 kW set was expected to be ready by 25 December.[20] Happily for us there were further delays, so we had Christmas 1945 at home.

18 WO 203 4410.

19 WO 165 111.

20 WO 203 5207.

A War Office report, in the same month, said that the RCA AR88 sets for receiving the BBC programmes for relay had been shipped. It also mentioned that Major Nutt was expected to arrive in Ceylon on 17 May. He was to be responsible for the installation and operation of the station, and would remain in Ceylon and act as liaison officer with the War Office. He was said to be taking all the War Office drawings essential for the buildings.[21]

A report to the War Cabinet mentioned above said that building started on 7 April, which suggests that building started without the plans, but outline plans had been sent much earlier via 'engineer channels' as mentioned in the previous chapter. The War Office report for May also said the first fifty cases containing the 100 kW transmitter had arrived in Ceylon, and the whole transmitter should be there by the end of August. Reference has already been made to the uncertainties entailed in expressions such as 'the whole transmitter'. Clearly, the building work had to be sufficiently far advanced to provide proper shelter before any transmitting equipment could be installed. The building work, which was the responsibility of Staff Sgt. Tom Cheetham, RE, could begin only when the site had been cleared of palm trees. Apart from what was to become the officers' bungalow, there were no living quarters for those building the station, so all personnel were accommodated at the high speed wireless station, Ja'ella, about a mile away.

Major Nutt had a week or two to settle in before the arrival of the Marconi engineer, Mr Jasper Caspard, who left England, with his wife, on 1 June 1945. At some stage he was joined by a trainee, John Sidebotham, who seems to have been paid little or nothing, but was there to gain experience. Whether he enjoyed the experience seems more doubtful, as Caspard found it necessary frequently to draw his attention to his shortcomings. Bill Reis, an AQMS in the REME, remembers John and these incidents well. We all remember John as being a man of extremely slender proportion, even skinny, but when Bill saw him again, twenty five years later, at Marconi, his frame was more than adequately covered.

Bill Reis recalls that once the building was sufficiently complete for installation of the transmitter to begin in earnest, there was always plenty to do. When considering the dates of various parts being completed (as obtained from War Office files) some of these seemed to be earlier than he would have thought. It may be that some optimistic anticipation took place when reports were compiled. However, there was a short period before it was possible to make any real progress because the building was not ready. At about this time he and others were flown to Delhi so that they could see an operational SWB18 transmitter at All-India Radio. He particularly remembers the large carved wooden sign bearing the words 'SUPREME ALLIED COMMANDER SOUTH EAST ASIA' above the entrance to what had been Mountbatten's headquarters before the move to Kandy. There was still an office which was described as a Rear HQ, which was probably for communication purposes, particularly with India Command HQ.

The packing cases containing the elements of the 100 kW transmitter were brought from the docks in Colombo on huge heavy lorries driven by Italians who may have been prisoners of war. The lorries were very wide, which made progress difficult along the relatively narrow roads that were often used by bullock carts, which had to make way for the lorries. This was a separate operation from the more routine transport tasks for which Sgt. Sam Beards was responsible, and which were carried out with the usual 3 ton and 15 cwt. lorries and a motorbike.

Opening the packing cases was a huge, exhausting, and time-consuming task, so everyone available had to assist. Some of the containers were very heavy indeed, and a crane

21 WO 165 111.

Figure 7.4 The station under construction.

was needed to lift them into the transmitter hall. The crane appears in the photograph of the station under construction, figure 7.4. On one occasion the jib was at too low an angle and nearly tipped over. It is interesting to note that this crane, on caterpillar tracks, took three days to travel to Ekala from the ordnance depot in Colombo. It was often necessary to man-handle equipment into position, and this frequently meant moving cases along the ground over steel pipes used as rollers.

Because one never knew how difficult it might be to obtain some small item, Bill gave strict instructions to his staff never to throw anything away. Any screw, nail or other item might come in handy when spares were so difficult to obtain.

The transmitting hall was essentially a single storey building. However, the floor was three or four feet above ground level, so there were steps leading up to the entrances to the building. The under-floor space was needed to run cables of many kinds between ancillary equipment and the transmitter itself, and between its several stages.

Installing those cables was a very uncomfortable job, because of the lack of head-room. In the conditions of high temperature and humidity always present, a pair of shorts was as much as anyone would want to wear. However, bodies were frequently moving beneath rough concrete beams, which meant that they were littered with sticking plaster. Fortunately, it was only on one occasion that one of these 'cables' was seen to move under its own volition. This was a snake, of course, and the cramped conditions did not permit of a swift retreat. Nobody knew whether the snake was dangerous, so there was great relief when it decided to retreat.

A War Office report included bad news about the aerial towers. Before they could be sent to Ceylon they had to be dismantled on the Isle of Man. (The six masts were up to 325 feet high). The work was behind schedule, and Marconi had been authorised to sub-contract the dismantling of two of the masts to a civilian firm. The report anticipated that this would allow sufficient time for the two masts on which the station would initially be operated to be erected by the target date.[22] Fortunately, in the event, all the masts were available when the 100 kW went live. A later War Office report dated 12 June, gave the reasons why the dismantling was behind schedule. It was said to be due to weather, lack of labour, and corroded bolts, which covered just about everything.[23]

Although masts is the term used quite often, they are more correctly described as towers, since they are constructed as such. They were not ready made and hauled up into position as on a yacht, but built up from the ground, piece by piece, the pieces being bolted together. Each tower rested on a two inch diameter ball bearing on a mounting set into a very large concrete block. The iron strips can be seen on photographs as a 'criss-cross' pattern.

At the next meeting of the I & CA committee, on 6 June, Joubert said that preliminary reports showed that Radio SEAC was putting down a strong signal. He understood that the station was being heard by the Pacific Fleet. It was hoped to commence testing the 1.5 kW (transmitter) on about 11 June. [24]

The phrase 'strong signal' hardly qualifies as a reception report. The service was not intended for the Pacific Fleet, although it was obviously good to know that it was reaching them, and Mountbatten will have been pleased. I think the navy 'listened to the wireless' via a number of loudspeakers in various parts of the ship. This network would have been fed by an amplifier, which in turn would have been fed by a communications receiver with an efficient aerial. Such an arrangement would have made the best of any signal available.

The 1.5 kW transmitter, mentioned in the minutes, was described earlier in this chapter. It operated on 88 metres, and produced a good local signal in Colombo, and quite a lot further afield in Ceylon. A War Office report said it was on loan from the RAF, and was intended to improve local service until the 100 kW was live. This is difficult to understand because the need for the local service continued after the 100 kW went live, as the big set was never intended to provide a local service.

The outlook for the largest transmitter was more worrying, as the minutes make clear:

> Sir Philip Joubert said the situation regarding the 100kW station was very unsatisfactory, and that the War Office were being very slow in this matter. He was taking back to London a brief from the Engineer-in-Chief and he thought it might be necessary to bring this matter to the attention of the Prime Minister.[25]

There is no way of knowing whether the War Office was being slow. It seems more likely the various suppliers were dealing with their orders in accordance with their own priorities.

The RCA AR88 receivers arrived in June 1945. Prior to that it seems likely the RC67 receivers in the high speed wireless unit will have been used. They also operated in diversity.

The next report to the War Cabinet, dated 26 June 1945, warned that the December deadline might not be met, and referred to the 100 kW as part shipped and part on route.[26] This neatly avoided the third part which was part nowhere. There was a welcome reversal of an earlier decision, and Marconi were lending skilled workmen to erect masts. Suitable skills are obviously needed when erecting something 300 feet high.

---

22 Ibid.
23 Ibid.
24 WO 203 5207.
25 Ibid.
26 CAB 78 – 27.

This was followed by another reception report which indicated that the 7.5 kW transmissions were very successful. Reception was said to be good at a radius of 900-1750 miles, which included Burma and Rangoon.

This may have been a summary of a report which indicated that reception had been good at Chugking, Rangoon, Calcutta, Jubbalpore, Delhi, Barrackpore, Vizag, and Secunderabad. Ranchi had apparently had good reception in the day and poor at night.[27] This implies a very wide beam, to say the least, and it would be surprising if Ranchi was the only place where reception was poor at night. Some of the other sources from which the report was compiled may have taken less trouble with their reports, or may have been using excellent sets well installed with good aerials.

The report for the Cabinet mentioned the importance of the transmitter to the Pacific Fleet. Two points arise from this. The Pacific Fleet was not part of SEAC, but it would be churlish to suggest they should have been left without radio entertainment. More to the point, when the 100 kW finally went on the air it was on a broad beam centred on thirty six degrees east of north, providing coverage of Burma, China and Japan. The further 7.5 kW transmitter that was eventually installed used an aerial system directed eighty degrees east of north, so almost due east. This was essential to provide a good signal for SEAC headquarters in Singapore, but should also have provided good reception for the Pacific Fleet.

The War Office file has a note in July 1945 that the first mast had been shipped and the second was due to go on the 5 August. The power house switchboard was expected to be ready for dispatch by mid-August. They were trying to get the four or five makers concerned to improve on that date. The start of the 1.5 kW local service on 23 July 1945 was noted, and the supply of receivers was also under continual review.[28]

The War Office monthly report for August confirmed that the switchboard had been shipped on 11 August, but mentioned that certain instruments that were not ready would be flown out later. Transformers, presumably also for the power house, were on the same ship. The second mast was shipped the same day. Two Marconi men were flown out on the 23 August to erect the masts. A third was ill and would follow. It was suggested that attempts should be made locally to obtain substitutes for the three erectors who had declined to go out by air.[29] (There are comments later about how impressive the men recruited locally were).

At around this time there is something of a gap in the SACSEA documentation. This may have been due, in part, to Joubert's return to the UK for consultations, from which he was never to return. His autobiography mentions going into hospital shortly after reaching England, and notes his final retirement in October 1945.[30] From an operational viewpoint this was a welcome development for Mountbatten, as serious disagreements had arisen between them about how to deal with a leader of the Burmese Army.

Apart from that, there was much to deal with at SEAC headquarters. The war in Europe came to an end, and in August the atomic bombs were dropped on Japan, which led almost at once to Japanese surrender on 14 August. Singapore was re-occupied on 5 September, and, during the weeks which followed, SEAC headquarters was moved there, although there was a period of two months in which the Kandy headquarters was retained as well. The main reason for having the 100 kW in Ceylon, rather than India, no longer applied, and essential

27 WO 165 111.
28 Ibid.
29 Ibid.
30 Joubert de la Ferté, *The Fated Sky*, p. 268.

ancillary equipment to make it work was yet to arrive. The last Cabinet report seen, after a longer gap (24 September 1945) was almost a repeat of the previous one shown above, and still mentioned two masts by mid-September.[31]

The war was over, and the original intention of keeping up morale to help win the war with Japan no longer applied. When it finally went on the air, the big transmitter was left with the slightly less important task of trying to keep the men in reasonably good spirits while they waited for their demobilization number to come up. The station attracted a large number of listeners. A handful of comments I have received from listeners makes it clear how important the station was for them at that time. So the work of building the station continued.

A message arrived from General Grover, Director Army Welfare Services, on 23 October 1945, for the attention of Maj. Gen. Sir Brian Kimmins, Director of Plans, at SEAC. It was mainly about the strikes at the docks in the UK. These started at the end of September as a small dispute about the unloading of pit props, but turned into extended unofficial action at most of the large ports, and lasted until November. The issues were higher wages and better working conditions. 40,000 dockers were on strike. 20,000 soldiers and others were used in their place. The message provides such an excellent overview of the position that it seems appropriate to include it in full:

> 1. Regret unable arrange tour before end November, but look forward to seeing you in Singapore.
>
> 2. Owing dock strike equipment held up in strike. Railways now refusing to carry to docks but although position somewhat obscure latest known information as follows:-
>
> A. Mercury Arc H.T.Rectifier Chambers. Mercury Arc collapsible earth switch assembly. Mercury Arc High Tension Switchboard. 1½ miles 7 pair screened /40 UG cable. All at S.S.Matheran at Birkenhead.
> B. PA AF and RF stages filament output control panels. Main RF feeder selector switch assembly. Heenan Froude secondary water cooler. Gents electric clock system. All at WOOLWICH depot.
> C. Antenna array materials for other than 36 degree beam. Part in S.S. Matheran, part en route Birkenhead, part at Woolwich.
> D. 25 line PABX not yet available.
>
> 3. Equipment now at Woolwich going by road to Newport by 2 November for S.S. Malaneka.
>
> 4. Studio equipment. Interim OB equipment officially released by BBC and MOS now procuring anticipate air shipment near future.
>
> 5. Transmitter technicians. NCO and 10 OR's now attending special course with BBC at PENRITH then proceeding MARCONI CHELMSFORD in 3 weeks for experience 100kW transmitter. Endeavouring arrange several courses of this nature.[32]

31 CAB 78 – 27.
32 WO 203 4410.

The thirty six degree beam was the most important aerial system used, as it covered the central part of the service area, including Burma. It was obviously sensible to erect this first. Item five was in response to a message dated 20 October 1945 from Noonan which had drawn attention to the need for the War Office to send adequate replacements for transmitter technicians who would be returning to the UK for their release. He was aware that they had heard that certain personnel were being trained for this work. We were those personnel, and like to think we were adequate replacements, but we never knew it had been intended that we should spend some time at Marconi in Chelmsford.

Paragraph two (A) of the message mentions the one and a half miles of underground cable still at Birkenhead. This screened cable was to provide the last stretch of the telephone lines carrying the programme into the transmitting hall. Laying the lines is described below. The reason for using this screened cable was that if the overhead lines had come into the station, or too near the aerial systems, the unscreened wires would have picked up a large amount of radio frequency signal which could have caused serious instability when fed back into the audio input to the transmitter.

The entry under 12 November 1945 in the War Diary item below is the only description found in the records of Ceylon Army Command of any part of the work of constructing the station:

> This date marked the completion of a Line Construction Route begun at the beginning of July 1945, which provided eight high grade overhead circuits from the SEAC Broadcasting Studio in Colombo to the new 100KW transmitter at Ekela. The route was surveyed during June and the first pole erected on 2nd July. The overhead construction of these speech circuits was carried out by 227(I) Line Construction Section, commanded by Lieut. D.G.Pyrke, R.Signals. Five of the circuits were brought into the station at Ekela by UG cable, and thus provided five high grade circuits over which programmes broadcast from the studio in Colombo could be automatically put on the air from Ekela - about 18 miles away. The remaining three circuits were continued to Horahena about 10 miles further on from Ekala through paddy fields and overgrown by-roads where they terminated at the BBC receiving station. Programmes received from UK and the Far East at Horahena could thus be relayed direct to the studio in Colombo. These routes were finally completed on 12 November 1945.[33]

The distance from Colombo to Ekela was actually shown as eight miles, which was probably a typing error. The phrase 'BBC receiving station' needs to be understood as the station for receiving the BBC. This simple account provides further evidence of the huge amount and variety of work involved in getting the station on the air.

In the War Office report for October 1945, the list of items still awaited included forty eight and a half miles of screened underground cable,[34] but it is not clear what this was for. Surely the overhead lines then under construction were supposed to provide the connection between the studios in Colombo, the transmitters at Ekala, and the receivers at Hora Hena.

Obviously, underground lines do not suffer from the sort of problem described to me by one of those on the station responsible for looking after the lines. They had to ensure that a line in good condition was always available to convey the programme from the studios

33 WO 172 9361.

34 WO 165 111.

to the transmitters. The test instrument used was a megger, which measured the electrical resistance, or insulation, between each of the pair of lines and earth. If this resistance was low it was likely that a wet palm tree leaf, for example, had fouled the line at some point. They then had to disconnect the faulty pair and use a pair that was working properly.

Hopefully the officer in charge of the overhead line construction never discovered that the lines his team had put up with such hard labour had been used for a relatively short time before being superseded. They will have been used for about a year, though, because a report in February 1946 states that the new cable was 40% complete, and one in May gives the figure 55%, so it was probably very late in 1946 before the underground cable was brought into use.

The monthly War Office report in November 1945 records that the mercury arc rectifier parts finally left England on three ships, on 10, 14 and 22 November.[35] Attempts were being made to get a third engineer to assist in their assembly on site. It was thought someone might be transferred from India. Another worrying delay was that two diesel generators in the power house were 60% complete. Four was to be the full complement, including one spare. The first aerial tower had been completed on 21 November and the second had reached twenty five feet. Only another 300 feet to go.

So we enjoyed our Christmas at home in 1945, unaware that the station we were to operate was still far from complete. The War Office files show when various parts were finally completed. The third aerial mast was completed on 23 January 1946, the fourth on 20 February and the fifth in March. All six were shown as complete in the April report.[36]

The reports concentrate on the erection of the masts. In some transmitting stations (often medium wave) the mast itself is the aerial. This was not usually the case with short wave stations, where typically a curtain of aerial elements is suspended between two masts. The installation of the aerials is mentioned in a report in February 1946, that array (seven, eight, nine) was 60% complete, and array (ten, eleven, twelve) was 40% complete. It is thought that aerials seven, eight, and nine were for India, and ten, eleven, and twelve were the main beam for Burma etc. This assumes they were numbered from west to east, so that one, two, three, four, five and six were for the two bays for UK/Australia, and that the Pacific beam would have been had aerials thirteen, forteen and fifteen. They obviously gave priority to the bay needed for the start of the 100 kW service.

However, in the early stages, Norman Shires sometimes actually worked with the team erecting the masts. He had great admiration for the local labour consisting of fisherman and climbers. The latter, in their usual daily work walked along loosely slung ropes between the tops of the coconut trees, and collected the sap from which 'toddy' was produced. So when it came to the big aerial towers, Norman remembered that height and lack of rigid supports meant nothing to them, and he saw instances where they would jump from one side of the structure to the other, irrespective of how far they were from the ground. Sixty years later, their brave agility was well remembered by Bill Reis, also.

Installation of the mercury arc rectifiers was also very late being completed, as has been mentioned. The last six cases of equipment left for Ceylon on about 10 January. Installation was said to be 40% complete on 14 February.

The least complicated of all the equipment needed was probably the ventilation system for the transmitter hall. The maker's drawings were reported as having been sent during

35 Ibid.
36 Ibid.

September 1945, and it was hoped to ship the plant late in October. It was certainly sent late, but not in October. As late as February 1946, this was in course of being collected, in the UK, from no fewer than nine sub-contractors. When it had all been assembled it was to be sent via fast passenger ship. The 100 kW set gave out a great deal of heat in an already very hot environment, so it was important, for the people, quite apart from the equipment, that the ventilating system should be working when the set was on.

This delay was mentioned at the twenty fifth I & CA meeting on 20 March 1946, during which Major Cronin announced that tests of the new Radio SEAC transmitter had begun on 14 March. A firm date for the opening of the new Radio SEAC could not yet be given owing to the non-arrival of equipment, particularly ventilating plant. The Supremo directed that a telegram should be drafted for his approval to GOC Ceylon asking him to arrange for every facility to be given to the quick unloading and transportation of the equipment for Radio SEAC when it arrived in Ceylon.

The telegram was sent the following day:

> For General Sparks from Mountbatten.
>
> The completion of the new Radio SEAC station at Ekela is being delayed by certain vital equipment, and in particular the ventilating plant. This is believed to be on the way or to have actually arrived at Colombo. Would be most grateful if you would give instructions that the unloading of this equipment to be given top priority and every facility given for this station to be completed and so get on the air as soon as possible.

The GOC replied the next day 22 March 1946:

> Situation EKELA as follows:-
>
> 1. 14 tons ventilating plant loaded in S.S.OBRA which is E.T.A.Colombo mid-April. Have given orders for priority unloading.
> 2. Spare parts for the third engine have been allotted priority two by ARMINDIA signal 416463 Q MOVS of 16 March. No intimation yet received here of a date departure or ETA.
> 3. Stores mentioned in first and second above must be installed before station can go permanently on the air. Will do my best to expedite completion when the stores have arrived.[37]

The installation of the 100 kW transmitter, during the twelve months which ended April 1946, was the work of a team under the following direction:

Capt. Thompson, Royal Signals, was the officer i/c the No.1 Army Welfare Broadcasting Station, the official title of the unit. As has been mentioned, Major Nutt, Royal Signals, represented the War Office, and Mr Caspard was the representative of Marconi Wireless Telegraph Company, with its headquarters in Chelmsford, Essex. He had John Sidebotham with him. AQMS Bill Reis was heavily involved in the installation of the transmitter itself.

The clearance of the palm trees, and erection of the domestic buildings, the transmitter hall and power house was directed by Staff Sgt. Cheetham, Royal Engineers. He also supervised the local labour. Staff Sgt. Stevens installed and maintained the diesel alternators, and had a name for each one.

37 WO 203 5207

Capt. Symington spent much of his time at the studios in Colombo. He supervised the installation of equipment as it arrived, and such work as was necessary to turn the building into a viable studio centre. The adjutant was Lt. Brian K. Foster, Royal Signals.

The decision to install a high-powered short wave broadcasting station in India or Ceylon had been made in December 1944. It went on the air officially on 8 May 1946, after a brief period of testing. In view of the huge distance everything had to be transported, and the fact that a global war was in progress for much of the time, this must be seen as a considerable achievement. Nevertheless, in terms of 'on time and on budget', a phrase much heard at the time of writing, it certainly was not on time, and with the original estimate of £100,000 and the actual cost said to be over £300,000, both suspiciously round numbers, the less said about the budget the better. £300,000 would be about £10,000,000 today.

8

Going on the Air

It may be worth describing, briefly, what is required to go on the air. There is the transmitter, supplied by mains electricity or other power source, and delivering radio frequency power to an aerial, via a feeder. There is a studio with microphones and turntables, or a more modern equivalent, the audio frequency outputs of which are mixed in a control panel. That electrical signal has to be sent to the transmitter, often by high grade telephone lines. The station is then ready for use by the people who devise, produce and present the programmes.

Part of the title of Doreen Taylor's book on forces broadcasting is a reminder of two things you must have, namely a microphone and a frequency. Radio SEAC's most important frequency was 15.120 megacycles a second, or as we now say 15.120 Megahertz, in recognition of the man who made fundamental radio discoveries.

In 1946, and for many years after, the intending listener at home turned a knob on the wireless set which caused a pointer to go round or along a tuning scale. Each point of the dial corresponded to a particular frequency. Wavelength which is directly related to frequency, was commonly shown on the dial. Nowadays, an LCD screen shows the frequency, although receivers of digital transmissions, which have recently become available, display the station name.

15.120 MHz was the frequency most used on the station's main beam, and determined where on the dial the listener would find us. As soon as programme input was applied to the signal, side-bands were added to the radio signal, with 15.120 being at the centre of a small channel of frequencies. This meant that other stations could not, for example, use 15.121, 15.122, and so on. The implication of this is that fewer stations could be accommodated in a given band of frequencies. So frequencies on the short wave bands are a scarce resource, which has to be regulated by international agreement. As with all forms of rationing, some people are disappointed.

A measure of the importance and difficulty which arose in Radio SEAC's case will be evident from the personal involvement of Mountbatten in obtaining frequencies in each of the wavebands in which it was thought the station might wish to operate. It seems the problem came to a head in March 1945, but this raises the question of what frequency was used for experimental transmissions which began in October 1944, and continued for some months. A previously quoted War Office message, mainly concerned with the Delhi/Ceylon argument, mentioned that one 7.5 kW transmitter had already been installed in Ceylon and was putting out a limited service, the message was sent on 14 December 1944.

This seems to tie in with the first sentence of S/Ldr Blakemore's account which refers to Radio SEAC coming on the air as experimental station ZOJ in October 1944, radiating only a few hours each day, on a borrowed transmitter and from borrowed studio space. Blakemore's name is listed in the preface to Doreen Taylor's book, as one of the many people who provided her with information. The following probably originated from him:

> ZOJ was the call-sign listeners were to hear. The aim was to move as soon as practicable into a white two-storied building in Turret Road, Colombo, already in use by the Psychological Warfare Unit.[1]

This ties in with his own reference to temporary premises. Other sources probably provided her with more information about programme production. She mentions a staff of four, and says that from November 1944 they produced four hours of programmes a day. The War Office signal refers to 7.5 kW and Blakemore talked about borrowed transmitter and borrowed studio space, so it seems possible this was a transmitter in Radio Ceylon at Welikade. Going back to the question of what frequency was used. If the studio and the transmitter were borrowed perhaps a frequency was shared.

When it came to the station going on the air officially as Radio SEAC, the question of frequencies had to be resolved. The problem emerged at the fifth I & CA meeting in March 1945.[2] Mountbatten ordered that a letter be drafted for him to send to Auchinleck. He further directed the Signal Officer in Chief to take the necessary action to obtain the frequencies needed for Radio SEAC.

On 19 March a message went from SACSEA to the War Office. This confirmed the call sign as Radio SEAC, and mentioned the need for frequencies. At the I & CA meeting on 5 April 1945, Lt. Col. Ducker announced that a 19 metre band frequency had been obtained.[3] This was stated to be 15220 kHz, and was thought to have been a typing error, as the one familiar to the author was 15120. In fact 15220 was used initially.

However, a frequency in the 25 metre band was still needed. There was mention of obtaining the agreement of All-India Radio to sharing their 11830 kHz frequency. 'Sharing' meant using it at different times of the day. The allocation of frequencies became so crucial that Mountbatten did what came naturally to him when he was sufficiently desperate – he went to the top. In a letter dated 21 March 1945, the man who was later to become the last Viceroy of India wrote to the then incumbent, Lord Wavell, as follows:

> My dear Lord Wavell,
>
> The question of frequencies for broadcasting from the new Radio SEAC station which HMG have erected in Ceylon for broadcasts to British Naval, military and air forces serving in India and South East Asia Commands is causing me much concern.
>
> A 100 kW transmitter for this purpose is now being installed in Ceylon and a 7½ kW transmitter has just been completed, and so far efforts to obtain the necessary frequencies have failed, although every possibility has been investigated and energetically pursued on lower levels.
>
> The requirements are for one frequency in each of the following broadcast bands:-
>
> 19 metres
> 25 metres

1 Doreen Taylor, *A Microphone and a Frequency - Forty Years of Forces Broadcasting,* London, Heinemann, 1983, p. 55.

2 WO 203 5207.

3 Ibid.

> 49 metres
> 90 metres
>
> and the objecting authority in this theatre in each case is All-India Radio. It may be possible to obtain the first two frequencies independently later, when German broadcasting stations are closed down, but I cannot wait for this. I am also seeing whether I can get a 90 metres frequency released from an Air Command operational frequency.
>
> I am now approaching you with the request that one of the frequencies in each band reserved for the above concern may be released for my purposes.
>
> I attach the greatest importance to this service for the upkeep of morale of all the British forces in this theatre, and I know you are fully aware of the attention and interest that British soldiers, sailors and airmen and the Women's services give to their broadcast programmes.
>
> The clearance of the above frequencies is the only thing that prevents the Ceylon service from going on the air on 1st April with 7½ kW output. This station will be superseded by the higher powered transmitter later and I am most anxious to get these broadcasts started on that date. The matter is therefore one of great urgency.
>
> I am sending a copy of this letter to C-in-C India as he is as closely concerned over this matter as I am.
>
> Yours very sincerely,
>
> (signed) DICKIE MOUNTBATTEN[4]

The Supremo had to intervene again about two weeks later in a personal message to Sir John Colville.[5] Apparently 11845 had been agreed by All-India Radio. This was not suitable, and Mountbatten went on to ask to share 11830, on the basis that Radio SEAC would have from 07.00 to 09.00 hours, and 18.00 to 23.00 hours. All-India Radio was apparently using only 10.15 to 17.00 hours. The reply was almost immediate, agreeing to the proposal, but for April, May and June only.

A message went to the War Office proposing testing on 13-15 April 1945, on 15220 from 11.30 to 12.30, and from 17.30 to 18.30, and on 11830 from 19.30 to 21.00.[6] The call sign was to be 'This is Radio SEAC testing'. If everything was satisfactory it was proposed to open the station on 21 April 1945, using an RCA 7.5 kW transmitter, and it was hoped it would provide an acceptable signal throughout most of Burma, Bengal, and Assam. In fact the station went on the air on 25 April 1945, as described in the previous chapter.

Having obtained the necessary authority to use certain frequencies, it is obviously important to ensure that the signal is on, or very close indeed to, one of those frequencies.

Many people have something generating a very stable frequency on their wrists. If the dial of a watch or clock has 'Quartz' on the face of it, it contains a thin slice of quartz crystal

4 WO 172 1809.
5 Ibid.
6 Ibid.

which determines, very accurately, the frequency being generated by a tiny transistor circuit. Digital technology converts this frequency to a much lower one which actuates the movement of the watch hands. Such crystals have been used in professional and amateur radio stations since the 1930s, to control the frequency of the oscillating circuit which is at the heart of every radio transmitter. Cutting such crystals is obviously very specialised work. One of the problems with such circuits is that the frequency can change with temperature, so where, as in Radio SEAC, a very high accuracy is required, the circuit is kept in a thermostatically controlled box.

A crystal needs to be available for each of the frequencies likely to be used. This is in contrast with the situation at the time of writing, when, as mentioned above, digital circuitry can produce large numbers of frequencies from one crystal. In 1945, simple valve circuits could be used to exactly double or treble the frequency. To cover the possibility of wanting to transmit on a frequency for which no crystal was available, a variable frequency oscillator (VFO) was available as well. In this, a coil and variable tuning capacitor were used instead of the crystal. Temperature control was still very important, as were other aspects of circuit design and choice of components. In spite of this, it would be expected that a VFO would be less accurate than a crystal circuit.

So in April 1946, with the aerials erected, the power house generating the electricity the 100 kW needed, and all its ancillary equipment finally in place, the big transmitter could go on the air.

That part of the story seems now to be reasonably well established. One of many gaps in the information available is concerned with the second transmitter. When the 100 kW service opened, mainly on 15.120 MHz, transmissions were also being made on 6.075 in the 49 metre band, a service directed north to southern India. It is assumed this was on the 7.5 kW RCA set that carried that service all the time we were on the station. That set was at the other end of the transmitter hall. A message has been found saying that testing on that frequency was to start on 1 May, so it seems reasonable to assume that the smaller transmitter had been installed by that time, and was used for those tests. At that time, the 7.5 kW set in the high speed wireless transmitter hall must have been continuing to carry the main transmission on 15.120. So when the 100 kW was tested on that frequency it either carried the normal programme, with the smaller transmitter off the air, or it tested outside the normal programme hours. When, in hospital somewhere in India for a couple of days, I heard a test transmission. It was in the 25 metre band, and reception was excellent on an ordinary domestic radio.

On Friday 19 April, Mountbatten sent the following personal telegram to Auchinleck:

> 100 kW opening 1 May hope you will join me in a brief opening broadcast. Subject to your comments I propose to broadcast:-
>
> When I spoke to you about a year ago at the opening broadcast of Radio SEAC, the station was broadcasting on a 7.5 kilowatt transmitter. I told you that a 100 kW transmitter would be added to the service later in the year. The building of the transmitter has taken rather longer than was expected, as there have been many difficulties to overcome. One of these difficulties was that all the equipment had to be specially manufactured for use under tropical conditions. But the Royal Engineers and Royal Signals staff of Ceylon Army Command, as well as a team of Marconi experts, who were

> sent out from England to assist them, have done a fine job. All difficulties have been overcome and the new transmitter is now on the air.
>
> I said last year that I hoped you would get the programmes you wanted presented in the way you liked best, but I told you this was largely up to you, and I asked you to send in any suggestions or criticisms you might have about how the programmes should be made up.
>
> The many letters that Radio SEAC has received in the last year show that you take a real interest in the station, and I hope you will continue to do so. The station's time on the air will now be greatly extended, and with the new transmitter, Radio SEAC will be one of the most powerful in the world, so the world would be listening to the programmes you are choosing.
>
> The broadcasts will be intended in the first place however for all English speaking service men and women in India and South East Asia, and the C-in- C India, General Auchinleck, is joining me in this introductory broadcast. You will now hear his voice.[7]

It is not known whether the general did add his voice to the broadcast. Although no confirmation has been found, it seems likely this was the text actually broadcast.

It is difficult to know what to make of Mountbatten's explanation that one of the reasons for the delay was that all the equipment had to be specially manufactured for the tropics. This may have impressed most of his audience, but Marconi, in particular, had had years of experience in making equipment for use in ships, and in land based installations in the tropics, so it was the sort of special manufacturing with which they were very familiar. It certainly was not true of the aerial towers, the bolts of which, as already mentioned, had gotten rusty on the Isle of Man.

Part of the twenty sixth I & CA meeting, held on 24 April 1946, dealt with the future of the station. Later in the meeting, at item twleve – Progress Report – Radio:

> Lt. Col. Noonan stated that Radio SEAC would commence broadcasting on 1 May. Satisfactory tests had been carried out, and reception in Singapore was extremely good. Trouble was still being experienced with the cooling apparatus, but it was hoped this would be overcome shortly after 1 May. The staff position would be satisfactory for the coming six months. Should the operation of Radio SEAC be required as a long term policy, arrangements would have to be made for civilian technicians to take over from service personnel now operating the station. The Supremo said that Maj. Gen. Kimmins should look into this matter. He also required suitable publicity to be given to the opening of Radio SEAC.

In his excitement, Lt. Col. Noonan (or the person taking the minutes) overlooked the fact that Radio SEAC had been on the air for a year, and so the reference to commencing broadcasting was inappropriate, and should have referred to the official opening of the 100 kW transmitter. The reference to cooling apparatus no doubt referred to the ventilation plant. The publicity was poor, as described later in this chapter. Fortunately the Supremo's broadcast was excellent.

7 Ibid.

However, two days after the 1 May date was given to the meeting on 24 April, the following message was sent:

> Radio Unit SEAC to SACSEA 26 APRIL 46
>
> COS states that May 1 will be 4½ hours with likelihood very early increase to 8 hours therefore May 8 will now carry Supremo's speech at 1500 hours and at 17.30 hours and official reception will also take place on May 8. Sure you will fully appreciate that all here coping with outside difficulty and deplore chaotic changes thereby imposed on you. ROSS PARKER asks when you are arriving here to add your strength to the struggle.[8]

Ross Parker's title was, I believe, 'Director of Programmes'. He was a composer of popular music, including musical shows in London's West End. He was perhaps best known for the music of 'There'll always be an England' and the hugely successful 'We'll Meet Again', which was featured by 'The Sweetheart of the Forces', Vera Lynn, amongst many others. The wording of the last sentence of the message suggests that Ross Parker may have met Mountbatten socially at some West End theatrical function or a nightclub perhaps.

Whilst writing the text of this volume I had assumed that Mountbatten had never visited the transmitting station. Many years previously, Andy Whetstone had given me the photograph, Figure 8.1, of the Supremo leaving the studios, but then Bill Reis provided the photograph Figure 8.2, he had taken of him walking past the transmitter, and Figure 8.3 of his entourage in the smoothing room, which also included Mr Caspard with his back to the camera. Bill's recollection was that the transmitter was operational at the time, so it was probably during the testing period.

Figure 8.1 Mountbatten leaving the studios. (C)

8 WO 203 5207

Figure 8.2 Mountbatten inspecting the Marconi transmitter, with Major Nutt on his left.

Figure 8.3 Mountbatten's entourage in the smoothing room.

Mountbatten kept a detailed personal diary of his movements, and substantial extracts were included in the daily War Diary which has entries for most days. As these files, known as the Mountbatten Diaries, are in the National Archives it was possible to look at the period from 1 March 1946 to the early days of May to try to identify his movements.[9] There was the hope that, apart from finding the date he visited the station, there would probably be a comment from him about the visit, as was often the case with such events.

9 WO 172 1804-10

During this period, the main activity for South East Asia Command was to close down the large and complicated organisation in an orderly fashion, whilst handing over ongoing responsibilities to other organisations, in particular Lord Killearn, the Special Commissioner who had been appointed. Many responsibilities were passed back to the governments of various countries, not least of which perhaps the most onerous and compelling was the need to do everything possible to avoid widespread starvation throughout the vast area. Statistics about the production, storage and distribution of rice appeared regularly in the Mountbatten Diaries.

Mountbatten was present on the 14 April as delegates from several countries arrived for a food conference held on the two days following. Prior to the conference he had been on a tour of Australia and New Zealand which started on 26 March and continued until 10 April. He and his wife Edwina were greeted by enthusiastic crowds, and although Mountbatten found it a great experience it was not one he wished to repeat. He found it very hard work meeting the demands on him for speeches and broadcasts.

It is against this background that one must consider the opening of the 100 kW transmitter. It must have been an unfortunate conjunction for Mountbatten that this was happening as he was preparing to leave.

By listing the dates, and noting the days when nothing was reported as having happened, it was possible to identify two short periods when he might have visited Radio SEAC. The second covered Monday 29 April to Thursday 2 May, and it seems possible he had a couple of those days pencilled in for a trip to Colombo to visit the station. He could have been present at the opening celebrations and might have broadcast his message live from the studios. The delay of the official opening until 8 May meant that he could not do this without cancelling long-standing arrangements to go to Nepal, which was clearly out of the question. So he may well have gone ahead with his intended visit, and recorded his message.

Further conjecture would suggest that if this was the case he would have put it in his personal diary, annotated to show it was not to be included in official records. This would be in line with the fact that no reference to Radio SEAC is made in his official biography.

If one follows this speculation further, and assumes he met the staff of Radio SEAC studios on 30 April, it may have been there that he heard the unofficial information that caused him to fire off an immediate shot across the bows of General Grover, Director of Army Welfare Services:

> I hear unofficially that the question of changing the name of Radio SEAC has been discussed. I hope no decision will be taken until my arrival home early June and I have time to discuss the matter with you.[10]

The name was not changed, of course, and when the station finally closed it still had that name. Obviously the point had some substance, because the closure was long after SEAC had ceased to exist. Having dealt with that matter, he may have found time to get in the car for the 20 mile trip to the transmitting station. We know he was there at some time, and the foregoing seems a plausible sequence of events.

The official inauguration of the broadcasts from the 100 kW transmitter was announced in *SEAC - All Services Daily Newspaper*. Its Tuesday 7 May 1946 edition had the following, on page three, beneath a picture of a pianist, guitarist and singer in the studio:

---

10 WO 172 1810

> RADIO SEAC Calling
>
> A trio from the Radio SEAC band broadcasting a number. Jack Read is playing the guitar, Wally Blackshields the piano, and Cara Thomas is at the mike. (See story below).
>
> Below the picture it continued:-
>
> Radio SEAC's new transmitter is ready.
>
> The new 100kW Radio SEAC transmitter, one of the most powerful in the British Empire and designed to cover India, SEAC and the Far East will be opened officially tomorrow. The transmitter, which has been under construction for more than a year, is a Marconi of the latest design. The construction, a SACSEA commitment, has been undertaken by Royal Engineers and Royal Corps of Signals of Ceylon Army Command, in conjunction with Marconi's experts who were sent out from England to supervise.
>
> The staff of Radio SEAC includes personnel of the Royal Navy, Army and the RAF.
>
> Daily programmes will commence at 06.30 and continue until 22.30 IST. Frequencies to be used will be 15120 k/cs in the 19 metre band and 6075 kcs in the 49 metre band. Radio SEAC will continue to operate its 7.5 kW transmitter which has been redesigned to give coverage to Ceylon and Southern India.
>
> In view of the vast area to be covered by Radio SEAC, listeners are invited to send in reception reports, giving the time, date and location at which the programme is received.

Programmes for the week commencing 8 May were on page two of the newspaper.

The paper was due to be discontinued within about a week, so morale was probably at a low ebb, but it is hard to imagine a less imaginative or appropriate piece of journalism. Perhaps they just printed what was sent to them by the person implementing Mountbatten's instruction.

Most readers would have had little interest in the fact that it was one of the most powerful transmitters in the British Empire. The questions more likely to have occurred to them might have been whether their unit had a suitable receiver, and whether they would get decent reception. They might well have wondered what the programmes were going to be like.

The request for reception reports should additionally have asked what short wave band was being received (19m, 25m, or 88m), and what was reception like (e.g. was there fading, or interference from another station?). It would also have been useful to know whether it was an ordinary welfare radio, with a bit of wire for an aerial, or a communications receiver. A report in May confirmed that there had been excellent reception reports from the whole of SE Asia, India, Japan, America and Australia.

The photograph was quite unsuitable. Most of the listeners would have been hoping to hear popular bands and singers, not some trio of people they had never heard of. There were few live broadcasts, so a more representative photograph would have been one of, say, David Jacobs seated behind four turntables and a microphone.

It was true that the staff of Radio SEAC consisted of people from the three services mentioned. Mountbatten's experience had made him an enthusiast for operations of that type, as mentioned previously. However, at the time that the newspaper piece was written was written it applied only to the studios, where it was obviously desirable to spread the net as far as possible to obtain the best people to present records, devise programmes, and so on. As a result the station had both Capt. Desmond Carrington from the army, and David Jacobs from the navy.

The transmitting station started out as 'No 1 Army Welfare Broadcasting Station', and representatives of the other two services joined the establishment later. The case for making this change seems less compelling, since the army could call on trained specialists from the Royal Signals, Royal Electrical and Mechanical Engineers, and the Royal Engineers. S/Ldr Bernard Blakemore was a special case because he was seconded from the BBC.

Mountbatten returned to England in June, unaware, of course, that he would not be assuming some sort of command in the navy as he hoped, but returning to Delhi to negotiate the handing over of the governance of India to its political leaders.

9

Power House Failures

If you ask anyone but a very old motorist what a starting handle is they will probably look at you as though you have gone mad. It is now many years since all private cars came equipped with a starting handle, which enabled you to turn the engine manually. A car might be started in this way if the battery was too weak to turn the starter motor.

When the diesel alternators in the power house at Ekala failed, two transportable diesel generator sets were brought in to enable the lower-power transmitters to be run, so that Radio SEAC continued to be on the air. They are shown in Figure 9.1. Ceylon is quite pleasant at about 5.30 in the morning, so the exertion of cranking a rather large diesel engine with its starting handle did not cause you to break out in too much of a sweat.

Figure 9.1 Mobile diesel alternators.

I had no idea where they came from, but found out, in discussion with Norman Shires of our high speed wireless neighbours, that each of their Marconi SWB 11 transmitters was supplied with one of these mobile generators. They were used until they were replaced by a custom built power house equipped with three larger diesel sets that came from Milwaukee,

USA. We were not alone in having alarming power house incidents. In their case one of the sets lost the pulley on its supercharger shaft. The pulley, which weighed many pounds, used five vee belts to drive the supercharger at about 2500 rpm. It careered along the floor and up the wall to the roof, before falling to the ground and trying to climb the wall again. Fortunately it did not collide with any equipment. Norman remembered that the generators were manufactured by a firm called Murphy, so one had to expect that his law would prevail.

When we did our nine week course at the BBC in Skelton, we saw the huge standby diesel alternators running on test. We were told that if the King or Churchill were broadcasting, these generators were running throughout, so that there should be no break in transmission in the event of a mains power failure. If the mains power failed at any other time the diesels were started up, and the transmitters were back on the air within a few minutes.

There was no mains power supply at Ekala, so a power house had to be built alongside the transmitter hall to provide electricity for the transmitters, and for lighting, refrigerators, and so on. A message sent on 11 January 1945 from the War Office to Ceylon Army Command estimated that about 600 kilowatts would be needed for the 100 kW transmitter, and three 7.5 kW transmitters. The power was to be generated by three 308 kW Bayliss & Morcom diesel alternators which were being diverted by engineers to Ceylon.[1]

This action, as early as January, meant that the project was being treated as urgent. Less than a month before, on 14 December 1944, the decision as to whether the station should be in Delhi or Colombo had yet to be made.

I am not sure who made the alternators actually supplied, but the eight cylinder diesel engines were supplied by Mirlees. Each generating set produced 200 kW output at 415 volts, three phase. A standby Lister generating set provided electricity to light the camp, run the fridges and so on, when the transmitters had been shut down for the night.

Figure 9.2 is a photograph of one of the diesel alternators, and figure 9.3 shows the line of four of them. Power from each alternator was fed into the switchboard via a circuit breaker. Figure 9.4 shows the switchboard, with meters which enabled current and voltage to be monitored. The engineer who started the engines was a civilian, as was a young local man who assisted. The control panel was usually manned by a Royal Signals radio mechanic. The main task was to get the diesels started, and the alternators were then connected to the live bus bars, one at a time. Before making the connection by swinging down the operating arm of the circuit breaker, the operator had to get the alternator about to be connected 'in synch' with the alternating voltage already on the bus bar. The additional alternator had to be running at the same speed as any already running. This was done by signalling to the diesel mechanic to adjust the speed of the engine concerned. The control operator watched a needle going round a dial, and when it slowed right down the operator waited for it to reach the top of the dial and immediately moved the arm of the circuit breaker to the 'on' position. Having connected two alternators, the work of the day was virtually complete. All that was required was to ensure that the dials on the control panel continued to show normal readings. It was the most boring job at the station because the men on the transmitters at least had the programmes to listen to. The power house was far too noisy for anyone to be able to hear anything.

1 WO 203 5207.

Figure 9.2 A diesel alternator. (C)

Figure 9.3 Four diesel alternators. (C)

Figure 9.4 The power house switchboard.

My hazy recollection was that there were three engines going, on the relatively few occasions when I was in the power house. However, wiser counsels have prevailed, and the usual number was two. Three could have been joined in the same way, had it become necessary for some reason.

Bill Reis was present when the first attempt was made to add the power from a second alternator to that already existing on the live bus bar, using the procedure described above. On each attempt the circuit breaker refused to complete the circuit, detecting a serious overload. Having satisfied themselves they had followed the routine properly, they were left with a fault-finding job. It was not too difficult to locate the wiring error which meant that the outputs from the two generators were effectively 'out of synch', and the circuit breaker would have none of it.

The diesel engines started to cause trouble at about the same time as we arrived at the station, so we knew very little about what was going on. I learnt, fifty years later, from a file in the National Archives, that the following message, dated 30 March 1946, was sent from Ceylon Army Command to HQ SACSEA:

> Colombo Welfare Broadcasting Station, Ekala 100 kW. Modifications recommended by makers to prevent water leaks in cylinders of Mirlees engines proving unsatisfactory. Testing of transmitter held up. Maker's expert who supervises project in addition to projects in INDIA is now at PADAM working under C in C India. Engineer in Chief requested in our 07341 of 30 March to send expert to Ceylon forthwith. Request your assistance in allotting priority for expert services.

SACSEA tried to prise the expert out of the clutches of C in C India by sending this message on 1 April, about five weeks before the 100 kW transmitter went on the air officially:

> Understand that Ceylon Army Command in their Q 7341 of 30 March have requested you send to Ceylon urgently expert on Mirlees engines to assist in modifications to engines now being set up there for new Welfare Broadcasting Station. Grateful if you can loan the expert for short period and assist in urgent dispatch to Ceylon as early completion of this station is highest priority.

If this message was seen by Auchinleck it may well have given him some secret satisfaction to read the reply from his command:

> C in C India to SACSEA 3 April
>
> Expert on Mirlees engines.
>
> Expert who previously assisted belongs Air Ministry, and is now fully employed on work of highest importance wireless installation which will not be finished before July. Regret no other suitably qualified expert in India.

HQ Ceylon Army Command sent the following message to the War Office on 5 April:

1. Water leaks have developed in engine cylinders. Modifications previously recommended by makers are no use. C-in-C India have been asked for expert but reply that he is not available before July. No progress on engines can be made without expert on Mirlees engines request you fly one out at once and instruct him to bring the Graphitoil joints.
2. Fourth engine expected to be on site mid-April. Spare parts for third engine already on site. Expert asked for in para. 1 could supervise installation and repair.
3. No satisfactory testing can be done until engines functioning properly.
4. 6th mast now complete.
5. Ventilating plant due mid-April.
6. Opening date for the station dependant on satisfactory solution of engine trouble by expert and on installation of ventilating plant. Estimate earliest date mid-May if all goes well.

Noonan had a rather less gloomy view of events in a note to Mountbatten's Secretary:

1. Called GOC Ceylon who explained that he is worried about modifications to the Mirlees power engines and requires a factory expert to visit Ceylon. A Mirlees engineer is at present supervising a job for the RAF at Paesam. The RAF have refused to release this man, and GOC Ceylon has signalled UK asking for an engineer to be flown out. This will take some time and I have drafted a suggested signal which SAC may wish to send.
2. Whilst I was in Ceylon last week, the RE's made minor modifications and we have been running the engines for the past week - in fact we have been running transmitter tests. I would, however, feel much safer if the RAF would agree to release the engineer for a few days.[2]

Whether Noonan's suggested message was used we do not know, but the one actually sent is very much in the Mountbatten style of trying to get his own way by an approach to

2 Ibid.

someone he presumably knew personally. In the course of this message he pulled out all the stops by including a reference to the War Cabinet, and probably understated the duration for which the expert was required as a few days.

> To C in C India
>
> Personal for Air Chief Marshal Carr from Mountbatten.
>
> I would be most grateful if you will allow the Mirlees engine expert now supervising wireless installation in India to make a quick visit to Ceylon. He is needed most urgently to carry out minor modifications on the power engines of the new 100 kW transmitter at Ekala. This project is TOP PRIORITY and has backing of Cabinet and all three service ministries. Am most anxious this Broadcast Station should open May 1. Understand he will only be required for a few days.[3]

There is no record of how this was resolved. It may be that the Royal Engineers or Royal Electrical and Mechanical Engineers (REME) were able to effect the necessary repairs. A War Office report in May 1946 said that the engine fault had been remedied, and that three engines were running satisfactorily, and a fourth had arrived. I remember standing just inside the power house door watching a warrant officer in the REME checking on the shims (thin pieces of metal) that had been inserted at the points where the engine casing was bolted to the floor, to ensure it had been accurately mounted.

This, then, was the crisis of which we were unaware. More serious problems were to follow about a year later, which resulted in the use of mobile generators, as mentioned at the start of this chapter. None of us could remember when this happened, or for how long the 100 kW was off the air. It started on 11 May 1947 according to a note in National Archives file WO 165/111, but no mention was made as to how long the 100 kW set was off the air. Our guess had been two to three weeks, but we now know the spares were flown out on 21 May, so it will have been about two weeks before they actually arrived on the station. They then had to be fitted, and the engines re-assembled, so it is unlikely the down period was much less than four weeks.

There was a sense of crisis about it which was very apparent when entering the transmitter hall without hearing the sounds of the 100 kW transmitter's ancillary equipment. Figure 9.5 shows the stripped down engines in the power house, and Figure 9.6 shows the apparent chaos. Those of us not closely connected with the state of the power house relied on information from various people as to the cause of the breakdown. Someone had told Andy Whetstone that the rapid variations in load, caused by the programme modulating the transmitter output and hence the power house load, could cause unusual amounts of wear in the diesel engines, which might lead to their breakdown. Of course, at that time, Paul Sollom had not had the experience he had from 1948 to 1951 of almost trouble-free running. With that in mind, the suggested reason for the breakdown does not stand up.

On the other hand, Peter Burland remembers hearing, on very good authority, that the problem was poor, and probably unnecessary, maintenance by the naval personnel who were working on the engines at that time. Presumably they had worked on marine diesels broadly similar to those in the power house, but may well have had only a short wartime course on a speciality which would usually have involved a much longer period of training and experience.

---

3 WO 203 5217.

Figure 9.5 Stripped down diesel alternators in the power house.

Figure 9.6 Power house chaos.

If Mountbatten had not been successful in getting the station set up in Colombo rather than Delhi, the problem would probably never have arisen because the mains electric supply should have been big enough to provide the additional power needed for the Marconi 100 kW transmitter. It might also have avoided the possibility of All-India Radio going off the air because of strike action by their technical staff. The struggle for Indian independence was, of course, reaching a crucial stage. The following message dated 24 April 1946 was sent by C in C India to SACSEA:

> Personal for Admiral Mountbatten.
>
> Reference your signal. In event of serious internal disturbances DELHI transmitters are considered vital. Lack of loyal technicians might result in it being impossible to operate the minimum DELHI transmitters without outside help. Only source of technicians might be Radio SEAC. My 101/COC of 131320 ** April suggested that if loan of technicians necessitated closing Radio SEAC then its importance relative to Delhi would have to be decided by COS at the time.[4]

However, the idea was disposed of in a memorandum from the Cabinet Office to C in C India.[5] It was considered undesirable that Radio SEAC should close down in the event of widespread disorder in India.

4 WO 203 5207.
5 WO 172 1810.

10

The Future of the Station

Following the unexpectedly early end to the war against Japan, the huge military machine had to be wound down. This was a difficult process because there were major tasks for the forces to undertake, particularly in areas which had been occupied by the Japanese. A reasonably smooth transfer of power to civil authorities had to be planned. Meanwhile, the civilian populations needed to be looked after as well as possible, often in chaotic circumstances.

Although the welfare facilities for the troops needed to be in place for some time, it was necessary to make plans for newspapers to cease publication, and for Radio SEAC's transmitting station to be disposed of in some way. In August 1945 there was a message from an Air Ministry Special Signals Officer to SACSEA. After mentioning something about winding down newspapers it stated that 'SEAC should forward request to HMG to state immediately the post-war policy with regard to the future of the 100 kW transmitter'.[1]

It is not known whether this prompted the discussion recorded in the minutes of a meeting of the SEAC Welfare Committee held during the autumn of 1945. This mentioned the background to the setting up of the station, and looked to the future:

> The erection of a high-powered transmitter for broadcasting to the forces in this theatre and the Far East was ordered by the Prime Minister and passed to the War Office for action. [After dealing with other matters the minutes continued]. Quite obviously, since the project is costing somewhere in the region of £300,000 the authorities must have had a long term policy in view. This, however, has not yet been defined by HMG.[2]

It seems far from obvious that a long term view had been taken, and one almost suspects sarcasm. It seems unlikely the prime minister was involved with anything as detailed as a high-powered transmitter. He probably approved the Munster recommendation, which was simply for additional transmitters. Even this was just one item in a long list of desirable welfare improvements.

When the installation was first mooted, a figure of £100,000 was mentioned. The need for a long term view would have been greater had the authorities known it was actually going to cost £300,000. This would be equivalent to about £10M at the turn of the century.

On 11 October, a message went from the War Office to SACSEA which indicated that negotiations had been started personally with Haley of the BBC. So far they were going well but it was too early to forecast success. In principle the idea was for the BBC to take over as much of

1 WO 203 4410.
2 Ibid.

army commitment overseas as possible.[3] Material reproduced below makes it clear there would, in any event, have been a gap of up to two years to allow time for the BBC's charter to be amended.

The following brief for Mountbatten was prepared in January 1946, and may have been intended as material from which he would prepare the letter to the Foreign Secretary which is quoted in full later in this chapter. However, this memorandum did not go beyond an assumption that the BBC would probably take over eventually, whereas Mountbatten's letter made a case for Radio SEAC being turned into a commercial, or semi-commercial station.

The memorandum briefly set out the station's history, and expressed the hope that the 100 kW would be operational in February. It continued:

> 1. Meanwhile, programmes being transmitted over 7.5 kW station, which, however, cannot include India. All-India Radio therefore allotting 6 hours daily to British troops in India, and will continue to do this until 100kW established in Ceylon.
>
> [Comment: The 7.5 kW transmitter could not cover India because the priority was to use a fairly broad beam, centred on Burma. This could not cover India as well].
>
> 2. Radio SEAC is run by SACSEA command - Unit Strength of 16 officers and 73 Other Ranks. These figures include studio and transmitter staff. All present personnel are radio specialists in civil life, and are due for release between now and midsummer. Men released must be relieved by personnel from UK if the station is to continue after May. Such personnel should be trained in UK.
>
> [Comment: Our party of Royal Signals radio mechanics was part of the answer to the manpower question. We were waiting to fly out there when this signal was sent. People were also needed for the studio centre. It would be interesting to know where the idea came from that all the present personnel were radio specialists in civil life].
>
> 3. Future policy is not known, but if the BBC take over in due course, gap of 18 months to two years is likely in view of Parliamentary procedure involved to alter its charter.
>
> [Comment: It is thought the BBC's charter did not provide for it to operate a station outside the UK, although its broadcasts *from* the UK covered most of the world.]
>
> 4. In view of immense importance of this station, not only for entertainment but for BRITISH prestige generally, essential this gap should be bridged. Best course appears to be formation by War Office in consultation with the Admiralty and Air Ministry of a Command Unit with director responsible to War Office, with a committee representing all services and commands. Establishment to be based on present SACSEA establishment but sufficiently flexible to permit interchange of civilians and service personnel to enable smooth hand over to BBC in due course. Australian Government may be able to assist in this.[4]

3 Ibid.
4 WO 203 5207.

Mountbatten needed to find out what plans the government had for the station. He decided to write to the Foreign Secretary personally, and took the opportunity of including his ideas for its future. As we have seen, he was never reluctant to go to the top. The letter, dated 28 January 1946, is worth quoting in full:

> Dear Secretary of State,
>
> In November 1943, a decision was taken at Cabinet level to erect a 100 kW radio transmitter in Ceylon, which was to cover the broadcasting requirements of the South East Asia Command, India, and the Far East. The scarcity of technical equipment, and various shipping delays, seriously delayed work on erecting this transmitter; but I am pleased to be able to say that it is now nearly finished, and should begin to operate within the next month or two.
>
> In the meanwhile, however, realising how essential it was that broadcast entertainment should be available to the services in my command, I gave instructions that a 7.5 kW transmitter should be used until the 100 kW was ready. This small transmitter, known as Radio SEAC, has been operating for the past 18 months; and the entertainment and news features which it provides have been eliciting about 1000 complimentary letters every week.
>
> The new transmitter will cover an infinitely greater area; and as it will have cost well over a quarter of a million pounds I am sure you will agree it should be made to serve a useful purpose.
>
> I see no reason why it should not capture the whole English-speaking audience in the Far East. But it can only do this if it puts out a news service and a form of entertainment which successfully compete with the high-powered stations which the Americans already operate, particularly as I am told that they are now putting up additional transmitters. It would be hard to deny that some of the programmes which are at present being put out from England are hardly of a quality to do this.
>
> We have been informed by the War Office that we shall have to operate Radio SEAC for at least 18 months before some other agency takes over, but I suggest it is not too early to begin discussions now on what the future policy is to be.
>
> I am sending Lieutenant-Colonel Noonan to London shortly, to discuss with the three Services the future policy for broadcasting and publications, and the possibility of the new 100kW transmitter out here being operated on commercial, or semi-commercial lines. Noonan has been responsible to a great extent for the present policy of Radio SEAC, and for the high standard of its programmes. He has had some years' experience in American methods of commercial broadcasting, having been in the film and broadcasting business in Hollywood since 1930. I feel confident that he is fully qualified to assess the standard that should be maintained, and the type of broadcast that should be provided, if we are to capture and retain the large audience

out here which will have the choice of listening to American broadcasts or to our own.

I should be most grateful if you could spare a few minutes of your time to grant a personal interview to Lieutenant-Colonel Noonan when he is in England, so that he can discuss with you the points raised in this letter.

[The letter was completed in his own hand:-]

Yours very sincerely,

DICKIE MOUNTBATTEN[5]

It was addressed to:
The Right Hon. Ernest Bevin, PC, MP.,
Secretary of State for Foreign Affairs.

There are a number of items that call for comment. The reference to November 1943 should have been to 1944. It mentions 'a small transmitter called Radio SEAC', but a transmitter is not a radio station. A broadcasting radio station includes people, other technical equipment, and so on. The quarter of a million pounds is significantly more than the original rough guess £100,000. One may speculate as to how appealing a commercial radio station would be to a senior member of a socialist government which was to mount a massive programme of nationalization. From the description of Noonan's background it seems possible he put the idea of a commercial station into Mountbatten's mind. The latter had a barely veiled dig at the BBC in criticising the quality of some of the programmes then being put out from England. There is no mention of Noonan in Doreen Taylor's book, and it does seem that he is being given too much of the credit which should have been due to Ross Parker, David Jacobs, Desmond Carrington and others. However, this was possibly justified as a means of persuading Bevin to see Noonan.

The minutes of the twenty sixth I & CA meeting on 24 April 1946 include a reference to a Special Commissioner responsible for coordinating broadcasting in SE Asia. A draft telegram was approved and sent from SACSEA to the War Office:

For DAWS for GROVER from KIMMINS

As steps now being taken to reduce this headquarters to small peace time establishment, Service Relations Division will shortly disappear. Will you therefore please confirm that War Office will take over entire responsibility for Radio SEAC with effect from 31 May. Noonan will be in London between 15 - 31 May for final consultation with you before he takes his release.

[This message has been quoted in previously in connection with progress on the 100 kW, so that part will not be repeated].

Confirmation that the War Office was preparing to assume control of the station was provided by the following message, dated 16 May 1946, from the War Office to C in C India, SACSEA and GOC Ceylon:

5 Ibid.

> Radio SEAC will shortly come under War Office control. Ceylon Army Command will be responsible for local administration. Request agreement all addressees visit Lt. Col. Wilson AWS 5 War Office to discuss details. It is proposed War Office to be responsible for overall policy provision, maintenance, spares, reinforcement personnel. War establishment to be transferred from SEAC to War Office. So that interests India and other commands are fully represented it is suggested Radio SEAC should include representatives India and SEAC in advisory capacity to Station Commander. Further suggested broadcasting coordinating committee comprising representatives all commands should meet periodically Singapore possibly under chairmanship LAWSON-REECE BBC representative shortly to go to Singapore under Foreign Office auspices.

This seems, perhaps, to acknowledge that India Command had not had much say in the running of the station while Mountbatten was in charge. The new arrangement was presumably intended to put that right. More importantly, perhaps, the BBC was finally getting some influence over the station, which was probably inevitable now the war was over.

Most of the SEAC HQ meetings mentioned have been those of the I & CA Committee, but there was, not surprisingly, a series of meetings covering the whole of the Supreme Allied Commander's concerns. The 333rd such meeting was on 23 May 1946, and the minutes included the following:

> The SAC asked that he should be provided with the views of all those interested in Radio SEAC in order that he might represent them to the appropriate authorities in London. The War Office had agreed to accept responsibility for the station from 1st June. Lord Killearn who was Special Commissioner in SE Asia (1946/48) said he was interested in the station, which had been discussed in London.
>
> The SUPREME ALLIED COMMANDER:-
>
> in agreement with the Governor General and the governors of Singapore and the Malayan Union wanted the Special Commissioner to form a committee under the chairmanship of his representative (Mr. Murray).
>
> a. to formulate proposals regarding the future of Radio SEAC which could be communicated to the Supreme Allied Commander in London.
>
> b. to consider and co-ordinate measures necessary towards the realisation of the projected high powered installation in Singapore, which it was understood had received Cabinet approval.

Those in charge of Radio SEAC were no doubt keenly aware that Mountbatten's departure could result in changes they might not wish to see. The following message was sent through HQ SACSEA to the Cabinet Office on 1 June 1946:

> Personal for Supremo.
>
> Respectfully offer on your departure our warmest regards. Thanks for everything. Our assurance, your policy and ideals for this station will be

> maintained. Bon Voyage Lady Louis and yourself from Smith, Ross Parker and all staff.

Mountbatten replied:

> Many thanks for your telegram of 1 June and for your good wishes to myself and my wife. I shall follow the future of Radio SEAC with interest and am sure you will make a big success of it.[6]

It is hard to imagine what was in his mind when dictating the last 10 words, although they should be read in the context that the high-powered Radio SEAC had been operating for only a month. He may still have hoped that something would come of his proposal that the station's future should be as an important, ongoing, popular service for English-speaking listeners in the Far East, but this was not to be realised.

6 Ibid.

11

The Transmitting Station

The station was an isolated community, requiring input of food, water, and other supplies for the men, oil for the power house, water for the cooling system, and programme input brought in on telephone lines. The water tower is shown in Figure 11.1.

Figure 11.1 The water tower.

On entering the camp, the main living quarters were on the left, the officers having a bungalow set among the palm trees to the right. The concrete road curved to the right and ran alongside the main buildings, passing the open doors of the power house, and finishing alongside the transmitter hall. The Heenan cooling tower stood in front of the hall, and the aerial feeder wires came through the rear wall, on their way to the aerial arrays, supported at intervals by metal frames. There is a general view of the station from an aerial tower in Figure 7.3, which shows two of the six aerial towers. We are also very fortunate in having the photograph Paul Sollom provided which shows a model of the whole station, with the possible exception of the living quarters, Figure 11.2. For this we are indebted to the unknown person, presumably employed by Radio Ceylon, who spent many hours creating this wonderful model, which was put on display in Colombo.

Figure 11.2 The model of the station.

The power house has been described previously, so the description which follows is of the transmitter hall and its contents. The plan of the hall in Figure 11.3 shows the disposition of the various transmitters and associated equipment.

The telephone lines carrying the programmes from Colombo were terminated in the line room, on racks which made them readily accessible for testing. Figure 11.4 shows Vern Pellen using a megger to test a line. The programme input from the lines went to the audio input console, which was used to check and control the audio signal, and pass it to the various transmitters. This is shown in Figure 11.5. If for any reason the programme from the studios was unavailable, the very small emergency studio could be used. The studio (at the left hand end of the plan) was the only place on the site which was air conditioned, but the transmitter hall had ventilating ducts throughout, to carry away the heat coming from the transmitters.

Before going on to consider the features of the various transmitters it may be useful to say what a transmitter is, and this at a time when a very high proportion of the population is walking around with one in a pocket or handbag. The segment of society most using mobile phones will be those least likely to have heard someone on the radio apologising for 'a break in transmission, due to a fault at the transmitters'. I cannot remember how many years have passed since I last heard that phrase, which I imagine is because most transmitters now are 'solid state', meaning they use transistor-like devices instead of thermionic valves, called tubes in the USA.

It is worth just mentioning that Marconi built up a world-wide business using radio transmitters before valves became available. Transmitters then were spark transmitters, which could be turned on and off to send Morse code, but were incapable of transmitting speech or music. They did telegraphy, not telephony.

An attempt will be made to describe what a transmitter does, and then to say something about how it does it. The input to a transmitter is a power source; battery, mains, hand-turned generator, whatever. Its output, delivered to its aerial system, is radio frequency power. That is not power as supplied by the mains, at 50 cycles (or Hertz, as we now call it), but at about 15,120,000 Hertz in the case of Radio SEAC's best known frequency.

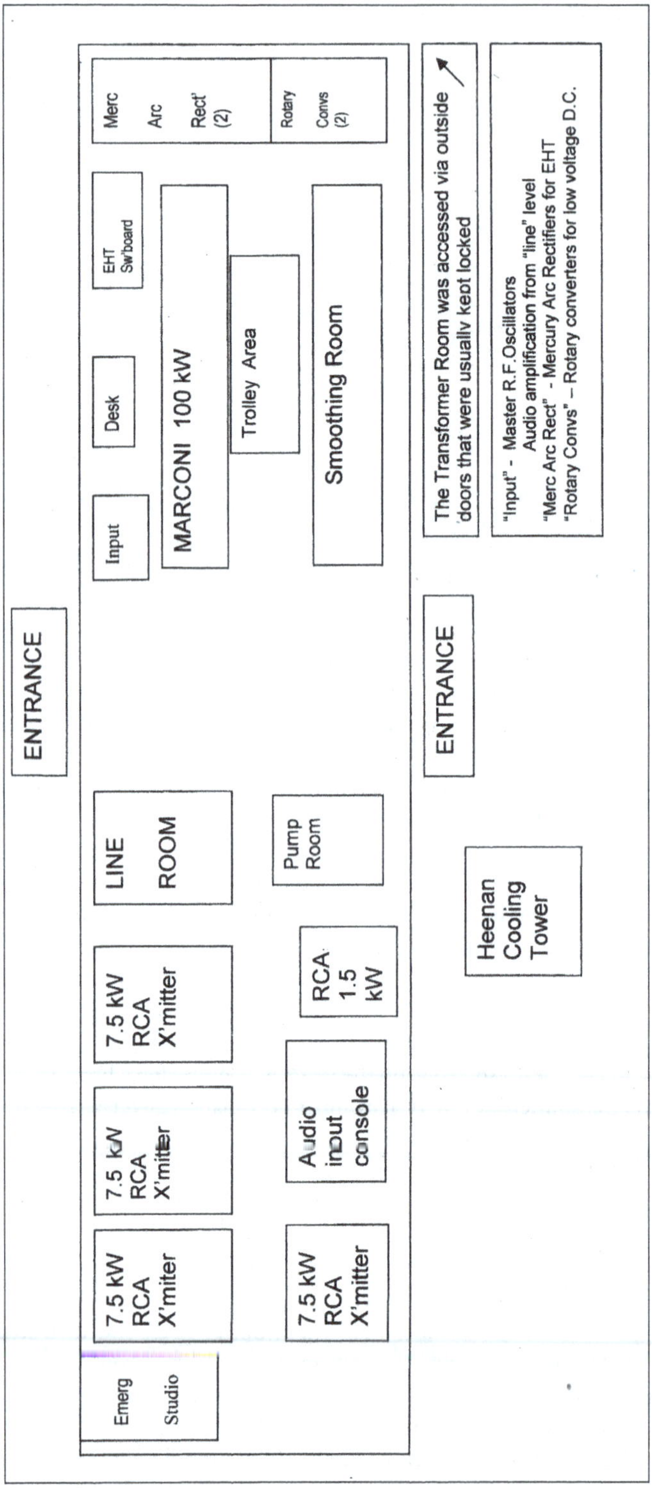

Figure 11.3 Plan of the transmitter hall.

Figure 11.4 Vern Pellen using a megger to test lines. (C)

Figure 11.5 The audio input control desk and its operator. (C)

That describes the full function of the transmitters used by our high speed wireless (telegraphy) neighbours in Ceylon. Their transmission started and stopped at high speed in accordance with the Morse code input supplied to it. The Marconi company produced a large number of telegraphy sets of that kind, but there was an option. If you wanted to use telephony (for phone calls or radio programmes) they could supply a 'bolt on' modulator.

The input to this was typically a very small signal composed of audio frequencies from microphone or record playing equipment. This was amplified, by the modulator, to the point where it was powerful enough adequately to modulate the radio frequency signal being generated.

In 1946, amplitude modulation (AM) was the type in question. Although frequency modulation existed, it was to be many years before announcers started saying 'FM', and more years still before the full glory of FM stereo arrived. That, of course is now old hat, and, at the time of writing, the British public is starting to express its displeasure at the prospect of 'going digital' and having to throw away two or three sets in the house, and a car radio, all of them in good working order.

Radio SEAC's transmitters produced amplitude modulated radio signals. Two things (at least) are common to valves and transistors. They allow current to flow through them in one direction only, and they are capable of amplifying an audio or radio frequency signal. The simplest valve capable of amplifying is the triode, so called because it has three elements cathode, grid and anode. When operating with no input to it, a steady current flows from the anode through the grid to the cathode. Put another way, the heated cathode releases electrons which pass through the grid and reach the anode. As part of a suitable circuit, a small change in the voltage occurring between the grid and the cathode results in a large change in voltage between the anode and the cathode. That is amplification. The general principal still applies in valves with more elements such as the tetrode or pentode.

Most amplifiers have several stages. Each stage consists of a valve (or now transistor) surrounded by other components and connections. At each stage an input is turned into a larger output. So, in an audio amplifier, the minute voltages coming from the microphone or pick-up are input to the first stage, and get larger from stage to stage, until the output from the last stage (output stage) is sufficient to drive a loudspeaker, or perform some other function. A number of the stages in the Marconi transmitter had two valves rather than one. However, they operated as a pair, in push/pull, each mirroring the function of the other. The final output stage with its doors open, in shown in Figure 11.6.

A radio frequency amplifier uses the same ability of the valve, and the main part of the transmitter is an amplifier of radio frequencies. However, it needs to have a radio frequency source to amplify. So the first stage is a valve connected into a circuit in such a way that part of its output is fed back to its input, and this causes the circuit to oscillate. The frequency of those oscillations will depend on the circuit connected to the valve. A suitable coil and capacitor can be used to determine the frequency. Alternatively, they can be replaced by a slice of quartz crystal, cut very precisely for a particular frequency. This will determine the accuracy and stability of that frequency to a much higher standard than the coil and capacitor. To improve the stability even further, the temperature of the crystal may be controlled thermostatically.

As with audio frequencies, the successive stages in the radio frequency (RF) amplifier at the heart of the transmitter produce ever greater RF power until the final stage, where it has reached the strength required to meet the design specification, (e.g. 7.5 kW). However, that final stage is crucial and unique. In addition to providing amplification, it has two other functions. It has to accommodate the high-powered audio signal coming from the audio amplifier, and combine the audio and radio frequency components into one modulated RF signal. The output part of the final stage has also to provide the means of passing that output to the feeder carrying the RF power to the aerial system.

Figure 11.6 The final stage of the Marconi transmitter with the doors open.

It is worth mentioning, at this point, that transmitters are less complicated than receivers. It would be stretching the point to say that transmitters are big and simple and receivers are small and complicated, but it does not seriously misrepresent the situation. It is true for the smallest transceiver carried by a WWII infantryman in a back pack, and remains the case if one compares the complexity of the RCA AR88 communications receiver, with the relatively simple RCA 1.5 kW transmitter used for our local service in Ceylon.

Needless to say, the devil is in the detail. In considering Radio SEAC's transmitters, the difficulties associated with conveying and installing the 100 kW Marconi transmitter were not that its circuit was complicated, but that so much of it was just plain BIG. The transmitter proper was literally surrounded by heavy electrical engineering. There were other significant differences between the Marconi and RCA sets.

We need not dwell on the fact that one was a plain grey box and the other had an art deco style front panel which was very 1930s. It is what was inside the boxes that made them so different. In the case of the 100 kW, what a smaller transmitter would have had within its cabinet was often in another room. Within its cabinet were its valves. It was mentioned above that the triode valve has three elements, one of which is the cathode. In pre-war domestic radios the cathodes in the valves were of two types. In the battery sets the heating filament, that glowed a nice orange colour and produced the electrons to enable the valve to work, was itself the cathode. In mains sets the filament heated a piece of metal which surrounded it, and this was the cathode. The filament operated from a transformer supplying typically 4 or 6.3 volts AC. If the filament itself had been the cathode it would have caused the most colossal mains hum you ever heard, even though the transformer winding was centre-tapped and earthed. The cathode was at or near earth potential.

So the valves on the 7.5 kW set had cathodes round their filaments, which meant the latter could be provided with AC from a transformer. However, the big valves in the 100 kW set had tungsten filaments rods which were the cathode. So these had to be fed with direct current. Because of the scale of things, the filament rods took huge amounts of current at about 35 volts. The most practicable way of producing that was to use a rotary converter, which was a large AC electric motor driving a DC generator. This needed associated control circuits involving big open relays with massive copper contacts. These became pitted, and it was one of our maintenance tasks to clean these with emery paper from time to time. As the set could not work without a rotary converter it was considered necessary to provide two, since it would have taken several weeks to get a replacement to Ceylon. Figure 11.7 shows part of a rotary converter in the lower left hand corner, and the DC switchboard through which its output was fed to the valves in the Marconi transmitter.

Figure 11.7 A rotary converter (lower L) and the DC switchboard.

The other difference between the RCA valves and the larger ones in the Marconi set was in how they were cooled. The output of the RCA set came from the pair of tetrodes supplying 7.5 kW of RF to the aerial. Such circuits produce heat, partly from the valve filaments and partly from the inevitable inefficiencies involved in converting the DC operating the transmitter to the radio frequency signal going to the aerial. Such heat had to be dissipated or the valves would have been destroyed. This was done by providing the valves with large metal fins, and directing a flow of air from powerful blowers to carry the heat away. This arrangement was neatly contained within the transmitter area shown in Figure 7.1.

The method used on the Marconi 100 kW was much more complicated. The task was the same – to cool the anodes. Marconi called a series of valves 'Cooled Anode Transmitting', and they were numbered CAT 14, CAT 17 and so on. Figure 11.8 is a diagram showing a cross section of a valve of this type. The solution was a cooling stream of water to flow around the outside of the anodes. Water on anodes with 11,000 volts on them. Surprising, perhaps, but it was distilled water, and this has a much higher electrical resistance than water with impurities. It is the impurities in water that kill people in their baths. This meant that stills had to be operational to produce it to replace that lost through evaporation and so on.

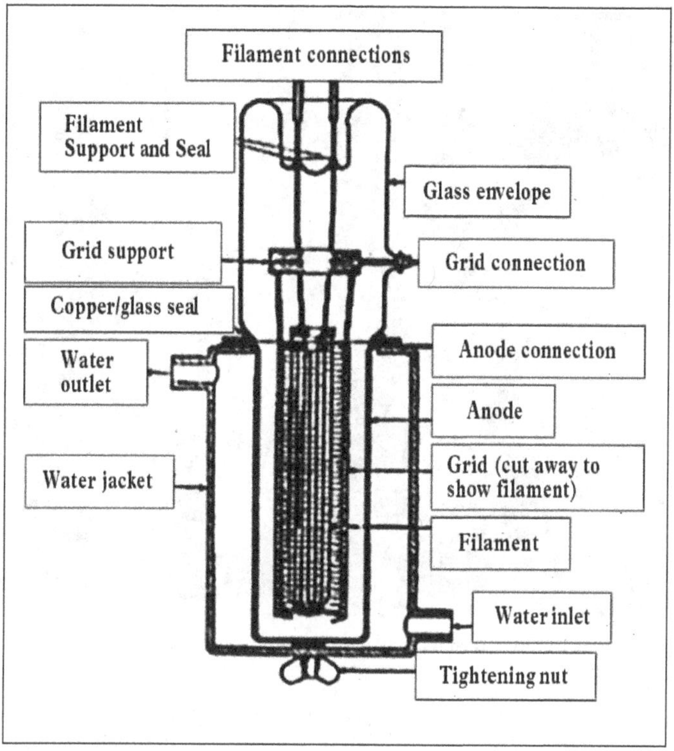

Figure 11.8 A cross section of a water-cooled triode valve.

Peter Burland found, on his return to the station, that they had changed to buying the water rather than producing it themselves. So there were stills, and there had to be big electrically driven pumps to push the water through the pipes that ran to and from the valves. Figure 11.9 is a photograph of the pump room.

Before the water was returned to the pumps, pipes carried it outside the building to the Heenan tower, shown in Figure 16.1. The purpose of this was to cool the water before it was again pumped to the valves. The water cascaded inside the tower in which a large fan blew through the water, taking away much of the heat.

The other difference in the valves used is that triodes were used in the high power stages of the 100 kW whereas the RCA sets used tetrodes. When triodes first appeared in the 1920s and were used in radio sets, it was realised they were very good as audio frequency amplifiers. However, they were poor at radio frequency amplification because the capacitance between the anode and the grid (whilst insignificant at audio frequencies) caused a serious drop in performance at radio frequencies. Towards the end of the 1920s, the screened grid valve (a tetrode) was introduced, which gave good RF amplification.

The first radio valve of all was a diode, which essentially was an electric light bulb with a separate metal plate inside the glass envelope. This refers to the old bulbs which are being replaced by more energy efficient devices. The invention of the valve occurred in just that way, when someone put a DC voltage across filament and metal plate. If they connected the positive to the plate, current flowed between plate and filament. When the connection was reversed, with the negative connected to the plate, no current flowed. The diode recti-

Figure 11.9 Pumps that circulated distilled water to cool the valves.

fier had arrived. The power to operate a piece of radio equipment has to be DC to provide the standing current flowing through the valves before any audio or RF signal is input. So, whether your amplifier uses valves or transistors, if it is to be plugged into the mains it has to be fed via a rectifier, which may be in the amplifier or external. Rectification is the process of converting AC to DC. Most homes now have several pieces of equipment that have a mains lead that includes a little plastic box. This has a transformer to reduce the voltage to the sort of level transistors need, and this is followed by solid state rectifiers. There are often smoothing components also, as described below.

In 1946, mains radios had transformers to produce the right voltages needed in the set, and one of those voltages was then rectified, using a double diode valve. The output from that was about 200 volts DC. Small transmitters could be powered in the same way. It is possible Radio SEAC's 1.5 kW transmitter had a similar arrangement, although the DC voltage would certainly have been much higher than 200 volts. Unfortunately it is not known what kind of rectifier was used in the RCA 7.5 kW sets.

Figure 11.10 is a photograph of the rectifier used for the Marconi set, so the type is not in doubt. It was a mercury arc device, which relied on the fact that current will flow in only one direction through ionised vaporised mercury. Whilst writing this chapter, a Google search on the computer for 'mercury arc rectifier' produced a number of hits. More than one of the sites had a colour photo of a very large glass vessel with several contacts going through the glass. Colour was an important feature because the apparatus produced a strong blue light. One text recounted how the doors of the cabinet could be opened to disclose this impressive sight. Sadly, perhaps, English Electric, the manufacturers, had seen fit to deprive us of this spectacular sight, by arranging for the process to take place in a black metal tank. As a very high voltage (called extra high voltage – EHT) was involved, the whole apparatus had a room of its own. As with the rotary converter, a serious failure in this department would

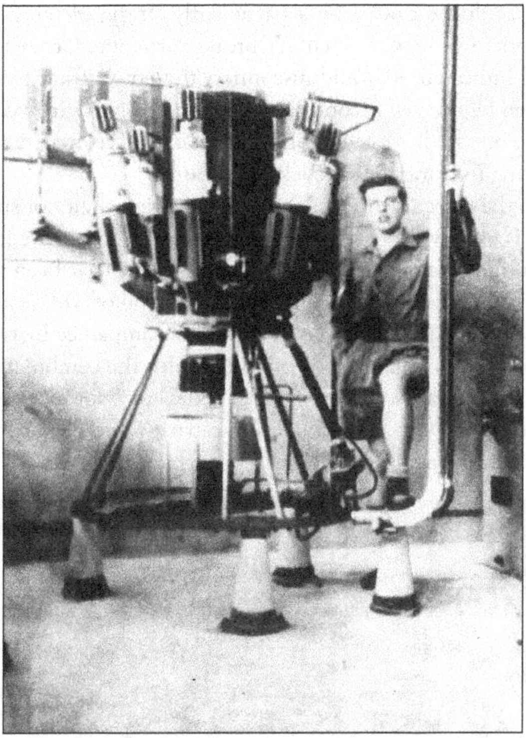

Figure 11.10 A mercury arc rectifier.

have put the transmitter off the air for several weeks, so the whole thing was duplicated. I believe this type of rectifier has been replaced by solid state devices, for most applications.

The electricity supplied to the rectifier started, in the power house of course, as three phase AC 415 volts. A transformer in the power house stepped this voltage up to 6,000 volts, and this was feed to the EHT switchboard in the transmitter hall. This was then fed to another transformer which stepped up the voltage to 12,000 volts. However, the secondary winding of this transformer was more complicated. It consisted of three windings each producing 24,000 volts, centre-tapped, which meant that the power actually supplied to the arc rectifier was 12,000 volts, six phase. Six connections are visible above the rectifier in the photograph. This second EHT transformer was contained in a room not accessible from the power house or the transmitter hall. I never saw it (or knew of it!) and there is no photograph. Both were oil filled. Paul Sollom provided all the information for this paragraph, and described how when he opened the door to this room 'it fell apart on me, the termites had got there first!' As with the arc rectifier, both these transformers were duplicated.

A point that worried me about the arc rectifier was the fact that when, out of curiosity, I looked at the circuit diagram on one occasion, I realised I had no idea how its control circuits worked, and they looked quite complicated. They were completely different from anything encountered in ordinary radio work. It was a comfort to know we had two of them, so that if one went wrong we could use the other.

The EHT switchboard contained the high speed relay circuit breaker, which rapidly disconnected the transmitter from that supply if excess current flowed. This was not all that uncommon. It could be caused by a particularly strong piercing note from a singer that created a very brief overload. The circuit breaker attempted a reset three times, and if an overload was still indicated, it would disconnect the power from the transmitter. Those operating the set then had to see if conditions changed to make it reasonable to bring the transmitter up again, or whether a fault within the transmitter needed to be found and put right before attempting to bring the set back on the air.

The output from the mercury arc rectifier was DC alright, but not smooth. It contained a 'ripple' residue, as is usual with rectifiers. I believe the use of 6 phase input to the rectifier meant that less smoothing was needed than would otherwise have been the case. The cure is usually found in the combination of a choke, which is a coil of wire wound on an iron core which offers a relatively high impedance to the ripple, accompanied by two capacitors which have a very high resistance to DC but lower to the ripple. The combination is described as a smoothing circuit, and is usually tucked away inside the box. Not so, of course, with the 100 kW. If you wished to see the very large choke and capacitors you had to visit the smoothing room which is shown in Figure 11.11.

Figure 11.11 The smoothing room.

The last unusual thing about the 100 kW set to be considered did not involve a separate room. It could be found in the heart of the transmitter itself. It has been mentioned that this used triode valves, whereas the RCA sets used tetrodes, and also that triodes are not good for RF amplification, and why. The way of overcoming the triode's disadvantage was neutralisation. Since two valves were involved, connected in push-pull, it was possible to arrange the circuit so that a small fraction of the signal at the anode of one valve could be fed to the grid of the other to offset the internal feedback of RF from the anode of each valve to its grid. It is an elegant solution, designed by one of Marconi's most loyal and able assistants, C. S. Franklin, and it is mentioned here because it provides a link with Marconi himself. Some idea of Franklin's standing can be judged from the fact that it is a photograph of him that is reproduced at the front of a well-known text-book of the 1930s.[1] Readers familiar with circuit diagrams may appreciate Figure 11.12 which illustrates the principal used.

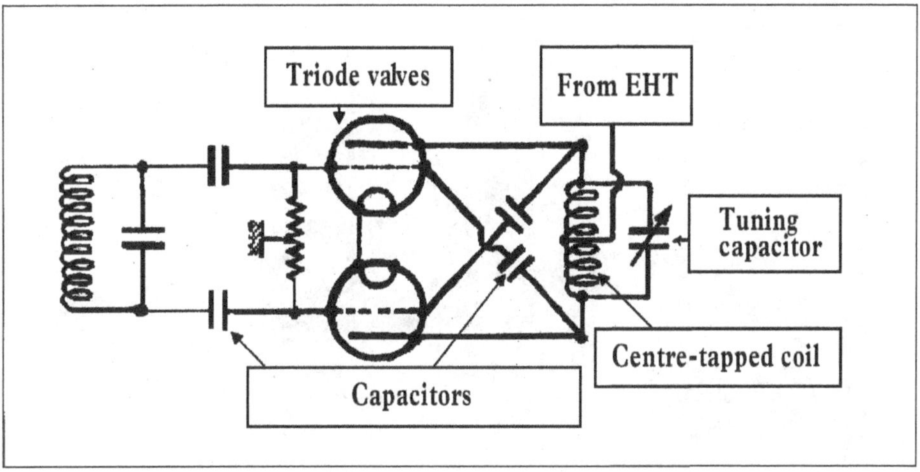

Figure 11.12 Neutralization of the final stage of the Marconi transmitter.

Franklin was responsible for numerous inventions and developments in radio, and an oscillating circuit is identified by his name. Other well-known circuits, Colpitts, and Hartley, use one valve. The Franklin uses two valves in a circuit designed to be more stable.

The three types of transmitter used are mentioned. The plan of the hall, (Figure 11.3, mentioned earlier) shows approximately where they were sited. Two 7.5 kW transmitters are shown that were not there during my time on the station.

The right hand half of the plan of the hall shows the Marconi 100 kW set with its ancillary equipment. There are photographs mentioned elsewhere in this chapter which include the main grey box containing the transmitter itself, the final stage, with doors open, and most of the ancillary equipment such as the mercury arc rectifiers, rotary converters, and the pump room.

On entering the transmitter hall, and passing the smoothing room on the right, one looked firstly along the rear of the 100 kW set. It was here that the coil trolleys for the RF output stage ran between guide rails when they were moved in and out of the set to change the waveband being used, (e.g. the 19, 25, or 31 metre band). Figure 11.13 shows a coil trolley behind the main transmitter enclosure, ready to replace the trolley in use when required.

Near the control desk was the small thermostatically regulated box housing the crystal controlled oscillator. A crystal was required for each frequency on which the transmitter was to operate, although the unit also included a variable frequency oscillator. In a similar rack was the equipment which formed the input audio stages, with controls to give the right sound level, and the capability of varying the degree of compression. This enabled a higher average level of audio to be input, by compressing the range of programme volume. This would result in soft passages of music being louder than they should be in relation to the

1 A. W. Ladner & C. R. Stoner, *Short Wave Wireless Communication,* London, Chapman & Hall, 1938.

Figure 11.13 A coil trolley behind the Marconi transmitter.

louder passages; a form of distortion. However, the facility could be valuable when broadcasting speech in a situation where an enemy might be jamming the frequency. Increasing the compression would increase the volume of sound relative to the jamming noise. It could also help in conditions where reception would not be good. Quieter passages of music were made louder and so were less likely to be lost under the 'mush' caused by atmospherics.

Another rack near the control desk contained monitoring equipment, which fed a high quality loudspeaker. A unit to measure total harmonic distortion was also available, from which one could directly read out the percentage distortion. This could be a valuable check, particularly if the sound quality from the monitor appeared to be suspect. It would, of course, only register distortion occurring within the transmitter, and not any distortion already present in the programme input.

When seated at the control desk, the final stage of the transmitter was in front of you, and to the left was the EHT switchboard, and beyond that the mercury arc rectifier bay. Figure 11.14 is a photograph of Peter Burland seated at the control desk and Harold Priestley standing in front of the transmitter taking readings from the various ammeters, each showing the current flowing through a particular part of the transmitter. He is writing the values on a sheet as a permanent record. Immediately in front of the control desk, on the transmitter cabinet, a large handle can be seen which had to be operated to gain access inside by opening any of the doors in the front panel. This was locked automatically so that the doors could be opened only if the EHT (11,000 volts) was run down to zero.

This may be a suitable point at which to mention how the set was put on the air. Assuming that there was no change in wavelength from that previously used, the sequence went as follows. The water pumps were switched on, which caused the distilled water to flow round the valve anodes. An automatic interlock ensured that nothing further happened unless the water was being pumped. The filament voltage was applied by turning on a simple switch on the control desk. This did not immediately apply a voltage of about 35 volts to the filament rods in the valves.

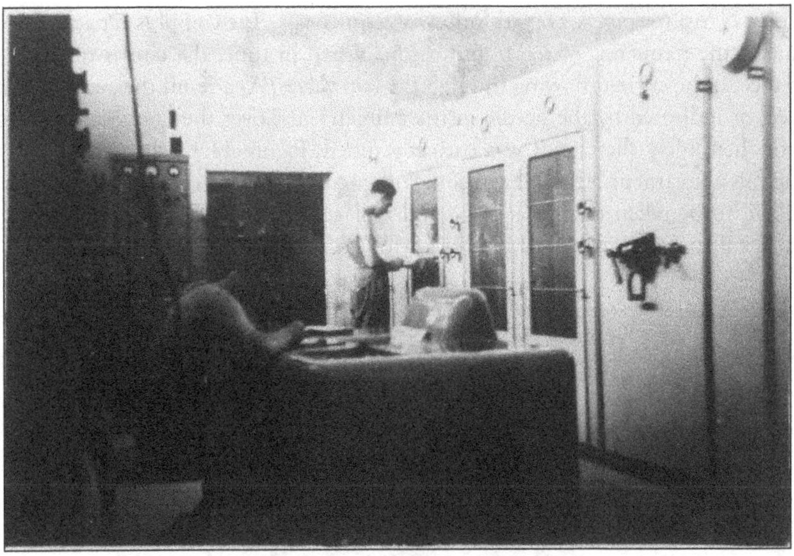

Figure 11.14 Peter and Harold operating the Marconi transmitter.

If the valve filament rods had been supplied with their full required voltage when they were cold they would probably have been destroyed. To avoid this, there was a control device which provided a steadily increasing voltage at start-up time. To reach the full voltage took probably more than a minute. This was achieved with a giant rheostat, driven by something looking rather like a bicycle chain, which ran over a toothed wheel driven by an electric motor. The CAT 17 valves, with the tungsten rod filaments glowing a warm orange colour, could then be seen from the control desk. The EHT could then be applied.

As with the 35 odd volts for the valve filaments, the EHT was applied slowly, to avoid damaging surges of power. Going on to full power added about 300 kW to the load on the power house, so the people working there needed to be aware that this was going to happen. Nothing could be simpler for the operator at the control desk. Pressing a red button caused the EHT voltage to start to rise, but unlike the filament voltage which increased automatically, the EHT voltage rose only whilst the finger was on the button. This enabled the transmitter to be checked and adjusted at low power, thus avoiding possible overloads. When satisfied that all was normal, the operator could then take the voltage up to the normal level by continuing to press the red button. Not surprisingly, an adjacent black button enabled the process to be reversed, and was the first step in taking the transmitter off the air.

The control desk had two glass areas, through which a number of meters were available to show voltages and currents in various parts of the transmitter. A large ammeter in the anode circuit of the final RF stage was also easily visible from the control desk, and this was a good indicator that everything was normal throughout the RF stages.

The tuning capacitor in the final RF stage was adjusted by turning a wheel, on the outside of the steel cabinet, which moved a large metal plate which was one half of the tank circuit tuning capacitor. As a result, the capacitance was varied, and the frequency at which that circuit resonated was adjusted. The other part of that circuit was a coil made of heavy gauge copper pipe. At the highest frequency the transmitter could generate (21 MHz), the coil was two 'turns', or less, of copper pipe about two inches in diameter, so it hardly looked like a coil. Narrower pipe was used for lower frequencies. The coil plus capacitor needed to resonate at the frequency of the transmission. When in tune, the circuit offered a higher impedance to the current flowing through the two valves. As a result the amount of current dropped, as indicated by the needle in the ammeter just over the doors of that stage. The operator then knew the circuit was correctly tuned. Figure 11.15 shows Harold Priestley making this adjustment. The coil and some other components were mounted on the trolley which had to be taken from that stage and replaced with another, when changing wavebands. A trolley was available behind the set for each waveband likely to be used.

Figure 11.15 Harold tuning the final stage of the Marconi transmitter. (C)

By moving a selector lever, the wheel mentioned above could be used to move the aerial coupling coil so as to be closer to, or less close to, the tuned circuit. As a result, the aerial system presented a larger or smaller load to this output stage.

When it was necessary to change frequency, the set, if it was 'on', had to be closed down by pressing the black button to take the EHT down to zero. The valve filaments could remain 'on'. With the EHT voltage at zero the doors could be opened in order to access the output RF stage. As previously mentioned, Figure 11.4 shows the lever which controlled the bolts which ensured the transmitter doors could not be opened while the EHT was on. The coil trolley was then pulled out and replaced with the trolley containing the coils for the waveband now required. Whilst this was going on, a line rigger was outside the building and disconnecting the aerial feeder from the aerial which had been used, and connecting it to one needed for the new frequency. Back inside the hall, the relative crystal would be selected on the crystal oscillator. Then the set would slowly be brought up, by applying EHT, using the red button as previously described. Some changes to tuning of the lower-powered RF stages would probably be needed, whilst the EHT was fairly low. The final stage would also need re-tuning. The EHT would then be brought up to the normal voltage, and further fine tuning would be made, if necessary.

The set was tested before I reached the station, and the first tests will have used the artificial aerial located in the smoothing room. This enabled the set to be run with the output radio power being dissipated as heat. Although Paul Sollom had no occasion to use the 100 kW dummy aerial, he recalls that this consisted of a number of carbon rod resistors, connected to present 300 ohms to the feeder line. The resistors were water cooled, and the water flow was measured and its temperature rise noted to work out the actual power dissipated. He mentioned that for the 7.5 kW RCA transmitters there was an array of thirty 250 watt filament lamps which were connected in series/parallel to present 300 ohms to the feeder. In his words 'it was good to see the RF power!', but Ceylon is hardly the most comfortable place to be standing anywhere near the equivalent of three 3 kW domestic electric heaters.

Testing with a real aerial took the form of music recordings, interspersed with special station identification to make it clear it was a test transmission. I was delayed in hospital at Mhow for a week or two, and later for a few days when I left the train 'somewhere in India' and reported sick to an army hospital. There was an ordinary domestic radio set on the ward, and I was able to pick up the test transmission. Needless to say it was a very strong signal.

There was another dummy load, out in the open, below the water tower. This is shown in Figure 11.1. This was to enable a mains power generator to be tested if a real load was not available. It was a steel tank that could have water in it. Three electrodes (one for each phase) were suspended in the water, through which current could pass, thus disposing of the energy by heating the water.

There are a few further points to be made about the RCA 7.5 kW transmitters. I cannot recall how these transmitters were switched on and off, probably a simple switch. Obviously they still had to be tuned, particularly after any waveband change. There was no coil trolley, and even the coil in the final stage was only about six inches in diameter, and made of silver plated strip metal. I think it was bolted in, which made wave changing fairly straightforward. It did not happen often though, because one of the sets was permanently on 49 metres, for southern India, and the other was rarely used on other than its 16 metre transmission to Singapore and the Pacific. They worked on three phase 415 volt AC, which was input to a large transformer. Typically, such large components, and the steel panels on which many components were mounted, were simply bolted to the concrete floor.

The audio input console was opposite the RCA sets. This Phillips device (shown in Figure 11.5) arrived while I was there, and I recall the disapproval of the ex-BBC men, who were particularly contemptuous of the programme level meters. They were considerably larger than the BBC 'peak programme meter' (PPM), and instead of the quick response provided by the BBC meter, the needles on the Phillips meters flopped about relatively aimlessly, instead of giving a quick peak response.

The emergency studio had a BBC input unit which showed how the job should be done. It also had a dynamic microphone, and a disk cutting machine. There was probably an ordinary record playing deck, also. It would have been possible to tap into the line from Hora Hena receiving station and take the BBC from London, and simply re-broadcast that, if all contact with the studios in Colombo had been lost for any reason. Station identification, and apologies for not broadcasting the usual Radio SEAC programmes, could have been announced from this little studio.

On leaving the transmitting hall by the back door you would have seen the aerial feeders, mentioned previously, disappearing into the distance.

For the most part, being on shift duty meant doing very little, and hoping nothing would go wrong, or if things got too boring, hoping something would go wrong. The transmitters had to be started in the morning, and any necessary waveband changes made until it was time to switch off again. The person at the control desk had the monitor loudspeaker switched on most of the time; partly for entertainment, and partly to listen for any falling off in quality, or loss of programme due to a studio or line fault.

A log was kept of everything that happened, such as HSR trips. It was easy to forget that one important member of the shift spent the whole time in the power house. The RCA transmitters had to be watched as well, of course. Although they were not 'built like a battleship' as was the Marconi set, they were very reliable.

As with motor cars, there was a maintenance schedule to be followed for the 100 kW set. Much of this was dusting and cleaning, rather like housework. This was done after closing down late in the evening, when the shift members were looking forward to bed. Some of us may have been tempted to follow the old saying 'if it works leave it alone'.

I'm not admitting anything!

12

The Receiving Station (Hora Hena)

Nearly all of the information in this chapter has been provided by Peter Burland, who was made responsible for Radio SEAC's operations at the receiving station, after spending the first half of his time in Ceylon on the transmitters. Figure 12.1 is a photograph of him.

Figure 12.1 Peter Burland at Hora Hena.

From the earliest planning stages it was accepted that some of the programmes broadcast by Radio SEAC would be relays from the BBC. In the event, there were not as many relays as had at one time been envisaged. There was a good short wave receiver at the studios (probably an RCA AR 88 as used at the receiving station). This had a reasonable aerial, and the set's output could have been fed directly into the studio control room if all the lines from Hora Hena failed.

Although this might have worked quite well for much of the time, the nature of short wave radio is such that the signal is quite often subject to fading (variations of received signal strength), and from time to time reception conditions are exceptionally poor. This was no doubt the reason for establishing a three-man unit in an existing army high speed telegraphy receiving station called Hora Hena, about eighteen miles from Colombo. The three men at the Hora Hena station did not travel out there from Ekala each day, but lived there, whilst remaining, of course, on the strength of the unit based at Ekala.

A fairly large, reasonably flat, ground area is needed for a receiving station of this type, which means that it will usually be well away from a city. This also has the technical advantage that man-made static interference from domestic and commercial electrical equipment is less strong because of its remoteness.

The site had to be large enough to accommodate the rhombic aerials which were chosen for this purpose. Viewed from above, these have the shape of a diamond on a playing card, and the outline of the diamond consists of aerial wires. Unlike the half-wave dipole, which is resonant at one frequency, the rhombic is a broadband aerial. Typically it might be designed to cover 7-14 MHz, although no record is available of the design actually used. This would have been a reasonable choice, since it would, in theory at least, have given an acceptable performance on the 19 and 41 metre bands, and rather better results on the 25 and 31 metre bands. The lengths of each side would be four wavelengths long at 40 metres, so, if this was something like the basis of the design, each of the four sides will have been 160 metres long. At 12 MHz the rhombic has a gain about 10 dBs better than a simple dipole. The angle of elevation is affected by the height above ground, so this should have been chosen to produce a low elevation, in view of the long distance reception required.

A rhombic aerial is directional. The feeder is connected to one end, and a terminating impedance (600-900 ohms) between the wires at the opposite corner. The optimum direction is based on a line from the feeder through the opposite corner, so this should have pointed to the UK. Peter recalls that the underground feeders were very heavy duty, and probably co-axial cable. As this has an impedance of about 75 ohms, some matching device would have been needed, and with rhombics used as transmitting aerials this usually takes the form of an RF transformer.

With this type of aerial connected to a good communications receiver, the signal should usually be about as good as one could wish for, but to improve the situation even more, three aerials and three receivers were in use at any one time. In this arrangement, called 'triple diversity', the Automatic Gain Control circuits in the receivers are specially linked to produce the situation where, at any given moment, the receiver producing the highest signal output causes the output being fed from the other two sets to be reduced. As a result, the signal being passed forward for programme transmission is mainly from the set getting the best signal at that moment. Although this is the way the system was intended to work, it did not always in practice produce the most pleasing result for the listener. What would, with normal reception have been slow fading, became rapid fading, which most listeners probably find less pleasant, particularly when listening to music. In view of the elaborate state of the art receiving equipment it is surprising that there were a few occasions when people at the studios complained that they were getting better reception from their own single receiver, with a modest aerial, than was coming to them from the receiving station.

The communications receivers used were American RCA model AR88, and arrived on the station in June 1945. This was one of the finest available anywhere at that time, and for years afterwards. It was a superhet, of course, with two tuned RF stages, a mixer and local oscillator, three IF stages and the usual demodulation and AF output stages. The operator could control RF and AF gain separately, and could select any of five available bandwidths so as to get the best sound quality consistent with keeping adjacent channel interference to a low level. These controls are shown in the diagram of the front panel of the receiver at Figure 12.2.

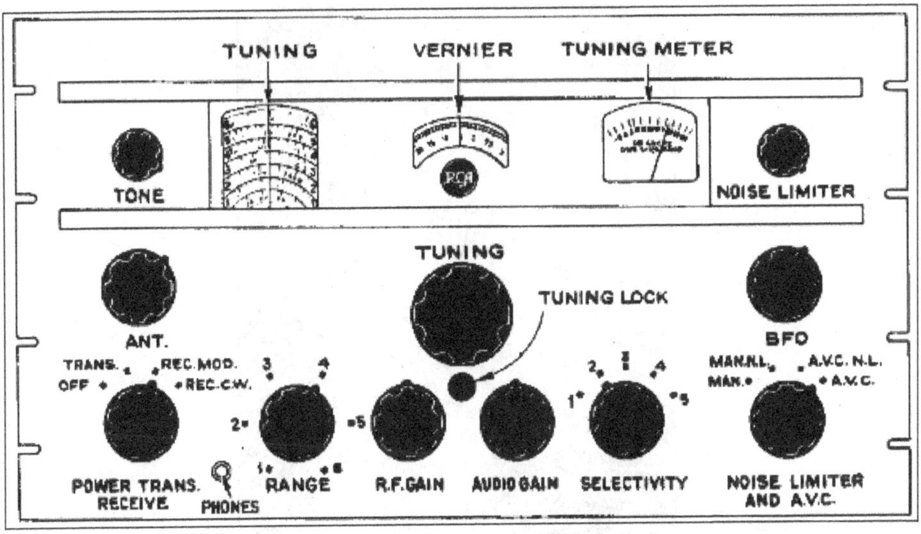

Figure 12.2 RCA AR88 receiver – the front panel.

In practice, the broadest setting was always used, which ensured the best available sound quality. The tuning drive was particularly good; very free moving, with a flywheel to make tuning even smoother. Backlash was virtually non-existent, and the vernier dial made it possible to tune back to the recorded reading for the frequency one wished to receive, and find the station virtually in tune. This was partly because the heaters of the valves were left on continuously, which meant there was minimal frequency drift due to changes in temperature.

The AR88 could be connected to a simple length of wire for an aerial, and an aerial trimmer was available from the front panel. Alternatively a feeder could be input, which would have been the case with the rhombic aerials, if special broadband RF amplifiers had not been inserted between the aerials and the receivers. Since RCA had, as they say, 'spared no expense' to provide the optimum useful amount of amplification, it is surprising that somebody decided that such amplifiers would improve reception. They seemed to make little difference, so they were left in place mainly to avoid someone coming along and complaining that they were not being used. Figure 12.3 is a photograph of the sets in a rack, with the RF amplifiers below.

The three Radio SEAC technician/operators worked shifts. Peter Burland recalls only one fault on any of the sets, namely one IF valve which had to be replaced. Not a bad record for six receivers over about eighteen months. He recalls another 'fault', for which nobody could really be blamed. It seems some of the local population had access to the aerial site, and, being unaware of the underground cables that carried the signal to the aerial to a receiver, dug a hole into which they disposed of what can best be described as sewage. This was no doubt a very practical and sanitary way of disposing of something best not left lying around, particularly in the tropics. In this instance the offending material had to be dug out again to effect a repair to the feeder cable which had been cut during the digging.

The BBC regularly provided a schedule showing the best frequency to use at any particular time, so it was always known in advance what frequencies were to be used at what times. Although three sets were in use together at any one time, there were another three standing

Figure 12.3 RCA AR88 receivers above preamplifiers. (C)

by. These were tuned to the BBC's frequency in the waveband next scheduled to be used. This meant that their output could be switched over to be the live output, without any break.

The Radio SEAC receivers were in the same room as that used for the high speed station's main functions. Excellent test equipment was available, including a frequency modulated signal generator and oscilloscope, so that receiver circuit alignment could be checked, and corrected if necessary, at any time. As this involves some compromise to get a reasonable signal over the whole of a band, advantage was taken of the fact that it was known BBC frequencies which would be used, and the trimming was adjusted to optimise the output at those frequencies. Other equipment enabled the sensitivity of each receiver to be measured to detect any falling off in performance.

Having arranged for a good quality signal to be obtained, a means of getting this to the Radio SEAC transmitters was needed. Special telephone lines had to be laid, as described previously. The receivers' output was actually sent to the studios, rather than directly to the transmitters, so that studio control staff could switch over to the BBC programme whenever they wished. From that point it became just part of Radio SEAC's programme, sent up another line to Ekala.

Radio SEAC opened officially, on 25 April 1945, using an RCA 7.5 kW transmitter. The special telephone lines were not installed until November, so it seems likely one of the high speed wireless lines between Hora Hena and Ekala was used until then. Alternatively, it is possible that a receiver in the studio building was used. In view of the comments about a receiver in the studios sometimes being considered to produce a better output than that from the receiving station, it may be that the resulting quality was usually acceptable.

Cricket test matches were played in Australia in the English winter of 1946-47. Radio SEAC's receiving and transmitting stations were well placed to act as a relay station for the commentaries from Radio Australia. Instead of using one long path from Australia to England, the two shorter paths were likely to produce a better signal at the BBC's receiving station, then at Tatsfield, in Surrey. This course was adopted, and the BBC reported the excellent signal strength by telegram. They also provided a check on the frequency of the 100 kW transmission, which Peter recalls was half a cycle out on one occasion, which, by anyone's standards, surely has to be an acceptable deviation.

When Peter Burland was on holiday in Sri Lanka in 1994 he visited the transmitting station, and went on in search of the receiving station which had been his 'home' for so many months. The taxi driver did not recognise Hora Hena as the name of a place, and Peter understands, from his contacts who worked on the station, that Hora Hena was the name of the station rather than any village or geographical area. Nothing remained except the pillars at the entrance to what had been the camp, with one empty building still standing.

13

Radio Receivers and Reception

The receivers available to receive Radio SEAC's transmissions fell into three main types.

The first type were those intended for operational use in the services. This included portable sets as used by the infantry, typically transceivers, and heavy communications receivers mainly used by headquarters or permanent establishments. Although more efficient in some ways than welfare receivers, they could have two main drawbacks. If they had a loudspeaker at all it was small and unsuitable for listening to music. Even more serious, they typically covered the short waves from about 2 to 8 MHz, which meant that they would only receive stations broadcasting in the 41 or 49 metre bands. In Ceylon they would have received Radio SEAC's 88 metre band transmissions, but this was low-powered and local. The 100 kW set broadcast mostly on 15.120 MHz in the 19 metre band.

The second type was welfare receivers. Receivers for recreational purposes were usually chosen from those which found pride of place in the living rooms of most homes in the UK. Although there were still plenty of battery sets in use, the thirties saw the more general introduction of sets plugged into the mains. This included 'all-mains' types which recognised that there were still areas of the UK where the mains was DC (direct current). The battery sets obtained their HT (high tension at about 100 volts) from a dry cell battery, which was quite expensive, but lasted a few months, with luck, and another dry cell battery for the valve filaments, which required 1.5 volts. There were reports that the welfare sets in India and SEAC were often unsuitable, but they did not say what made them so. One simple reason could have been the absence of any short wave band. Apart from this, the principal cause would have been inadequate sensitivity to pick up relatively weak signals. This would sometimes have been because of the set's design, but may also have been due to a fault in the set, such as a valve needing to be replaced. Sometimes, no doubt, the receiver could have been installed better. A good aerial might have worked wonders. In 1946, a better type of set started to be issued which was more efficient and easier to use on the short wave bands.

The third type was probably rather rare, but when available could be ideal. They existed only when someone knew enough to construct a set, using components acquired from wherever they might be found. A case is described later in this chapter where a receiver was built by someone from spares they could 'acquire', and designed to cover the short wave bands they wished to receive.

The most suitable kind of operational set was a communications receiver, which would not have been generally available. Its high performance would have made the best of whatever short wave signal was available, and it would have covered all the usual short wave broadcast bands.

A suitable speaker could easily have been connected (provided one had the speaker, of course). Typical of these sets were the Army 107, RAF 1155, and the Naval Marconi CR100.

It is easy to forget, as I did, how many army units operated in areas where there was no mains electricity. For some time I took all references to 'battery sets' as meaning the dry batteries. The other kind of battery set was like a car radio, in that it was powered by a 12 volt lead acid battery, as used in vehicles. This covered the LT requirement directly, and there were ways to get the 100 volts or more HT that was needed. Of the various ways this could be done, the most practicable was a vibrator pack. The vibrator provided a mechanical way of rapidly, and repeatedly, reversing the direction of the current flowing from the battery through the primary coil of a step-up transformer. The resulting alternating HT output from the secondary winding of the transformer was then rectified and smoothed in the usual way.

The records mention that, even if the set was of a suitable type, they were, all too often, not in good working order. The question of repairs is dealt with later in this chapter, but we should first consider a more fundamental difficulty, namely the shortage of sets, and what was done about it.

The War Office welfare section was aware of this problem as early as November 1942 (and probably before that). It was a matter of priorities. The production capacity of the radio industry as a whole could only be expanded so far, and its priority had to be radio equipment for military purposes. It was not only communication equipment (transmitters/receivers) that industry had to produce, but an increasing range of radar sets. Some of these were vital to success in the battle of the Atlantic, against the U-boats, that so nearly starved Britain into defeat. Small wonder then that welfare receivers could not be produced in anything like the numbers needed until the war was over.

Of course, it is not being suggested that British industry had to produce everything that was needed. Much came from the USA and elsewhere. For example, I was surprised to find that some welfare sets came from New Zealand. The 48 set mentioned earlier was designed and built in the USA.

Sir Robert Watson-Watt was quoted, in the *SEAC* daily newspaper of 11 April 1946, as having said that Britain had spent £1,000,000,000 on radio in the war years. About half of that was for radiolocation, later known as radar. Such a round figure makes it pretty certain this came from a very rough calculation, but, even so, it gives some idea of the huge resources involved. This would be about £50 billion today, using the now generally accepted US definition of billion. Sir Robert is sometimes credited with having invented radar, but, although this is debatable, he certainly made a huge contribution in providing a form of radar, and associated organisation, that was particularly effective in the Battle of Britain.

After fifty years of improvements in radio receivers, it may be worth mentioning how receivers were manufactured in the 1940s, since this provides the reason why they were so time-consuming to produce, and therefore costly. All radio equipment used thermionic valves, since transistors did not come into general use until the 1960s, the age of the 'tranny'. There were no silicon chips or printed circuits; all components were discrete. Every component (capacitor, resistor, coil, valve holder, and so on) had to be connected into the circuit on a production line by workers armed with soldering irons.

So, as mentioned above, many items came from overseas. At the fourth Army Broadcasting Committee meeting on 29 March 1943, it was reported that 15,000 sets had been ordered from the USA.[1] This was intended to bring down the ratio of personnel to radio

1 WO 163 200.

sets to 70:1. A directive was being issued to units that it was in their interests to take good care of them. However, at the next meeting it was noted that the US had not been able to supply the sets, but no reason for this was recorded. Washington was asked for more details of what it could supply.

Mountbatten was aware of the serious shortage of receivers at the time of Lord Munster's visit. At their meeting, attended by numerous very senior service officers, Mountbatten pointed out that, as things stood, new transmissions were being arranged, but there were too few receivers for them to be enjoyed.

During the Christmas season of 1944, some of the recommendations of the Munster Report, were starting to reach the Civil Service. The one of immediate concern here was for the provision of more radio receivers. Someone in the Ministry of Production came back to his desk on 28 December 1944, after a rationed wartime Christmas, to write the following:

> Receivers for welfare purposes and for education are very similar. Total Service requirements were recently increased to about 40,000 for 1945. This could be covered from production arranged. It is now possible the 1945 requirements will be doubled, and subject to certain reasonable conditions about type, and diversion from other sources, it seems possible these requirements (if formulated quickly) can be met from production in the UK, Canada, and France, although at the expense of civilian sale in the UK.

Notes of a meeting in Downing Street in April 1945 include this about the supply of receivers:

> The scale of initial provision, maintenance and spare parts for wireless sets for the Far East has been agreed. 1945 production prospects are better than expected, and it now seems unlikely that it will be necessary to procure any sets from the USA. Some sets are coming from the USA in the 1944 programme.
>
> The total production forecast for January and February [1945] was 800 in each month. 490 and 1553 were actually delivered. In addition it is anticipated that 12,000 will be obtained out of a contract originally placed by the Ministry of Information. 4,500 have already been obtained from that source.[2]

It is appreciated that the figures are pretty meaningless when not related to some sort of estimate of the needs to be met. Nevertheless, they are sufficiently large to give some idea of the size of the operation, and the serious lack of provision until then.

In view of the shortage of receivers, the importance of repairing any that were faulty was addressed, in June 1945, in the recommendations from the third meeting of a signals standing sub-committee:

> 1. That the attention of all concerned should be directed to the recommendation of the G.S. Development Policy Committee, of the 32nd meeting, which was as follows:-

2 PREM 4 13/2 Part 2.

> It is realised that the maintenance of receivers broadcast in a proper state of repair is desirable and is a definite requirement of the India/SEA Commands. Nevertheless the maintenance of any warlike stores, whether required for operation or training purposes, must in all cases take precedent over this requirement.
>
> 2. For 'Amenity Wireless Sets' substitute 'Receivers Broadcast' (this is the correct nomenclature recently agreed on and in use in the UK).
> 3. (a) No change in the existing procedure for the provision and distribution of Receivers Broadcast is desirable except that A.G. Welfare should pass a copy of this issue instruction to MG/OS.5 to enable the latter to check the distribution of types of sets by Armies/Commands. (b) India Office should be asked to limit the number of different types of Receivers Broadcast sent to this theatre to a minimum, and, so far as is possible, different types should be segregated so as to ease maintenance commitment.
> 4. An instruction should be issued to Armies and Commands ... that maintenance of Receivers Broadcast should be carried out by IEME or Signals units, whichever were most convenient in local circumstances. If neither ... were conveniently located then the trade should be employed according to existing procedures.[3]

The remainder of the document covered the provision of maintenance spares, the distribution of spares, and the provision of servicing instructions.

These sections include a requirement to list the vulnerable parts of the five main types of receiver that had been received to date, and to estimate the quantity and type of spares needed. Units were also to investigate the possibility of cannibalising obsolete service sets for components. Available servicing instructions were going to be reprinted. Not as easy as it sounds today because photocopiers did not exist.

So it was recognised that sets were scarce and expensive, and so usually worth repairing if they became faulty. Radio repair involved diagnosing the fault, by a process of elimination. This meant finding which of the dozens of components (valves, capacitors, resistors, etc.) had failed, and removing and replacing it. Our training, as radio mechanics in the Royal Signals, was intended to give us the knowledge to do this. Knowledge, but not experience. This is why the document quoted above recommended limiting, if possible, the number of different types of welfare sets in any particular area. It also explains why there was a suggestion of listing the vulnerable parts of the five main types of receiver seen to date. A quick check of the likely faulty components might avoid the need for a more time consuming search for the fault.

Receivers (like other radio items) were adversely affected by the combination of high temperature and high humidity found in many tropical areas. Even the 100 kW set, in a well built concrete building eventually showed a few signs of this. Where the equipment was less well protected (e.g. under canvas in jungle conditions) the damage could be much worse. The station manager of the AFRS station in New Caledonia reported that it was necessary to blow the fungus out of the microphones with a bellows twice daily. He also mentioned that fungus, along with frequent periods of 99.999 percent humidity, limited the useful life of receivers to about four months before their innards simply rotted away.[4] (There may have

3 WO 203 2118.

4 Trent Christman, *Brass Button Broadcasters*, p. 44.

been a few too many 9's in his assessment of humidity). The shortage of receivers was also mentioned, so it was not just the British forces that suffered from this deficiency.

Radio components that were not sealed were vulnerable. The wave-change switch wafers, with many little pieces of metal, could easily become corroded and cause trouble. This is just one example, but happened to come to my notice because an uncle of mine was employed, late in the war I believe, in designing a totally closed in (sealed) wave-change switch. Whether it ever went into production I do not know. I do not recall seeing anything like it in catalogues of radio components. The UK domestic radios, issued quite often as welfare sets, were certainly not designed to operate in these conditions, and this could well have been the reason why some of the sets were faulty.

There was concern about the shortage of receivers at the highest level. When Major Noonan was reporting, to the eleventh Information and Civil Affairs meeting in May or June 1945, on the reception of the Radio SEAC's 7.5 kW transmitter, Mountbatten evidently asked about the availability of receivers:

> In response to an enquiry from the Supreme Allied Commander, Major Noonan said that receiving sets had arrived in India, and were now being allocated to forward areas. There had been some difficulty over the dry cell battery sets, and it had been found more suitable to send the American sets forward.[5]

It is tempting to suggest that the so-called difficulty with the dry cell battery sets could have been the complete absence of a short wave band.

When the war was over much operational equipment was presumably put back into store. Approval was sought, in the message quoted below, for some of these items to be made available for entertainment. The message was from the 12th Army to ALFSEA (Allied Land Forces South East Asia) in September 1945:

> 1. Due to the acute shortage of Receivers Broadcast it is suggested that all obsolete and obsolescent receivers fitted with loudspeakers and now held in Signals or Ordnance be released for distribution to units as Welfare Sets.
> 2. Will you please give early approval of this as the position regarding wireless sets and spares for welfare purposes is critical.[6]

Earlier in this chapter, reference was made to receivers constructed by people with the necessary knowledge, and access to suitable components. An example of this came to light in a letter I had from Tony Martin (with 298 Squadron in 1946):

> I was stationed at RAF Baroda (about 240 miles north of Bombay) from the middle of 1946 to December 1948. Part of that time the next room was occupied by an amateur radio ham who had built his own set, and during September to December he used to pick up on short wave. I seem to remember a radio programme from Ceylon, but only after dark. Was that Radio SEAC and did you only transmit in the evening? I remember the programmes cheered us up a lot as we were all waiting for our demob and felt very depressed and deserted. The radio link became even more impor-

5 WO 203 5207.
6 WO 203 2118.

> tant after the roof of the camp cinema blew off one evening during a performance. The dust, muck and bird droppings of the past years descended on the audience!

Of course we broadcast all day, but they had been listening to the lower-powered transmitter on 49 metres, as the 100 kW set was beamed principally on Burma. At that distance, reception of the 49 metre transmission will have been possible only after dark. A later letter confirmed this, and added:

> As the amateur made his set from parts no doubt scrounged from the radio section, the resulting set was no doubt more powerful than anyone else's.

Earlier in this chapter it was said that a better type of radio receiver started to be supplied early in 1946. It seems possible this had come from USA, because (as mentioned elsewhere) the Americans delivered their broadcasting on medium wave, wherever possible, but accepted that there would be circumstances in which their personnel would need to use short wave receivers to pick up the AFRS transmissions directly from USA. For those cases it is thought they supplied a set more suitable for short wave operation than the usual domestic radio with a single short wave band.

The remainder of this chapter is concerned with reception reports. None of the reports gives the sort of information amateurs provide on QSL cards. The basic details of aerial and receiver are very important if the report is to be really useful. Too often in the cases below, all that is reported is that reception was good, or perhaps very good, in a certain location. This ignores the obvious fact that reception on a set with four or five valves and one short wave band is going to be very different from that provided by a six-band, twelve-valve communications receiver. With that in mind, we can look at some of the reports that have been seen and noted.

No doubt many reception reports were received at the time, but the following have been found in various places. Some reports were so vague that they tell us very little. Soon after the start of the 7.5 kW service, for example, Joubert said at the tenth I & CA meeting on 6 June 1945 that preliminary reports showed that Radio SEAC was putting down a strong signal. He understood the station was being heard by the British Pacific Fleet.[7]

We do not learn where it was putting down a strong signal, other than the Pacific Fleet. The main target area was intended to be Burma. The reception in the Pacific was probably down to good luck, and, more importantly, excellent communications receivers on the ships, rather than welfare radios.

A message from SACSEA to the Air Ministry, sent later in June, included the statement that:

> Results of reception tests show good reception in Chungking, Prome, Toongoo, Pegu, Rangoon, Meiktila, Calcutta, Ranchi, Vizog, Secunderabad, Jubbalpore and Delhi.[8]

It went on to say the 1 kW set was being tested, and early reports showed good reception. This was intended mainly for local reception in Ceylon. It would have been unsuitable for most welfare receivers, because if they had a short wave band it will have covered, say, 16 to 49 metres. The 1 kW transmitter was on 88 metres.

7 Ibid.
8 Ibid.

The minutes of the I & CA meeting on 2 July 1945, record that Air Commodore Hunter mentioned more good reception reports. Incidentally, he said the troops were well satisfied with the programmes, and were particularly interested in the coverage given to the election speeches. It was, of course, to be the election when the people seem to have decided that Churchill had been great for the war, but they wanted a change for peacetime.

At the I & CA meeting on 25 July 1945, it was announced that the 1 kW transmitter had gone into regular service two days previously. At the next meeting, on 1 August, it was reported that it was well received in Colombo, Diyatalawa, Kandy and Trincomalee.[9] There is no doubt a good signal was received in Colombo, and there would have been hell to pay if the strength of the 88 metre transmission had not been good in the headquarters of SEAC in Kandy, as it then was. Kandy is about sixty miles from Colombo. They probably had very good receivers which will have helped.

When this report was first read, it was difficult to believe that Trincomalee should have been included among places where the signal was well received. A report seen much later, in a War Office file, made it entirely plausible by adding the words 'in the evenings'. Other evidence has been found of the 88 metre transmission being received much further away than that after the sun had gone down. (The reason for this was explained in the first chapter). During the hours of darkness it will have been heard well outside the area it was intended to serve. An old friend heard it whilst spending the night in a military hospital in Caloba, Bombay.

The opening of the 100 kW transmitter transformed reception in the areas it served. However, the wide and deep area to be covered meant that more transmitters, with a better choice of frequency bands to provide an optimum path, were really needed to provide a fully satisfactory service. S/Ldr Bernard Blakemore, the Chief Engineer, made this point in the piece he wrote at the time.

The situation during an important twelve months, from May 1945 to April 1946, was that Radio SEAC was broadcasting on medium size transmitters to an intended audience whose receivers were generally in short supply and of poor quality.

9 Ibid.

14

The Programmes

Although this volume is mainly about the transmitters and other technical features of the station, it might seem strange to make no reference to the programmes, the delivery of which was our sole concern. Doreen Taylor has given an excellent account of this aspect of Radio SEAC. What follows is the work of a technician with very little special knowledge of what went on at the studios.

Forces broadcasting generally tried to cater for its audience as it was; not how one might wish it to be. Having said that, Radio SEAC provided serious as well as popular music, but with an emphasis on the popular, since that, by definition, was what most people wished to hear.

How much Mountbatten listened to the programmes we shall never know. He had much else to occupy his mind. There is evidence, though, in a letter to Norman Collins, BBC General Overseas Service, that he was prepared to compare the programme quality favourably with the BBC's output, which Mr Collins may well have felt was pretty cheeky. The letter was dated 11 December 1945, and dealt with other matters before saying:

> I know that the BBC at present supply special programmes, and that these are much appreciated; I am anxious they should continue. My latest information records the fact that Radio SEAC is becoming increasingly popular, both within and outside South East Asia Command, and I therefore hope that in the event of its passing to the control of the BBC every effort will be made to preserve SEAC's present standard of programmes.[1]

Until the war ended, the station had the benefit of being able to broadcast recordings of complete programmes featuring American stars. These transcriptions were produced for the Armed Forces Radio Service. Some of the most remarkable radio programmes ever made featured Hollywood stars who were keen to support their forces by performing without a fee. As a result, the programmes could include several stars whose usual fees would have made the programme too expensive to produce. Radio SEAC could no longer use the programmes after the war ended.

Appendix A is a copy of a *SEAC Forces Radio Times*. When reading this after a lapse of half a century, it was noticeable that the balance of the types of programmes was not as I had remembered it. As a jazz and swing fan, I was surprised to find very much less of that kind of music than I thought there had been. Perhaps memory retains the items we most enjoy. Listening to the monitor for several hours every day was an education, in the same way that listeners in England listening to the American Forces Network found themselves enjoying American popular culture. I started out with a liking for British popular music, but turned into a jazz fan, and learnt to enjoy *Swing with Scott*, presented by Roger Scott.

1 WO 203 5207.

As the late Benny Green sometimes reminded his Radio Two listeners, popular music is often very evocative of a particular time in a person's life. The recordings listed below will surely remind former Radio SEAC listeners of their time in the Far East. They featured strongly on request programmes.

Bunny Berigan	*I can't get started.*
Harry James	*Trumpet blues & cantabile.*
Tommy Dorsey	*On the sunny side of the street* and *Opus One.*
Glenn Miller	*Juke Box Saturday Night.*
Fats Waller	*I'm going to sit right down and write myself a letter.*
Spike Jones	*Cocktails for two.*

For the big band fans, there were Basie, Dorsey, Miller and Kenton to be enjoyed. Even more exciting to me was the music of the Woody Herman band, with numbers such as 'Apple Honey', 'Wild Root', 'Northwest Passage', 'Your Father's Moustache', and the great flag-waver 'Caldonia'. I was slow to grow up and appreciate Duke Ellington. Having become accustomed to the sort of chord changes found in popular songs and show tunes of the 1930s, I shall not forget the shock of hearing a Charlie Parker recording for the first time from Radio SEAC, and wondering if the world had gone mad. It was some time before the strange new bebop improvisations started to make any sense. Tito Burns, a jazz accordionist who died in September 2010, made an important contribution to the programmes, and was quicker than most to master the new music. He became well known later for his BBC broadcasts in the 1950s, before starting on a long career managing famous artists.

It seems less likely that Ross Parker (for some time Director of Programmes) got involved with the bebop influences. He could certainly play the piano, and composed the music for West End shows. He may be most remembered for 'There'll always be an England' and 'We'll meet again'. The latter became associated with the 'forces sweetheart', Vera Lynn.

Special programmes included an occasional outside broadcast. One such was a commentary on a festival in Kandy called 'Perahera'. Figure 14.1 is a photograph of the outside broadcast van. Plays were performed quite often, and there is a photograph of one such occasion. (Figure 14.2). Unfortunately the only person I am able to identify (assisted by his three pips) is Desmond Carrington. He was, of course, to feature later in a very popular, long-running television drama for the BBC, amongst many other successes.

Figure 14.1 The outside broadcast van at the studios.

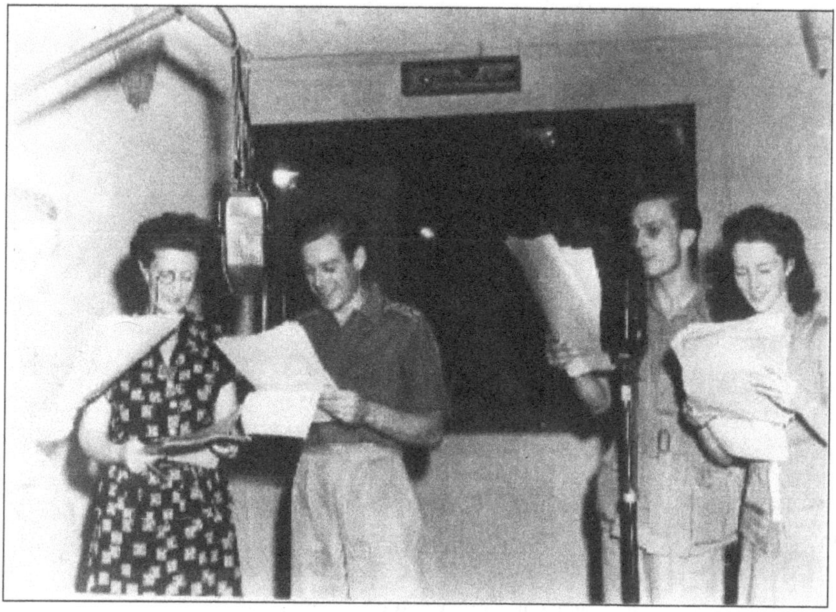

Figure 14.2 Performing a play, with Desmond Carrington (2nd from L).

He no doubt learnt a lot about presenting record programmes which he is still doing in the present century. Record programmes were an important part of the station's output. There is a photograph of Joy Allen selecting a record, (Figure 14.3) and another of an unknown presenter operating a playing desk with four turntables (Figure 14.4).

Figure 14.3 Joy Allen selects a record.

Figure 14.4 A record presenter.

As time goes by the number of people who have ever played a gramophone record will be very few, so it is worth saying something about what is involved. The crucial point is when the fingers have to lift the pickup arm and move it to just inside the edge of the record. It then has to be lowered gently until the 'needle' is in the record grove. It is a fiddly job. If you are a record presenter, trying to say interesting or amusing things to thousands of listeners, probably the last thing you want to have to do is put the needle gently and precisely into the record groove.

Fortunately, the makers of record playing equipment provided a neat answer. They produced a pickup arm that was mounted on a device that held the playing arm in a carefully controlled way, with a small lever to operate it. It moved straight across the record rather than in an arc as with the ordinary pick-up arm. Most importantly, the arm could be in one of two positions up or down. The latter meant the needle was playing the record. So the presenter did not touch the pickup, but simply flipped the arm down, which caused the needle to go down gently on to the record. There was another important feature. It was possible to find where exactly on the record you wanted the needle to descend, in instances where you wanted to start part way through the record. You 'cued it up' and left the arm in the up position. The playing started where you wanted when you moved the lever down to cause the needle to go down to the record at the right point.

The record library in the studios had a type of record that was not available to the general public. It is thought it was sometimes called a platter, because of its exceptional size – sixteen inches. It operated at 33 rpm. However, they did not have the microgroove of the familiar vinyl LP, so the quality was inferior to the then standard 78 rpm recordings. However, the sixteen inch disks had the advantage of being able to hold a complete half-hour programme without the need to change disks. Eight sides of a 78 rpm disk were needed for a half-hour show such as the BBC's *ITMA*.

Ingenious use of several gramophone turntables, linked by mixer/faders, enabled sound effects to be mixed with records. One such programme was called *Make-believe ballroom*, and included applause between dances, and other sounds. The most ambitious programmes technically were probably the film adaptations by Desmond Carrington. Excerpts from the actual film sound track were put together with narrative links. Needless to say, this would have been very much easier if tape recording had been available. As it was the programme had to be assembled by using a film projector, disk recorder and gramophone turntables. Many films received this treatment, but the only one I remember was *Brief Encounter*. Desmond Carrington featured also in plays, but one wonders if he could ever have imagined the long acting career in BBC television drama that was to come, not to mention his long running, much appreciated, record programme on BBC Radio Two that continues to the time of writing. This features an extraordinarily broad selection, including a few little-known performances which are well worth hearing. David Jacobs also still has a very popular record programme featuring what he calls 'our kind of music', much of which is sometimes described as being from 'the great American song-book'.

When the allied forces occupied Germany they found that tape recording there was much more advanced. When Andy Whetstone was demobilised he joined his brother in a recording studio in a Bond Street basement. This had open-reel, fifteen inches per second tape recorders manufactured in Germany. It is worth recalling other technical developments we now take for granted which were yet to come. Stereo was many years hence, although Walt Disney had used his version of it in the film *Fantasia*. The long playing record was not so far in the future, and many 'mono' LPs were later to be produced before stereo became standard. Of course, all this has been swept away by digital sound recording.

On a number of Sunday evenings a special broadcast was directed to the UK, and also to most of the SEAC areas covered by the regular transmissions. The signal in the UK was so strong that ordinary domestic sets could provide clear reception, so long as the set had a short wave band of course. These programmes included some routine Radio SEAC programmes, so that listeners in Britain could sample what was being provided for regular listeners. There were also record requests, and messages for those at home.

One of those broadcasts was outstanding as it included a recording made live, from a theatre in Colombo, and featured a variety of entertainment, including a large live band. A recording was made of parts of it which Andy Whetstone eventually transferred to cassette tape. As far as is known this is the only recording of the station's broadcasts. He gave me a copy, and a copy of that was accepted by the Imperial War Museum sound archives. Another copy was kindly accepted by Jerry Berg, an author of several books on short wave radio. The recording is in his archive of articles, recordings and other items at: www.ontheshortwaves.com.

It was very surprising to find, in October 2012, that somebody has given it a much wider distribution. This was brought to light by a Google search for 'Radio SEAC'.

Harry Moore was on the adjacent high speed wireless station, and was one of the lucky ones who were able to send a message home. I, too, was fortunate, and instead of having a request played I was allowed to play something on the piano, which I pre-recorded at the studios. I have no idea what I played, but well remember the strange experience of playing the piano in a room where virtually no sound was reflected back from the walls. The walls of studios are usually lined with sound absorbent material.

The question arises of how our parents knew that we were going to be broadcasting, and when. Harry provided the answer by sending me a copy of the letter sent on the 3 February 1947 to his parents by someone in the office of the Director of Army Welfare Services in the War Office:

> Dear Sir and Madam,
>
> 1. We have been advised by:-
>
> The Station Director,
> Radio Unit SEAC,
> Forces Broadcasting Service,
> 191, Turret Road,
> Colombo, Ceylon,
>
> that an item of request music is being played for you in a programme specially directed to this country called "Radio SEAC Calling the U.K."
>
> 2. This programme is broadcast on behalf of men and women of the three Services now serving in South East Asia and who send requests to Radio SEAC for tunes to be broadcast in this programme to their relatives and friends in Great Britain.
>
> 3. The programme may be heard at 6.30 p.m. our time on Sunday evening, 9th February 1947, in the Short Wavebands of 19 metres on a frequency of 15.12 megacycles, and 41 metres on a frequency of 7.185 megacycles.
>
> 4. Should you be unable to hear the broadcast and would like to have details, perhaps you would care to write direct to the Station Commander, Radio SEAC.
>
> Yours faithfully, etc.

There were people in authority alive to the danger that others might wish to use the station for purposes which might have encroached on its prime function of forces broadcasting. As early as August 1945 there was a message from an Air Ministry Special Signals Officer to SACSEA. After something about winding down newspapers, and the need for finding out what the Government had in mind for the station's future, it continued:

> Until such time as future policy is declared, Radio SEAC should confine itself solely to welfare programmes. As Radio SEAC is likely to be only 100 kW outside India for at least one year, pressure may be brought to bear to devote part of the time to Civil Affairs and propaganda purposes. This would have serious repercussions on the entertainment output, and should be resisted. All-India Radio should be able to help in this respect.[2]

This warning proved to be far sighted. About nine months later, minutes of a staff meeting in SEAC HQ held on 9 May 1946 included this:

> The Chief of Staff directed that [someone] should dispatch a reply to a telegram received from the War Office and to assure them that every assistance would be given to Mr. Murray in arranging for Radio SEAC to broad-

2 WO 203 4410.

> cast short items, up to three quarters of an hour daily, connected with the production of food.[3]

The background to the message can be provided by quoting Mountbatten's words during a TV programme many years later:

> The original SEAC area was 1 million square miles; now it was 1.5 million. It contained 128 million people. There were still nearly three-quarters of a million Japanese at large in it. There were 123,000 Allied prisoners of war and internees.
>
> The whole of this vast area was in a state of utter administrative chaos, and much of it was facing imminent starvation. The reports which poured into my headquarters every day were more and more depressing.[4]

It is hardly surprising that messages about food production were considered to be important enough to disrupt the usual programmes. I do not recall hearing any such messages going out. Such matters would probably have been discussed at a morning conference. Figure 14.5 is a photograph of such a meeting. Bernard Blakemore was taking part, and W/Cdr Smith, the station commander was no doubt in the chair. The latter rarely had cause to go to the transmitting station, but one instance was when the station was being visited by the distinguished *News Chronicle* journalist Vernon Bartlett. Most of the photographs in this book were taken by others. However, I am sure I took the one at Figure 14.6 because I remember my embarrassment when deciding to stop these very senior people so that I could photograph them. Unfortunately the quality of the picture leaves much to be desired.

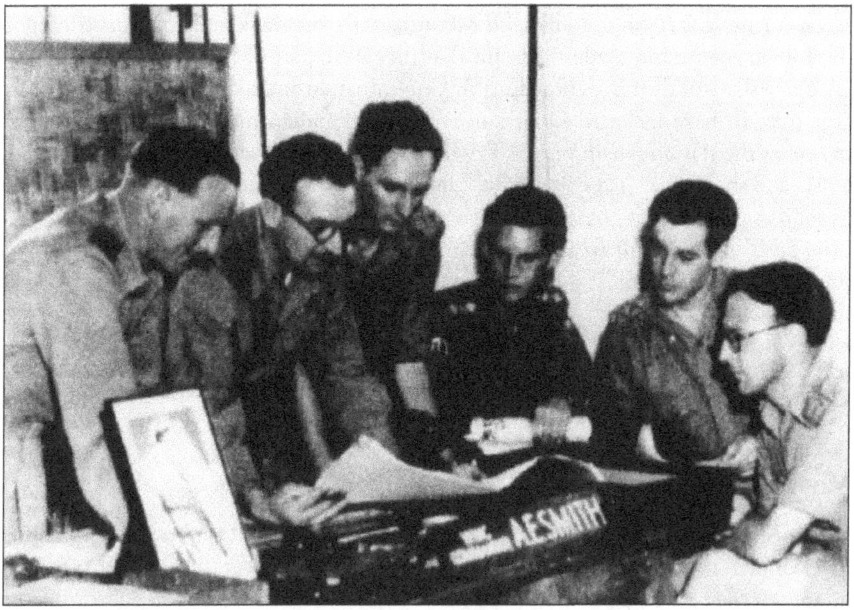

Figure 14.5 A morning conference at the studios.

3 WO 172 1811.

4 Terraine, *The Life and Times of Lord Mountbatten*, p. 132.

Figure 14.6 (L to R) W/Cdr Smith, Vernon Bartlett, and B. Blakemore.

It is worth remembering why forces broadcasting was perhaps even more important in SEAC than in the European theatre. The answer, of course, lies in the gulf between eastern and western culture. Most of the music broadcast by All-India Radio sounded strange to western ears. No doubt the reverse applied also. At one time this became a bone of contention between Auchinleck (C in C India) and Mountbatten. Auchinleck was a staunch supporter of the Indian Army, and made the point that they were part of the allied forces, and were entitled to a share of the forces broadcasting. Mountbatten and his assistants argued strongly against this. To have included significant amounts of Indian music would have detracted from one of the station's main purposes, which was to remind services people from the UK of music and shows they had enjoyed back home, which was where most of them wanted to be as soon as possible.

The *SEAC Forces Radio Times* for December 1947 also provides the basis for information about programme sources. At that time the station was broadcasting from 06.00-12.05, and from 15.30-21.45, a total of twelve hours twenty minutes a day. Of this, the content was as roughly as follows:

BBC relays of news, news related items	1 hour 10 minutes.
Other BBC programmes	1 hour.
BBC Transcription Service recordings	30 minutes.
Overseas Recorded Broadcasting Service	30 minutes.

In percentage terms, overall BBC relay was almost 18%, and the transcription services were 4% and 4.3% respectively. They varied, as between days, over the week. The remaining programmes were produced in the Radio SEAC studios, and made good use of the very large record library. The figures do not include Sunday evening broadcasts to the UK.

Listening to Radio SEAC in the transmitter hall, for hours at a stretch, certainly affected my taste in music. I still have a rather guilty feeling when I remember wasting precious resources by cutting a disk of Woody Herman's 'Caldonia'. I think I risked copying one other which was Dizzy Gillespie with the Lucky Millinder band playing 'After You've Gone'. The programme line failed one day, and I rushed down to the emergency studio and put on 'Caldonia'. I thought I had done quite well, until a BBC man pointed out my error. Apparently, in such circumstances, you should not use a recording which features a singer.

15

How It Was for the 'Other Ranks'

Files in the Public Record Office, (now National Archives) and books were the sources of most of the information in earlier chapters. What follows is the story of a few Royal Signals radio mechanics sent to Ceylon to operate and maintain the transmitting and receiving equipment of Radio SEAC.

Most of us arrived at the transmitting station at about that time. We joined a unit about forty strong which had run the transmitting station from the outset. They included not only radio mechanics, but linemen, riggers, drivers, and administrative staff. It was described initially as an Army Welfare Station, so all were in the army, and most were in the Royal Signals. We now know that from 31 May 1946 control of the station passed to the War Office, and the command structure was changed. One of the results of this was that personnel from the other two services joined the unit, although not in large numbers. The studios had always included people from all three services, and this obviously made sense because it provided the widest possible source of suitably talented people. That consideration did not apply to the transmitting station, where army tradesmen could undertake nearly all the jobs.

Most of our group were conscripted in 1944. They came from all over the United Kingdom, and from a variety of occupations. The Royal Signals men had joined infantry regiments for their basic army training of 'square bashing' (drill), looking after one's kit, maintaining and shooting with the standard rifle, firing a Bren gun, throwing hand grenades, and so on. This lasted for six weeks. Towards the end of this course there was an aptitude test, which formed part of the process of deciding where soldiers were to be posted for further training. The test included mechanical aptitude, for example, assembling a bicycle wheel hub with its ball bearings and other components. Presumably the person's education, civilian employment, medical grade, and other factors were taken into consideration. It might be supposed that men who had been civilian radio mechanics would have been selected for that work, but, although this sometimes happened, it was by no means always so.

In the Royal Signals there were two quite different kinds of job involving radio communication – 'operators' and 'mechanics'. The former had the very onerous task of learning to send and receive messages in the Morse code at speed. Anybody could learn the code in a matter of hours, but it took many weeks to build up the necessary speed. The use of Morse was officially discontinued in 1998. Telephony had finally triumphed over telegraphy. Telephony was, of course, widely used in the services in WWII, but in difficult reception conditions Morse was more reliable than speech. Radio amateurs still use both.

Those selected for training as radio mechanics had a more interesting time. Many went to Catterick Camp, in Yorkshire, where they had a seven months course in electrical and radio theory, and practical work. The practical side was not confined to radio work, but he had a couple of tame radio mechanics on call to operate the transmitter, and if necessary repair it. As he did not want his system to fail while his technicians were somewhere in the queue of 2000 getting dinner, he issued special passes which took us to the head of the line. This privilege did not find favour with those who had already been waiting about an hour for their dinner, and they sometimes made their views on queue-jumpers absolutely clear.

The transmitting hut, which served also as a rather spartan bedroom, was at the far side of the parade ground, and it served the more important function of concealing a gap in the hedge much favoured by those confined to barracks on the last couple of nights before going overseas.

Once again, a reasonably pleasant spell came to an end, and, on a wet miserable February day, half the team found its way to an airfield, and a Douglas DC3 Dakota, waiting to take us to the mysterious east. Peter Burland reminded me that we went in two groups, for security reasons. Although one of the most successful aircraft ever built, its services version could hardly be called luxurious. By today's standards it flew at low altitudes and had a relatively short range. The first stop was an airfield in the south of France (Bordeaux perhaps), and the second in Sardinia. This was followed by a bumpy flight over North Africa into El Adem, for a lunch of tinned sausages, presumably a recognised treatment for air sickness.

Two or three days acclimatisation were allowed in Palestine (now Israel). After years of wartime shortage of fruit, the unlimited availability of oranges was the most memorable thing. Some of our party were unwise enough to pose in front of a tent wearing their bush hats for the first time, and Figure 15.1 is a photograph of this unfortunate fashion event.

Figure 15.1 In Palestine. L to R: P. Burland, A. Whetstone, P. Foot & E. Hitchcock.

As the team was split between two aircraft, the tale of the bumpy ride followed by tinned sausages applied to only half of us. The party I was in did not experience the rather alarming incident remembered by Harold Priestley. They had just taken off in Palestine when they noticed a smell of burning. They drew the crew's attention to this, and were soon told they

Figure 15.3 The party at Mhow, except Peter (photographer).

Figure 15.4 The 'other ranks' canteen at Ekela.

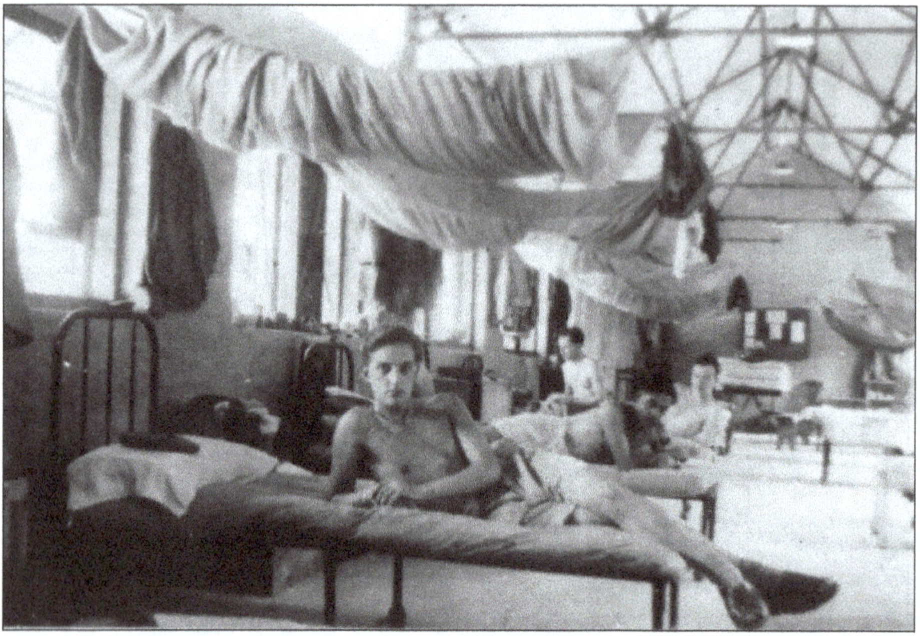

Figure 15.5 Barrack room at Ekela.

Life could be rather boring. Andy Whetstone found shifts on the transmitters more boring than I did, so he was very pleased when someone told him his name was on the notice board, instructing him to report to the studios in Colombo. Before he could get packed up and ready to go, someone came to tell him the order had been cancelled, but he decided not to know about that, and went anyway. He never returned, and never looked back, because the work was more interesting and he eventually became a studio manager. Rank did not mean much at the studios, and he was amused to recall that he had a Lt. Colonel working for him at one time. His experience was to form the basis for his lifetime career and hobby, as a sound engineer. Another man who started with us and was moved to the studios was Geoff Shaw. He came from the BBC, and returned there to make a distinguished career in TV engineering. Peter Burland spent the later half of his time at the Hora Hena receiving station, as previously described.

The climate was humid and 95°F, with marginal variations when the monsoon was on. There was air conditioning in one room – the emergency studio, which was about ten feet square. Elsewhere we did a lot of sweating. Allowing for this, the conditions were as good as anyone could expect. Building block barrack huts had been erected on concrete slabs, with glassless window openings with shutters. Similar buildings served for the men's mess and canteen/recreation area and the sergeant's mess.

Not surprisingly, there were radios available. There was a very worn-out piano which was not improved when it was left out in the monsoon. Sergeant James repaired it by taking out all the keys, sand-papering the edges where they had swollen up, and generally refurbishing and tuning it. Another piano arrived later, which was in much better condition, and stayed like that because it was kept away from the recreation area, with the risk of the occasional beer spillage.

Bill Reis recalled that James was the only man he ever met who had a piano tuning key in his kit bag. This is a kind of spanner that enables adjustments to be made to the tension on the piano strings, and thus varies the pitch. Less happily, he remembered one morning when he was trying to sleep (after working all night long) and the pianist was playing double forte. Eventually, and knowing full well that he was making himself very unpopular, he just had to go and put a notice on the piano, to the effect that it was not to be played again that day before 4 pm.

There was a full sized snooker table, and table tennis. As one sweated almost continually the snooker cue would not slip along the skin between the thumb and first finger. The cure was a liberal sprinkling of Johnson's baby powder on the piece of skin between the thumb and forefinger. This provided a smooth surface on which the cue could slide.

Army transport was occasionally available to travel into Colombo, where a light meal could be had, to make a change from the army diet. There was also the Galle Face hotel which had a fine swimming pool, with very salty water. Learners could hardly fail to swim. Mount Lavinia was further away, with surfing, and coconuts straight off the tree. These were smooth and green, in contrast with the hairy brown appearance they have when they finally reach the UK. They were not for eating. The seller just chopped of the end and you enjoyed a large drink of juice. Then there was the American canned beer. As I drank this, with no very great pleasure, I never imagined that fifty years later I would discover that the War Cabinet had discussed, at some length, how to get more beer to the men in the Far East. Apparently English beer would not travel, and the reason for this was probably that English breweries did not can beer until some years later. We were quite glad to make do with what Americans like to think of as beer.

I discovered something else about half a century later. Mention has been made previously to the lack of female company, but we were not aware at the time, that our predecessors had been more enterprising in actually persuading a few ladies to venture out to our jungle location. Bill Reis was appointed to the role of entertainments officer, a challenging responsibility under the circumstances. It was not difficult to find out what the lads would like, and some of their suggestions were fairly easy to meet. A football team was assembled, and at least one game was played against local Singhalese, playing barefoot of course. Cricket was also suggested, so Bill organised a game against the people at the studios, who were not all that keen to venture out into the jungle. David Jacobs declined to play, but did the scoring.

The lads also wanted to see films, and this was easy enough to organise once it had been established that there was an occasional open air cinema show at a nearby naval camp, and a proper cinema at RAF Negombo. Many of the films were American, and any love scenes will have been scripted with the restrictions imposed by the Hays Office very much in mind. This ensured they remained love scenes, and did not develop into what the tabloid press now likes to call 'sex romps' amongst other things. Even so, the audience had mostly been deprived of female company for months or years, and when love scenes were on the screen, there were shouted words of encouragement, and suggestions for ways in which the action should develop. These trips continued during our time in Ceylon. Bill remembers their being offered rum in generous quantities at the naval camp, but I think they may have drunk it all before we got there.

The final long-felt want of the lads was female company. The studios had that very rare welfare amenity. Bill's biggest challenge was therefore to persuade them to venture out into the jungle, when they almost certainly had a good choice of male company in Colombo. He succeeded in getting them to come out to a dance on about three occasions. Only on the first occasion did he offer what I believe the advertising specialists sometimes refer to as a 'unique selling proposition'. The gathering of women in the WRENS, WAAF, and ATS were to be transported nearly to Ja'ela by truck, but the special attraction was that they were then transferred to an elephant for the last part of the trip. It had taken the animal three days to walk from Kandy. Whether it remembered the unusual outing we shall never know.

My recollection was that we did not arrange anything as enterprising as that, and I do not recall ever seeing a woman at the transmitting station. Fortunately Peter Burland's memory was more reliable, and he recalls two dances while we were there. However, we probably missed the best ones, because Peter felt the two he went to were not well attended or particularly enjoyable, and no more were arranged.

There was plenty of time for hobbies. Radio technicians have often found the subject so interesting that their day job has also been their hobby. Some did some radio construction work, and were able to get components very cheaply from the market in Colombo which was selling war surplus equipment. Recent miniature valves sold for less than older larger types, because, without technical knowledge, the traders could only work on the basis that bigger items must be worth more.

Captain Sollom ran an amateur radio station from the officers' quarters on the station, and was able to speak to his family in the UK. Harold Priestley remembered sitting with him on one occasion, and became an amateur transmitting enthusiast after returning home. Andy Whetstone had probably moved to the studios before Paul Sollom arrived, but he took up amateur radio when he got home. He was in his 'shack' when he suffered the stroke which sadly proved fatal. He and Harold used to make contact on the air occasionally.

Fortunately there were a few people doing photography. Perhaps 'taking snaps' would be more accurate, but they have been invaluable for this volume. I did some developing and printing, but they were only contact prints of course, because I had no enlarger. This activity ceased when stains started to appear on the prints, which, years after, I decided had been caused by using an unglazed pottery vessel as a rinsing bowl. This probably accumulated chemicals and eventually caused unwanted reactions. Amateur photography in those days was mostly monochrome.

Apart from these interests, people passed the time in the usual ways, by playing card games, chess, snooker and table tennis, and writing home. Mention of home brings to mind another matter which was often in our thoughts – when was that demob number going to come up. The demob number was the designation of the group you were in for demobilisation. You watched as men with lower numbers left to get the boat home, and tried to guess how long it would be before your number came up. We had been flown out, presumably to save time, and because it was a very small party. Thousands were going home, and it did not matter how long it took – except to us, of course. Somebody decided to make a demob chart which is shown behind Bill Reis in a photograph taken in his room, (Figure 15.6). The chart plotted demob number against projected date of leaving for home.

With the 100 kW set fully operational, Bill Reis was keen to get home and prepare himself for a career in broadcasting technology, based on the start he had already made with the BBC, followed by his time on our station. However, some men had already gone and others were keen to be on their way. Those in charge were reluctant to let Bill go without an extended hand-over period during which his intimate knowledge of the 100 kW set would still be available. He was therefore told that his departure would be delayed for three

Figure 15.6 Bill Reis and a 'demob' chart.

months. He made it clear this was very unwelcome, particularly after the exceptionally hard work he had done in installing the transmitter. S/Ldr Bernard Blakemore had recently taken over the technical direction of the station and had begun to look at the available resources, particularly spare parts. He was concerned at some serious deficiencies, and soon made a list of items he felt should be kept in the stores. W/Cdr Smith, the Station Director, managed to arrange for Bill's delayed departure to be set aside so that he could take the details of the spares requirements back to the UK, and justify them if necessary with the authorities.

So it was not all that long after we arrived on the station that Bill left for the boat. He completed a degree course externally, at Imperial College. This led to his working on the development of television transmitters and studio equipment with EMI Research Laboratories at Hayes; a job of absorbing interest, but inadequately rewarded, as has so often been the case in engineering. His subsequent career took in both BBC television and the IBA. A few years ago he embarked on a long-felt ambition and set about making a violin; he had had many years experience of playing violin in an orchestra.

Being back in 'civvy street' would mean trying to find a job. Some of us had had jobs involving radio work, and might be hoping to go back to something similar. Others had done an office job, and hoped to move into radio work, perhaps after further training. The stories of what happened to a few of our party of Royal Signals radio mechanics are picked up in the final chapter.

16

Maintenance and Repairs

The 100 kW transmitter was being tested when our party of Royal Signals radio mechanics arrived in Ekala. Once the testing phase was over, and the transmitter had taken on its role of main transmitter for the station, it was reasonable to expect that a more or less trouble free period would follow. This proved to be the case, but any account given here relies on the memory of two or three people over half a century, so there were probably long forgotten minor problems. The only serious disruption in the use of the transmitter was caused by the complete breakdown of the power house, as detailed in an earlier chapter.

Bill Reis, who had a major role in the construction of the station, recalled one rather unexpected problem that came to light quite early in the set's operational use. The commutator on the rotary converter was examined because of undue wear of the brushes which connected the commutator segments to other circuits. Wear of these brushes appeared to be caused because some of the mica insulation, which separated the copper segments, had become slightly proud. Guidance was sought, and the treatment prescribed consisted of running the sharp edge on the back of a broken hacksaw blade along the length of the insulating segments. We do not recall having to do this as part of ongoing maintenance, so that problem was probably caused by a slight over-tolerance in manufacture.

Peter Burland emembered the painstaking repair of more than one loudspeaker. He also recalled the failure of the small unit which generated the RF input to the main RF amplification stages. He volunteered to find the fault, but Mr Caspard's assistant John Sidebotham was very keen to do it himself, and Peter felt he made rather a meal of it. The systematic checks he would have made, when fault finding in his radio repair work before being called up, would have pinpointed the fault more quickly.

Peter did take over when there was an HSR trip much later on. Although the breakdown had been caused by a huge capacitor (2 Mfd at about 15 kV) his fault finding routines enabled him quickly to identify the very large component which had failed. He remembers it as being a decoupling capacitor in one of the stages of the intermediate RF amplifier which fed the final output stage. He got a spare from the stores and laid it close to the faulty one, switched over the leads, and was able to bring the set back on the air in about twenty minutes. It seems likely the stores had not managed to get a replacement by the time Paul Sollom needed it much later, because he was faced with having to repair the capacitor, as described below.

As the 'demob' numbers came up, the Royal Signals radio mechanics, and other servicemen, gradually left for home. They had arrived to find a brand new Marconi 100 kW transmitter, and after less than two years service it had yet to be fully tested by the high temperature and humidity in which it had to operate.

Paul Sollom arrived on the station a few months before men started to go home. He was responsible for the technical operation of the station, and as time went by the unfavourable circumstances of the installation began to take their toll. This chapter deals with some of the difficulties he encountered. Not least of these was the fact that proper spares, if not actually in the storeroom, were likely to be several thousand miles away. That could mean a wait of several months. Fortunately, as we shall see, he was often able to find alternative solutions.

Paul provided almost all the information for the remainder of this chapter. It was not long before he realised that maintenance would have to be improved. The aerial towers, and the cables which held them up, were certainly in need of attention. They had to withstand blistering sunshine, torrential monsoon rain, and salty sea breezes.

Tower maintenance called for a budget, and the engagement of suitable contractors. The red and white paint had begun to peel off, and rusting had become significant. Paul was able to leave this to others to organise, but unfortunately the first firm engaged turned out to be cowboys. They made noisy hammering noises when they thought someone was watching, and no sound at other times. There was no evidence of scraping off old flaking paint and rust, or of successive coats of paint. One final camouflage coat and the job was done. Happily, another firm did rather better.

The other item was the corrosion of the heavy steel cables, the stays of the masts. A pulley rode on the stay cable with a large bucket dangling beneath, in which a workman travelled, winched up and down by assistants on the ground. He applied what was probably a tallow and grease mixture to prevent the salty sea air from doing further damage.

The aerial towers were not only susceptible to corrosion. At certain seasons of the year, there would be a thunderstorm regularly every evening for a couple of hours, and the masts attracted the lightning. It was necessary to phone RAF Negombo to let them know the hazard lights at the top of the masts were not working. Replacing the bulbs became a daily maintenance task.

Radio SEAC suffered programme interruptions because of flash-overs in the final RF stage. These were noisy and alarming, and potentially damaging, besides being an unwelcome surge on the power house.

Another item of equipment which stood in the open air, gathering rust, was the Heenan Cooling tower. Figure 16.1 is a photograph of this. The cooling process required that water should pour down the inside of the tower, so there was rust deterioration internally. Treatment with red-oxide paint was used to delay the process. The plant was essential for the 100 kW transmitter, and was not duplicated, so the problem had to be solved. It seems likely a new fan-blade system was made locally. This would have provided a spare so that a replacement could be effected without delay.

High humidity and very high voltage could not always be kept apart as well as one might wish. The 11 kV output from the mercury arc rectifiers was conveyed to the EHT room by a very well insulated cable. It was probably lead sheathed, and insulated with umpteen layers of cambric tape. The same cable connected the modulated voltage (22 kV peak) to the final RF stage. The humidity got into the ends of this cable, and failure occurred far too frequently, a few inches down inside the end of the lead sheath. The immediate remedy was to cut back the cable and re-connect it. Eventually this treatment resulted in the remaining cable being too short, so it was all replaced by a rubber-insulated cable supplied to withstand both voltage and climate.

Water found its way into other places where it was not wanted. The high-powered transformers were oil filled. This included the two stages of voltage step-up from the 415v

Figure 16.1 The Heenan cooling tower.

three phase on the power house switchboard to the input for the mercury arc rectifiers.. The smoothing choke and the modulation transformer in the EHT enclosure in the transmitter hall were also oil cooled. (Fig 11.11 is a photograph of the EHT enclosure, sometimes called the smoothing room). As a routine check, Paul had the oil tested by the Electricity Department who found it sufficiently contaminated with moisture to need treatment. They undertook the work using hoses to their mobile dehydrating plant while the transformers were live. It is thought they had to supply some extra oil to top up. Water and very high voltage came together by design in the final RF stage of the main transmitter. The distilled water connection to the anodes was by rubber hoses wound on formers in such a way they were effectively RF chokes as far as leakage currents at RF were concerned.

The rubber insulation was relied upon for the 11 kV DC (plus 11 kV modulation), which was quite a demanding specification for the hoses. Of course they failed from time to time. It was noticed they always failed a few inches from the anode, which was probably due to a local concentration of RF stress. Anti-corona rings were fitted found the stress points, and this seems to have prevented further trouble. The hoses can be seen in a photograph of the final stage with the doors open. (See Figure 11.6)

Other components to suffer from the effects of humidity were metal rectifiers in the filament generator room. One of the sets failed, and there were no spares. Replacements from the UK would have been available in months rather than hours. A motor generator was found with little difficulty in Colombo, and was up and running as soon as the concrete had set hard enough to mount it.

Failure of a capacitor is easily remedied by removing it from the circuit and replacing it with a new one. This is not so easy when it fails in Ceylon and the nearest spare is in the UK.

There would, of course, have been spares in Colombo, had the item needed not been rated at 2 microfarad, 24 kV. The remainder of this paragraph is based on Paul Sollom's description of the event. The only evidence of something being wrong was EHT overload in the audio driver stage. This was resistor-capacitor coupled to the output modulator stage. Disconnecting things eventually traced the culprit. As it was a push-pull stage, loss of drive from one half was not fatal, and the set was on the air again quite quickly, but with only half the modulation level. Turning up the audio gain produced an acceptable output quality, but it lacked the usual punch. The capacitor (about 24 x 24 x 18 inches) was similar to the EHT smoothing capacitors in the smoothing room. In the workshop, blowlamp treatment was applied to the soldered brass case. The contents, apart from much insulating jelly, consisted of probably 576 small capacitor units each (say) 8 microfarad at 500 volts working, arranged in series chains of forty eight units (to get 24 kV working) and twelve such chains in parallel (to get 2 microfarad capacitance). It is likely the paralleling was done at each of the forty eight levels of the series chains. However, one unit had failed at each level and thus provided a through track which was short circuiting the EHT. So forty eight units were removed, and the remainder were reconnected to provide 1.8 microfarads at 24 kV. The jelly was put back inside, and the case re-soldered. The capacitor was still in service long after the long delayed replacement spare finally arrived.

The heavy RF tuning trucks were wheeled in and out of the final RF stage of the main transmitter whenever there was a change to the waveband being used. Potholes eventually developed in the floor, and a permanent repair was effected by covering that area with steel plate, one eighth of an inch thick.

The high grade telephone lines between the studios and the transmitters were vulnerable to being tampered with. This refers to the lead-sheathed 7-pair screened cable which Paul Sollom remembers, and which probably became operational in late 1947. Crossing the Victoria Bridge over the Kelani Ganga just north of Colombo, the cables could be seen emerging from underground to enter pipe ducts across the bridge, and going underground again at the far end. Thieves wanting the lead would cut the cable at each end of the bridge and pull it out. They could be away with their booty before anyone realised the programme had failed. Unfortunately the control telephone line had failed too. There was a 1 kW transmitter at the studios in Turret Road which carried the Radio SEAC programme, so an AR88 at Ekala could take that off-air for retransmission, at least in daylight. This was practicable until the commercial broadcasting multiplied the number of languages being broadcast simultaneously. When the new studios were opened at Torrington Square there was no emergency transmitter, but the medium wave station at Welikade could be used in daylight. The noisy transmission made it unusable at night.

Telephone lines were laid overhead from the Colombo automatic exchange to Ekala. In the event of trouble, the authorities who were able to help with repairs could be contacted immediately. As a last resort, it was possible to dial the Studio's control room and have a programme sent up the phone line.

When Paul Sollom arrived on the station there was a 7.5 kW RCA transmitter under construction. This earned the nickname 'the smoker' because whenever it was switched on to test it, something went up in smoke! Eventually he ironed out the bugs and made it serviceable.

The AR88 receivers at Hora Hena started to suffer from the heat and humidity combination which caused such a variety of problems throughout the station. The test room at Ekala was set up to service AR88s and realign if necessary. The performance did deteriorate with time. The IF coils were not proof against the humidity, and gradually the 'Q' of the coils lowered. Although they could, with benefit, have all been removed from the circuit and baked in an oven, this would have been a major undertaking which was not attempted. A more common cause for reduced performance was the humidity getting into the decoupling capacitors. Not all sets were made with the same components, but if the manufacturer of the decoupling capacitors was Micamold, it was worth checking every one with a megger, as most would have become resistors. The name was misleading. They were actually paper capacitors. Fitting capacitors which really used mica worked wonders, but there were a lot to replace. It was not unusual to find screen voltage dropping resistors with about ten times their marked value of resistance. As screen grids were also decoupled, there were two possible causes for low screen voltage.

Type D AR88s were by far the most common, but Paul favoured the LF type. It was not its coverage of long wave and even lower frequencies that appealed to him, but its IF of 735 kHz. The type D had an IF of 455 kHz, which meant that the 100 kW, on its usual 15120 frequency, produced an image right in the middle of the 20 metre amateur band.

He looked at the AR88s at Hora Hena, following a report from the BBC's Tatsfield monitoring station of poor quality re-transmission of BBC programmes by Radio SEAC. Apart from the receivers, and their operation and alignment, he checked on the equalisation of the lines, and took some action on the line equalisers as the main suspect. On another occasion he went to inspect the lightning damage. A particularly violent electric storm had put the station partly out of action. One rhombic aerial had melted into short pieces of wire about six feet long after a direct hit.

Although a lightning strike on an aerial is rapid and devastating, it is not in the same class as the terrifying self-destruction of a diesel engine in the powerhouse. There was an exhibit of a crankshaft which had fractured or cracked. It had presumably been found on inspection, because no other damage was associated with its history. The warning had been acted on, and meticulous care was taken with the alignment and scraping of all crankshaft bearings thereafter. It is not known how long it had taken to get a replacement crankshaft, but it certainly took a long time to get a complete replacement diesel.

During coffee break one day there was the sound of an explosion in the power house, and everyone rushed to the scene. Fortunately no one was hurt, but there was all hell let loose. One of the connecting rods had snapped. The piston had dropped onto the crankshaft, and been thrust out through the crankcase. Shrapnel and oil were flying everywhere as the remainder of the connecting rod flailed everything it could hit. As the switchboard was not provided with reverse current trips, the damaged engine was being driven also by the other generator. The staff had fled. It was necessary to get to the switchboard, open the switches, and shut down the diesels. When silence had descended the station was off the air. The two good diesels could not be restarted because the compressed air bottles used to start them were empty. In the event the station was off the air for about half an hour.

There were occasions when Paul was able to make small but useful improvements. The 7.5 kW set called 'the smoker' was mentioned earlier, and this was the first set to which he fitted a continuous modulation depth monitor – a small cathode ray tube with RF output on the Y plates and audio modulation on the X plates, giving a trapezoid display. This was at a time when such improvements could be made very cheaply, thanks to the surplus stores selling ex-services equipment. The tube cost one rupee from the junk market in Colombo. It was not only in Ceylon that such bargains were to be had. In the years just after the war, surplus stores in the UK were a happy hunting ground for radio construction enthusiasts without much money.

The same source provided the components for a useful modification to an AR88 receiver which also provided a check on modulation depth of a transmitter, but remotely. An output was needed at IF to display against the audio output on an oscilloscope. A miniature valve acting as a buffer, with a suitable socket outlet, was mounted inside the set. Although not a perfect arrangement, it enabled a first check to be made on a poor quality transmission before investigating further. Other modifications were made to this type of receiver, such as the addition of a signal strength meter.

17

Aerial Arrays

Earlier chapters have mentioned the importance of increasing the strength of the signal reaching the listener's receiver by directing the signal towards the area it is intended to service. Marconi seems to have been the first to seize on the importance of doing this, in order to offset the effects of fading and static interference which can never be eliminated from short wave broadcasting.

When we did our Royal Signals radio mechanics' course we were told about aerials, but they were of the simplest possible design. It was accepted that you often would not know the whereabouts of the person with whom you wished to communicate, so the signal had to be sent in all directions. The answer was a vertical rod, about two or three metres long. This aerial was used by infantry soldiers and tank commanders, amongst others. In medium wave broadcasting, the equivalent of the vertical rod is a single vertical mast, several hundred feet high, with a big insulator at the bottom to separate it from the ground. The mast is the aerial, and any wires you may see are just to keep it in place. This type of aerial is sited towards the middle of the intended reception area, thus making use of its omni-directional properties.

Another simple aerial used by the infantry was the long wire. Harold Priestley used a version of it at home for his amateur radio hobby. This is a very flexible device that can be adapted to all sorts of circumstances, but its directional properties are not very strong. Infantrymen may have used it in preference to the rod when it was necessary to work longer distances.

The last aerial I remember from the Catterick days was the half-wave dipole. Now we are starting to get technical. If you were a radio amateur wanting to listen or transmit on the 20 metre amateur band you could take a length of copper wire ten metres long (hence the 'half wave') and cut it in half. Then attach each five metre half to either side of an insulator an inch or two long, and suspend the whole thing so that it is more or less horizontal, with its length at right angles to the area to which you wish to send the signal. It has useful directional properties, but not all that strong.

One way to connect this to the receiver or transmitter is to run a length of co axial cable (the same as that behind the television set at home) up to that insulator at the centre of the dipole, and connect the centre of the cable to one side and the outer element to the other. The role of Marconi's distinguished assistant C. S. Franklin in the basic design used in the final stage of the 100 kW set has already been acknowledged. Franklin was also responsible for the idea of a concentric feeder. The most widely used example is the cable connecting the aerial to domestic television sets. Inside the plastic cover there is an outer conductor consisting of a mesh of copper wire, normally earthed, and at the centre of this, and separated from it by insulating material, is a wire carrying the signal. In Franklin's original design, the mesh of wire was a metal tube, and a metal rod ran through the middle of the tube.

Returning to the subject of the simple dipole, it may be wondered what relevance this little aerial has to the wonderful systems Marconi dreamt of that would focus a beam much more precisely on the target area. It is because (like many other short wave stations) Radio SEAC's aerial arrays consisted of numerous half-wave dipoles in a variety of configurations.

Back in the 1920s, when engineers were looking for ways to improve the beam effect, some extraordinary arrangements had been tried. One American writer at the time compared the results to a spider's web. This may have been meant as a derisive comment, but anyone looking at the curtain of wires making up a Radio SEAC aerial array might have noted some sort of resemblance. It has to be remembered, though, that the 'web' was not all aerial. The actual aerial wires had to be held in place between the masts. So many of the visible wires were not copper aerial wires, but steel hawsers, separated from the aerial wires by insulators. These supporting wires kept the actual aerials horizontal and straight. In descriptions below, of various arrays it should be assumed that all active elements were isolated by insulators. The photograph of the model of the station shows the wires of both types, and may help to explain why somebody thought it looked like a spider's web. (Figure 11.2).

The directional effect inherent in a single dipole can be increased by using two in line, side by side. The beam can be made narrower still by using four side by side. These arrangements result in a beam in a horizontal sense (e.g. roughly speaking, east for Singapore and the Pacific, north-west for the UK). Figure 17.1 shows the relative positions and heights of the masts, and the directions in which the signal was sent. However, although four dipoles side by side produce a good beam in this horizontal sense, it leaves huge amounts of energy going to waste. Some of the signal would be going parallel to the ground and some would be radiated vertically. More energy would be radiated at unsuitable elevations in between. So the beam as so far described could still waste large amounts of radio energy.

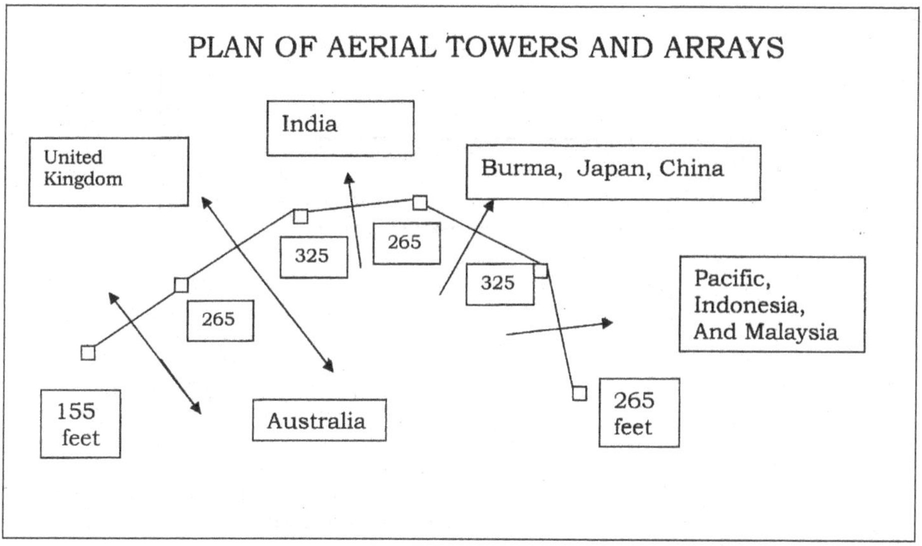

Figure 17.1 Plan of aerial towers and arrays.

This can be minimised. As we have seen, a narrow beam, in a horizontal plane, may be produced by having two or four dipoles side by side. The equivalent effect in the vertical plane can be produced by 'stacking' dipoles one above another. In fact in the early forties, the BBC, for its short wave stations seems to have standardised on four stacked one above another, and four such stacks side by side, thus producing a fairly concentrated beam in both horizontal and vertical respects. Radio SEAC's UK/Australia arrays followed this layout because the long distances involved meant that by the time the signal reached the service area it was more than broad enough to cover that area. For example, the beam to the UK was wide enough to provide a good signal in Sweden.

The four stack arrangement, in the version described, results in a concentrated beam with a very low trajectory, about fifteen degrees above the horizon, provided the lowest part of the array is a suitable distance above the ground. This produces a strong signal at long distances. Even with a single dipole, the height above ground affects the radiation pattern. If it is low the radiation is sent at a high angle, and vice versa. All this goes to explain why Radio SEAC's masts had to be so high.

So the typical BBC stack mentioned above could be described as 'four stack, four wide'. The layout is shown in Figure 17.2, in which the thick horizontal lines are the 16 dipoles, each half a wavelength long. The thinner lines represent the feeder. A broader beam is sometimes needed, as was the case with the station's array for Singapore and the Pacific, and this was achieved with an array 'four stack, two wide'. This could be represented by half the diagram just mentioned, divided vertically, of course. As the dipoles need to act in phase, thus supporting each other, the vertical distance between them will have been half a wavelength. As shown in the diagram, the feeder changed left to right as it ascended, for the same reason.

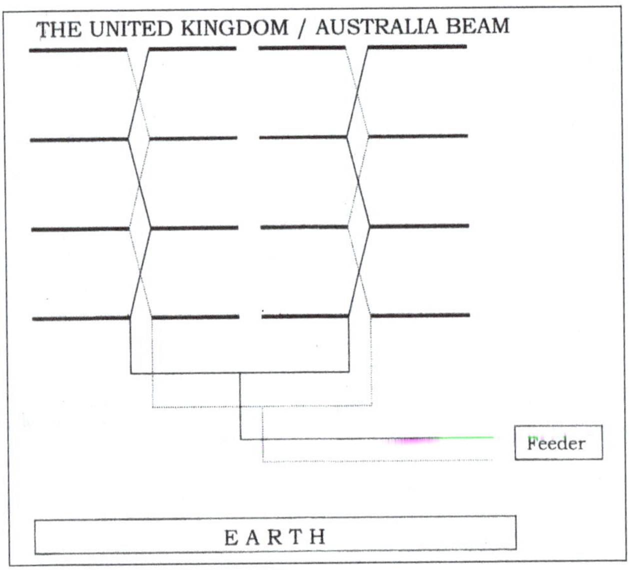

Figure 17.2 An aerial array, four stack four wide.

As India was very close to Ceylon the beam for India needed to be very broad. This was achieved by with 'two stack, two wide' (a quarter of the diagram just mentioned).

Radio SEAC's most important aerial has not yet been mentioned because it was fundamentally different in being three stack, one wide, which meant that it produced a very broad beam. The Marconi 100 kW transmitter was usually connected to that aerial array. It covered Burma, China and Japan, as intended, and much of the United States which would be expected in view of the direction of the beam. What would not have been expected was that the station also had listeners in Australia. This was well outside the area the main beam was intended to cover, and can only be explained by the sheer power of the transmitter. When I returned home and constructed a receiver I was able to hear the station with an indoor aerial a few feet long, although it must be said it was a weak signal with a lot of fading. Any transmissions intended for the UK were beamed in a completely different direction, and used a four stack four wide array which produced a much narrower beam. Listeners with ordinary domestic receivers had good reception, as long as they had a short wave band.

Figure 17.3 is a diagram of the aerial which illustrates how it differed significantly from all the other aerials. It was described as a Krauss dipole in recognition of the American aerial expert who was associated with its design. It used folded dipoles, and each was centre-fed, which meant it was being fed at a low impedance point, which was close to the characteristic impedance of the feeder. It is thought this minimised the need for impedance matching devices.

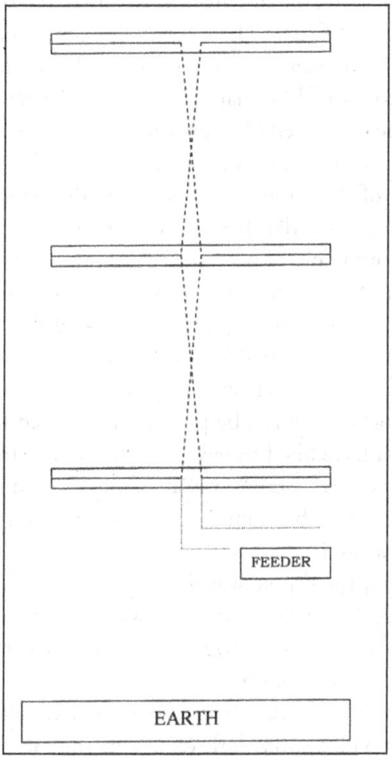

Figure 17.3 The main beam aerial array.

One thing more was needed to make the beams about as good as could be achieved, given the practical restrictions imposed by the sheer size of the arrays. As already mentioned, in this kind of array, the signal goes off at right angles to the aerial wires. This means of course, that the arrangement so far described would have produced a good signal in Singapore, and an equally good one in equatorial regions of Africa. This back beam is undesirable for several reasons. It means that half the signal is wasted. It also means that people over a huge area will be sent a signal they do not want, and which may interfere with stations they actually wish to hear. It is also possible, given the right conditions, for the back beam to go right round the globe and be received in addition to one which has usually travelled a relatively short distance. The two signals are likely to reach the receiver at slightly different times and so provide an echo effect. So there are compelling reasons to eliminate the back beam as far as possible.

The earliest experiments with radio waves in the laboratory, showed that they were reflected from certain objects. This was half a century before radio waves were bounced off bombers, and picked up by radar. The television aerials that decorate so many of our rooftops nearly always have a reflector element at the opposite end from the direction of the transmitter. This boosts the signal going down to the set, and acts as a screen against unwanted interference from the opposite direction.

A reflector for the basic single dipole mentioned on the first page of this chapter consists of a second wire, the length of the dipole (i.e. half a wavelength) positioned a quarter of a wavelength behind the other dipole, relative to the service area to be covered. This wire will reflect the signal back to the active aerial wire and reinforce the strength of the signal going in the required direction. The experts will be muttering by now that the dipole should be cut slightly shorter than half a wavelength and the reflector slightly longer, but there are books with formulae and tables for stuff like that. However, the aerial arrays mentioned earlier, such as four stack, four wide, consisted of many dipoles, and the reflector curtain was virtually the same as the curtain being fed by the transmitter. In the case of the reversible UK / Australia beam the change of direction was effected by disconnecting the feeder from the active curtain and connecting it to what had been the reflector curtain.

We should pause for a moment, to note that the simplest dipole and reflector arrangement was the basis of Radio SEAC's first aerial in 1945. Norman Shires kindly provided a detailed plan of it, and the diagram in Figure 17.4 is based on that plan. He remembered the aerial well. The diagram shows feeders going to both dipole and reflector, because both elements were driven, which meant that care was needed to ensure the correct phase difference, if a reasonable forward lobe was to be produced, directed to the right area. He never met the designer, but would have liked to have had the chance to discuss with him the fact that some of the supporting wires were too hot to touch, even when running only half a kilowatt. This suggests, of course, that some of the energy which should have been radiated as a radio signal was being wasted.

Very early in this chapter, the dipole was described as a half wave dipole. Therein lies a serious limitation. The intention, in the example, was to transmit on 20 metres, and used a piece of wire ten metres long. But if you then wanted to transmit on 30 metres you would need another aerial which would be fashioned from a wire 15 metres long. So, Radio SEAC transmitted to Singapore and the Pacific on 16 metres, but if it had been found that a better signal could be provided after dark on 25 metres, it would have been necessary to have another aerial alongside the first, and connect the transmitter to that for evening transmissions. For this reason, the five 'aerial bays' (a bay being the space between adjacent masts) mostly had three aerial arrays to provide for broadcasting in three possible wavebands. Unfortunately it has not been possible to assemble a complete picture of all the bands covered in the various directions.

As its title indicates, this chapter is about the aerial arrays used by Radio SEAC, and at this point there is no more that can usefully be said on that subject, with the information

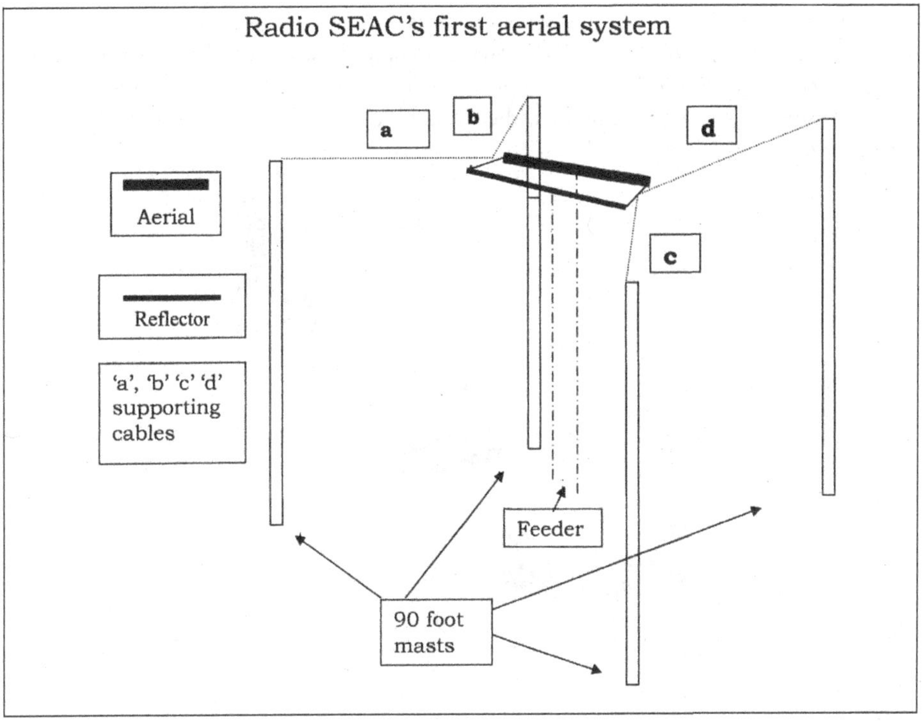

Figure 17.4 Radio SEAC's first aerial.

available. A general description of the transmitters has already been given, what remains is to consider how the radio frequency output from the transmitter was conveyed to the aerial. The only feeder mentioned so far has been a length of coaxial cable connecting a transmitter to the middle of a simple dipole.

When considering how to join pieces of equipment operating at mains frequency of 50 Hz, or audio frequencies from 20 Hz to 20,000 Hz, a cable containing a pair of wires of suitable thickness is all that is usually required. Once you start connecting bits of wire in a simple fashion to a transmitter operating at several million Hertz the wires start acting as aerials, and very bad aerials at that. The ratio between current and voltage, in the cases mentioned at the start of this paragraph, is constant throughout the length of the connecting wires. At radio frequencies, this varies regularly along the length of the wires. A feeder is what is called a 'transmission line', and the theoretical considerations, expressed mathematically, can be found in textbooks, but have no place here. It is sufficient to say that the feeders, stretching sometimes for hundreds of metres into the aerial field, look like neatly suspended wires. Their apparent simplicity is misleading.

We should therefore consider what a feeder needs to do, and some of the factors involved. What a feeder should not do is act like an aerial and radiate a signal. In this respect it is helpful that the type of feeder being considered is an open wire, balanced feeder, so that the current in one wire tends to nullify the effect of the current in the other wire alongside it. If a feeder is not connected in the right way to the transmitter or to the aerial, excessive 'standing waves' will exist which can give rise to radiation, and other problems. Figure 17.5 is a photograph of a piece of equipment called a standing wave meter, hanging from the feeder. I saw such a device being used on one occasion, but did not fully understand what was involved. Suffice it to say that the meter is literally hooked onto the feeder wires, and, with the transmitter on low power, the meter will indicate the level of standing waves. If the results indicate excessive amounts, the cause needs to be established, and appropriate corrective measures taken.

Figure17.5 A standing wave meter on an aerial feeder.

The use of coaxial cable for feeders was mentioned earlier in this chapter. The best known example of this use must be the lead that connects the TV at home to the aerial in the loft, or on a chimney stack. This cable has a characteristic impedance of about 75 ohms, and makers of TV sets and aerial systems have that fact in mind when designing their products. When something has a relatively low impedance as this does, it means that the power is delivered at a high current and a low voltage. With a high impedance the situation is reversed,

Loudspeakers typically have an impedance of about 8 ohms, so the current going to them is high, but at a low voltage. When buying good quality speakers from a specialist shop the salesman may suggest buying good quality leads capable of handling the high currents without undue loss. They can be very expensive.

An open wire feeder consists of a pair of wires kept a fixed distance apart by using insulated spacers at regular intervals. Such a feeder typically has a characteristic impedance of about 600 ohms. In Radio SEAC's feeders, where each 'wire' was in fact two wires, one above the other, the figure was 300 ohms. The calculation to arrive at this figure takes account of the diameter of the wires, and the space between them.

With a station such as Radio SEAC, with a number of transmitters feeding a variety of aerial types, it is sensible for this impedance value to be standardised throughout. So an identical type of feeder went out from every transmitter and was carried on supports which looked something like the frame of a child's swing. Ideally, it should have been possible to connect any transmitter to any aerial. (It is not known whether this was fully achieved). The layout of the feeders therefore included switching arrangements. They were not switches as one would normally think of them. The wires each had a special hook on the end which hooked onto the end of the feeder going to the aerial to be used. Such connections had therefore to be made by hand, and a lineman went out into the aerial field when the daily change was made from 19 metres to 25 metres for the main transmission at the start of the evening. (Not made later in Radio SEAC's years on the air). Obviously the transmitter had to be taken off the air, set up for the new frequency, and then restarted on the new frequency. There was a ten minute break in transmission to enable this to be done. A lineman changed the connections back again before transmissions opened the following morning on 19 metres. In modern transmitting stations, the transmitter operator can operate specially designed switches remotely from the control desk.

It has been mentioned that Radio SEAC's feeders had an impedance of 300 ohms. The final output circuits of all the transmitters were therefore designed to enable them to deliver their outputs effectively into 300 ohms. In the case of the 100 kW set, the final stage of the transmitter, with its pair of massive triode valves, included a large tuned circuit (most often tuned to 15.120 MHz) made of heavy gauge copper pipe. The radio frequency power had to be taken from that 'coil' and passed on to the aerial feeders. A smaller coil was inserted in the centre of the main coil, so forming a transformer. As the number of turns in the main coil was more than those in the smaller coil, a step down in impedance was effected, as well as the required coupling, which meant the feeder was supplied from a source having a matching impedance.

The coils mentioned above were on a demountable trolley, so a trolley had to be available for every waveband used. When a change had to be made, the set was taken off the air, and one trolley replaced by another.

The matter of impedance becomes more problematic at the aerial end when different kinds of aerial array are used. The design of most of Radio SEAC's aerial arrays was such that it was the ends of the halfway dipoles, rather than the middle, that were fed. These are high impedance points, even though not as high as they would have been had the arrays not had reflectors, which reduce the impedance. The main beam, on the other hand, used Krauss dipoles which are fed in the middle, but are 'folded'. This has the effect of changing the impedance, and it is thought this brought the impedance nearer to the required 300 ohms.

Fortunately, various solutions were available to solve the matching problem. Typically these involved the use of what were called stubs. No information is available on the types of stub used for the various aerial arrays, and without the detailed knowledge Paul Sollom had, the omission can not be remedied. The main purpose of this discussion of feeders has been to provide a general idea of the sort of issues involved. Getting the power from the transmitter to the aerial was nothing like as simple as it might appear to be any illustration showing the feeders.

18

The Station After Radio SEAC's Closure

Paul Sollom arrived on the station in August/September 1947, and I returned to the UK for demobilisation a month or two later. Paul took over the technical direction of the station, and when Ceylon became independent on 1 April 1949, the station passed to Radio Ceylon, the name by which the Ceylon Government's Department of Broadcasting became known.

The negotiated agreement included the requirement that the BBC would open an office in Colombo, and would have eight and a half hours airtime daily. Peggy Archer and John Wing from Radio SEAC became part of the small BBC programme unit, which was headed by James Mudie, who had been a prisoner of war.[1] The relay of the General Overseas Service continued until the relay transmitter in Singapore was ready for service.

Paul's amateur radio was not used only for the usual amateur activities. As he wrote:

> My ham radio was useful in obtaining reports of Radio SEAC reception around the Pacific. There were many American amateurs on the air from all over the Pacific area, and it was clear that they appreciated the SEAC broadcasts. In exchange for their reception reports I would sometimes arrange for their request records to be played.

It was not too long after his arrival on the station that he had to introduce a more rigorous level of maintenance. He also had to recruit local staff to replace the army personnel going home. Most of the new staff needed to be trained.

Eventually there were about one hundred staff, of whom roughly half worked on ground maintenance. Their work involved ground clearance to keep the snakes at a distance from the paths to the aerials, and monsoon drain clearance. They could also be called on for any physical work. Some could operate the winches for the aerial arrays, and others were permanently attached to the team of aerial riggers for general assistance. They worked under a foreman who spoke English and took instructions from Paul. The Chief Rigger spoke English well; was expert at his job, and had assistants. The foreman was called Kangani, and the Chief Rigger was 'Sonny' Nannakera.[2]

So far so good, but there was obviously a need for people who knew something about radio. Paul had made some initial contacts with local radio amateurs, and many of the technical staff eventually came from that community. His own amateur activities included

1 Taylor, *A Microphone and a Frequency*, pp. 63-4.

2 Any errors in the spelling are regretted.

keeping in touch with home on 10 metres, and making local contacts on 40 metres; a good place to meet for a Sunday morning chat. Paul wrote:

> Ernie Perera was one of the first radio hams I recruited. VS7EP was his own call sign. He put out an exemplary signal from his home in Moratuwa, and was highly intelligent. I trained him in the theory and practice of aerial design, and he was my most senior assistant.

The website of the Radio Society of Sri Lanka includes a brief history, which mentions the time in 1947 when torrential monsoon rains caused floods. Most of us have photos of flooded roads. Up-country was completely cut off from Colombo. The history mentions that up-country hams played a very important part in maintaining communication with Colombo. It also includes this:

> VS7EP Ernie Perera and VS7PS Paul Sollom were working at the Radio Ceylon transmitting station. They discussed the formation of the radio society with other hams on their 40 metre Sunday morning chats. VS7PS sent a notice for a get-together. It was called a HAMFEST.

This occasion seems to have played a part in encouraging the formation of the society. Sunday morning news bulletins started on 40 metres, read by Paul Sollom, or in his absence by Ernie Perera. Paul remembered that:

> Over the months, I recruited a large number of Singhalese radio hams, who at least knew what a valve was – though they had hardly met CAT 17's, but then I had'nt either! I guess we had about a dozen licence holders by the time of Independence in 1949. I think recruitment was largely by personal recommendation and interview.

The transmitting station itself had grown between 1947 and 1949. Paul wrote that there were rather more lower-powered transmitters than in 1947, but added that memories are confused as to where those transmitters came from. It has not been possible to assemble a reliable account. However, I was fortunate in contacting Adrian Peterson, of Adventist World Radio, who believed there were five. His organisation used air time on the station for about thirty five years, and he visited the station and remembered seeing the 100 kW set. Four or five is probably about as close to the truth as we are going to get.

Paul mentioned that commercial sponsorship began for programmes to southern India and Malaysia. He also wrote that:

> In 1951 there were overtures from the Voice of America to set up a station at Ekala. I was party to the discussions which were about building a new transmitter hall to the north of the present one, and installing three 35 kW transmitters. There was a lot of discussion about the aerials that would be required and how they might be integrated with existing arrays. I left before any work was started, but understand the transmitters were installed much as planned, and aerials must have been available for them.

By that time the station was being powered by mains hydro-electricity, which was installed in 1951, just after Paul left for home.

When the War Office handed over control of the station to Radio Ceylon, Capt. Paul Sollom (REME) and Capt. Alex Oulianine (REME) became civilians working under contract. The contracts provided the remaining two residents of the officers' bungalow with an entitlement to a rather better standard of living than had been afforded when the bungalow was furnished as considered suitable for army officers. This translated into a better standard of refinements such as fans, refrigerators and furniture. They lost no time in effecting these improvements; most of the work being carried out by the staff of the station.

The bungalow had been shared with Mr Bonong (a BBC man) who very kindly wrote a letter of introduction for me to the BBC. He was replaced by a Mr Fletcher who was seconded from the BBC and who left when the station was handed over. Paul's responsibilities under his new contract included the medium wave transmitting station at Welikade, 'Colombo Radio', and later an involvement in the design and production of studio equipment for the new studios at Torrington. This was undertaken against very tight deadlines, because a great deal needed to be done.

The Marconi SWB18 100 kW transmitter proved to be very durable. In visits to the station, (unknown to each other) Bernard Blakemore (in February 1986) and Peter Burland (in 1994, January 2001, and November 2004) heard about some of the changes made over the years. Peter phoned me in February 2001, shortly after he and Lesley returned, and in the next paragraph I have attempted to summarise the main points he mentioned.

The military security evident on the first visit had gone, because the soldiers were needed for the continuing civil war in the north of the country. There were transmitters of 1, 10, 25, and 35 kW rating, in addition to the 100 kW still in use on 15.120 MHz. He was told the Marconi set was the cheapest to run, because its reliability meant that fewer spares were needed. Japanese spares were expensive and more prone to breakdown. Japanese valves had been used where necessary, to replace the Marconi ones. Transformers had been mounted above the transmitter housing to supply the valve filaments. The rotary converters were no longer used, and only one of the two mercury arc rectifiers was in use. The master oscillator had been replaced by one with caesium frequency control. The stills had been removed, and distilled water was brought in as needed. Two of the original Mirlees diesels were still in the power house, the other two being used for spares. The officers' bungalow was being used for administrative staff. Peter was shown a small museum that had been set up, and he gave the superintendent copies of a considerable number of our photographs, many of which are in this volume.

19

Paul Sollom's Aerials

After Radio SEAC closed, Paul had to design and build aerials to meet new requirements which arose from the change of ownership, and the need to handle work on a commercial basis. For a while there was also a need to meet requirements arising from the BBC connection. The next few pages are concerned with these challenges, and the first to be mentioned was for the BBC.

Inevitably perhaps, the situation arose where the test match commentaries from England needed to be re-broadcast to Australia in a waveband for which there was no array in the UK/Australia curtains. (Paul did not mention what that waveband was). Bearing in mind the differing waveband requirements between day and night, it is worth remembering that while the players were taking their lunch interval in England it was around dusk in Ceylon, and Australians were mostly in bed. So the path from Ceylon to Australia was dark during most of the transmission. Perhaps the 25 or 31 metre band was needed. It was decided to extend the line of aerials for that direction by erecting a three section (105 ft) cigar mast (there were a number available) and suspending a curtain between one of the 325 ft masts and the cigar mast. This was a communications task, as opposed to broadcasting, so the beam could be as narrow as practicable. The layout of the Blighty beam was therefore followed, in being 4 dipoles wide, but with space limitations vertically, it had only two dipoles stacked, one above the other, rather than four. Obviously this was not so effective, but by using a 7.5 kW transmitter, and with a professional receiving station at the Australian end, reception was very good.

Radio SEAC did not transmit on medium waves, as the great majority of its listeners were hundreds or thousands of miles distant, and only short wave would reach them. An additional medium wave channel was brought into use some time after the hand-over of the station to Radio Ceylon. The intention was to provide an additional language broadcast for people on the coastal plain running north/south from Colombo.

All the dipoles we have considered so far have been horizontal, but in this case it was more suitable to suspend them vertically. An array of four, side by side, (without reflectors) had the effect of providing a beam in both directions, but with very little radiation east or west. (West being across the sea, of course). The dipoles were suspended from a triatic cable attached at each end to a 325 foot mast. Only a small transmitter was available which had been made from spares in the stores, so the transmissions lacked power, but provided a service some people were able to enjoy.

As will now be evident, Paul needed to bring technical skill and ingenuity to his task of shoehorning additional aerials into the very rigid structure he inherited. A further 'one-off' requirement arose when there was a commonwealth conference of foreign ministers in

Colombo. The band required for reliable reception was 31 metres, used only occasionally by Radio SEAC, and not provided in the Blighty beam arrays. The transmissions were to be aimed at Toronto, Canada. An atlas will provide readers with no clue as to what connection that has with Blighty, but a toy globe will disclose that a line from Ceylon to UK will, when continued, pass not all that far east of the eastern side of Canada. Paul drew on his amateur experience and erected a Yagi aerial, consisting of a director about an eighth of a wavelength in front of an active dipole. In this instance, there was insufficient spacing in the curtain to use more than one director, and no reflector, because of the spacing between the already existing aerials and reflectors. The width of the beam produced was not as narrow as one might ideally have preferred for a communications rather than a broadcast transmission, but the direction was slightly wrong. This arrangement resulted in the aerial impedance being as low as 20 ohms. A four wire Krauss type folded dipole was therefore used to give a 16:1 impedance increase to match the usual 300 ohm feeder. Other technical devices were incorporated to avoid possible trouble in feeding such a small aerial with 100 kW. Although there was some anxiety about this, all went well, and a satisfactory signal was provided.

Much more often than not, short wave has been used for long distance transmission, whether broadcasting or communications. This was certainly the case with Radio SEAC (apart from the low-powered 88 metre transmissions). Most of the BBC's UK national and regional programmes, and hundreds of small AFRS stations, were on medium wave. However, Paul Sollom experimented with short wave skybeams for local broadcasting whilst in Ceylon. The aerial was always designed to avoid ground wave, as far as possible, and to send the signal vertically, and thereabouts. Essentially he took an arrangement similar to the Radio SEAC array directed almost due east to Singapore and the Pacific. This was 'four stack, two wide', and described previously. The curtain was laid out on the ground and then raised by suspending it from palm trees, so that every point on it was about twenty feet above ground. At this distance the wave was reflected strongly from the ground, and thus went vertically. There was still some breadth to the beam, of course, so this meant the signal went up at angles approaching ninety degrees.

This first skybeam was used to broadcast a weekly news bulletin for radio amateurs in Ceylon, using his amateur transmitter, running about 100 watts on the 40 metre amateur band. He did this every Sunday morning for a time, and apparently people started to ask why the signal was so much better than that from the broadcast service.

Another skybeam was assembled in response to a crisis. There was a threat of a serious national strike, and the plan was for the station to be defended by the army, so that broadcasting could continue to the whole of Ceylon. A skybeam was erected on the football field. This had been created in the mid-forties for the army by clearing a suitable area of a coconut plantation. A 31 metre band frequency was to be used, and the array was to be fed by the 100 kW Marconi set. The same configuration of 'four stacked, two wide' was used. Not surprisingly, the aerial, when tested, showed that a very strong signal would have been provided, had the arrangement been brought into use. Fortunately the crisis was resolved, without the aerial needing to be used. Paul wrote an article about his experiments for the RSGB Bulletin.[1]

In sending a signal vertically using a skybeam there was some similarity with the experiment carried out in 1925 which provided radio engineers with the first detailed evidence of

1 P. H. Sollom, 'Skybeams, Moonbeams and Howitzers - Part 1', *Radio Society of Great Britain, Bulletin*, July 1952.

the various layers of ionised gas which make up the ionosphere. In that pioneering experiment the signal was a very short pulse, so that its going and then its return could each be displayed on a CRT (and photographed as a record). Paul conducted a very similar experiment. At first sight this might appear to have been an interesting but fairly pointless exercise. However, the ionosphere varies from region to region all round the globe. As we now know, there are differences in the various ionised layers between the temperate zones and the tropics. In the late forties there was still quite a lot to be learnt about these differences, and regular soundings were being set up in many countries at around that time.

Paul conducted another experiment to get an echo back from the moon. This was not successful. His amateur transmitter was nothing like powerful enough to ensure that the reflected signal would be detectable above the background noise. He established this when he made the appropriate calculations. He was probably unaware, at the time, that an American amateur had attempt this some years earlier without success.

While he was still in Ceylon, Paul wrote about his amateur station VS7PS in the *Radio Society of Great Britain bulletin* of May 1949. He mentioned the problems of the climate which is not kind to radio equipment. He also had the unusual difficulty of sharing the site with a 100 kW transmitter, and others. So he had to take technical steps to avoid unwanted signals interfering with his amateur activities. These included making regular contact with his family in the UK on 10 metres, and getting to know local radio amateurs. He was fortunate in being there when the sunspot activity was very high, so the 10 metre band was an obvious choice. The aerial he erected was a straightforward three element array which included a reflector and a director. As mentioned earlier, this reduces the impedance, so he used a folded dipole to offset that problem. On the ten metre band the half wave element is of course about 5 metres long so director and reflector could be of one inch copper tube, which avoids flexing. He also used wooden supports. As it was folded, the dipole was 10 swg copper wire. The whole array was mounted on top of a galvanised pipe about thirty two feet above ground level. The result was that with relatively low power he was able to send a good signal to the UK. He seems to have been particularly interested in aerial design, and in his article he mentions a more complicated array he built and tested, but found was no improvement on the three element array. He also mentioned the hazards of being 'sought after'. Amateurs like to talk to small countries with few amateurs, so that to have a QSL card from someone in Ceylon was a much greater prize than one from UK or USA.[2]

Paul was a practising Christian while in Ceylon. He wrote:

> On Sundays the 15cwt lorry took me, and some others, to St Lucia's cathedral at Colombo for mass, where English was the language for sermons, and the church was equipped with familiar furniture. The local church had a bare earth floor and no furniture, and singhalese sermons! But I went to its services on a number of occasions.

Although I have only a very slight knowledge of his life story after his time in Ceylon, I know that he died at Douai Abbey, near Reading in Berkshire. He was known there as Father Wilfred. While we were communicating he told me on one occasion he would not be available for some time because he was going on a retreat. It seems he was at the Abbey for many years, teaching science at the school associated with the Abbey, and later becoming headmaster.

2 P. H. Sollom,'The Station Behind the Call – VS7PS', *Radio Society of Great Britain - Bulletin,* May 1949.

He was an active radio amateur to the end, and also had a hand in the Abbey's website. When I looked at it there was a section in which he gave very precise constructional details of a device for measuring electrostatic charges. This was intended as a tuition tool and was made mainly of household objects such as drinking straws.

After he died, the website contained a number of very touching tributes from former pupils, and from other radio amateurs who had had contacts with him on the air. One, from New Zealand, said how he would miss their weekly contacts.

20
Postscript

Since WWII, the British Forces Broadcasting Service has continued to serve the forces throughout the world. As mentioned elsewhere, Doreen Taylor's book provides an overview of its activities from its inception until 1982, a year before her book was published. Unfortunately it is long out of print, but in recent years it has been possible, from time to time, to obtain a second hand copy from Amazon or its associates.

Towards the end of her book, the author mentions the start of television (BFBS-TV) on 18 September 1974.[1] This was perhaps the biggest change made since WWII, but technology had been moving forward in other important ways, and satellite communication has provided the means to deliver programmes instantly from the UK to other parts of the world, with no significant loss of technical quality.

Bernard Blakemore was, of course, aware of all this in February 2005, when he decided to see just how it all works now in practice. Whilst avoiding the English February weather for a week's break in Sotagrande, he decided to visit BFBS Radio Gibraltar (about 30 kilometres to the south-west) to find out at first hand.

A station on the Rock was broadcasting to the forces several years before Radio SEAC went on the air. The official start of forces broadcasting was in North Africa on 1 January 1944, although there was some earlier activity in the Middle East. Gibraltar, however, was very much a special case because the Rock had had its own radio station since 1934. This was a rediffusion system using cable and rented sets. In 1940 it was requisitioned to provide a service for the forces.

The story thereafter is fascinating, but too complicated to summarise here. In 1982 the Services Sound and Vision Corporation (SSVC) was formed, from the merger of the BFBS with the Services Kinema Corporation (SKC). Their headquarters is in Chalfont St. Peter, Gerards Cross, Buckinghamshire, which is often referred to simply as 'Chalfont'.

When Bernard visited BFBS Gibraltar on the 15 February 2005, he spoke first to Jacqui McGuire, a reporter whose husband was a lieutenant commander in the navy in charge of the Gibraltar squadron. She said that her task was to report local things going on, and local interest stories. They tried to keep the forces community aware of what was happening locally, in sports clubs and youth groups, for example. They used the local paper as one source of information when compiling a local news programme that goes out on BFBS 1 at 10 am and 4 pm each day. She explained that Annwen Smith, Programme Director, was at the airfield with a camera, covering a story for BFBS TV. The TV pictures would be sent on DV tape by post to the UK, where the material would be edited for their Forces Magazine programme called 'BFBS Reports'. This would form part of the twenty four hours of

1 Taylor, *A Microphone and a Frequency*, p. 195.

TV programmes sent every day by satellite. The Gibraltar station relays this on cable to the viewers. The use of cable ensured that it would be seen only by the Services community.

She went on to say that the TV programmes included some taken from the BBC and some from independent television. The 'soaps' were well covered, but the episodes were usually a few days behind those being transmitted in the UK.

Bernard also spoke to Surgeon Lieutenant Commander Nick Martin, who explained that he was there to be interviewed for a programme about welfare. They were setting up a 'well man' clinic. Bernard introduced the doctor to Alberto Navarro, and said he was staying for a week with Alberto in his lovely villa in Sotagrande. The doctor spoke French, and so did Alberto, so they chatted briefly. When asked how many people were in the community, he replied that there were about 500 members of the forces with their families. This was some 2,000 people altogether, and he looked after about 1,800 of them.

Bernard interviewed Annwen Smith when she arrived back from the airport. He commented on the important position she had on the station, and expressed interest in her unusual name. She explained that she had come from Wales originally, but had spent the last four years travelling with BFBS.

In order to explain her role it was necessary for Annwen to define the three services going out from the station. The TV channel was simply a relay from HQ, although, as mentioned earlier, she had just been working on some programme material which would be sent to their HQ over the satellite. BFBS 2 was a VHF radio channel, and, as with the TV, the programme was produced at HQ and sent to Gibraltar by satellite for relay. Programmes on BFBS 2 came from various sources, including BBC Radio 4.

Annwen was mainly concerned with the other radio channel, BFBS 1. This was produced locally from their studio which was equipped with up to date production equipment. Recorded music was held on computer rather than CDs. She explained that BFBS 1 was live and local from 7 am to 2 pm. This included the Breakfast Show, Morning Programme, and Lunch Show. Programmes were relayed from the HQ at Chalfont between 2 and 4 pm, and then it was local again until 7 pm.

These schedules had not applied when everything 'kicked off in the Gulf', and they had gone into 'escalation mode', which meant that output was live '24/7'. Annwen agreed that this had been 'quite challenging'. She had been in Bosnia at the time.

As Programme Director she was responsible for local output. This meant making sure that local promotions were going out OK, and that all the features, and the new packages and shows were sounding alright. Annwen emphasised that they worked as a team. The presenters could come to her, and she was the point of contact. If necessary she could go to Aidan Donovan, the Station Manager, if a problem came up. However, she played down any sense of hierarchy, which was not important. She felt that what was nice about being [illegible] was pulling together as a team to keep the listeners happy. Clearly Annwen was happy, not only with her job, but because she had met her fiancee in Gibraltar for the first time. He was in the navy, and they had become engaged at the New Year.

Bernard mentioned that he found the operation to be very slick and professional, and Annwen said there was competition, partly from commercial radio stations, but she felt that BFBS tended to stand out from them in terms of professionalism. She introduced Bernard to Ben Lynch, the lunch time presenter in the studio.

Bernard mentioned the fading he had noticed when listening during the day at Sotagrande, and Annwen introduced him to John Brookes, an engineer who was able to answer the technical questions. He said that their remit was to cover the Rock. They were licensed to use 1 kW which was fed into a two element yagi, well positioned on top of the Rock, and pointing almost due north. As a result it was quite a wide beam, but they had to accept that reception was not always perfect. They had trouble with a Spanish station which Bernard described as being right on top of their frequency.

BFBS Gibraltar is just one forces station among many, and there are differences, no doubt, between stations. However, the overall structure of the organisation seems to ensure that economies are achieved by using satellite technology, so that the same BFBS 2 programme material is used by many stations. Nevertheless, it is evident that the local radio element is important for the service men and women and their families.

Attempting to predict the shape of forces broadcasting in 2044 (its hundredth anniversary) is a particularly foolish pursuit, especially since the technology involved with entertainment in all its forms is changing exponentially. In 1945, requests went forward for more wind-up gramophones. We had one at the transmitting station, and a few 78 rpm records, to be shared by fifty men. Today, every soldier could have a few thousand tracks of favourite music in digital format on a very small device. It would be unwise to say how small it might be because they are getting smaller all the time. The choice of entertainment, selected personally, on demand, anywhere and everywhere, will surely be a continuing development, and this must have an impact on forces broadcasting.

Among all the changes since 1948, one radio device stood out unchanged in the Gibraltar interviews. The Yagi aerial is by no means obsolescent, and as it happens, Gibraltar's two element VHF version is not unlike Radio SEAC's first short wave aerial in April 1945.

Early in the present century, a considerable amount of information about Radio SEAC has already been accumulated on the internet. A search for Radio SEAC, using a search engine such as Google, produces several hundred 'hits', many of them duplications. The BBC's huge website includes, for example, references to David Jacobs and Desmond Carrington. A notable new hit arose when an article appeared in an Indian magazine *Frontline* (January 14-27, 2006 issue) which dealt with the alleged decline in the fortunes of the Sri Lanka Broadcasting Corporation. The article mentioned the passing of SEAC's transmitters to Radio Ceylon, which, in the words of the former Director General, Eric Fernando, resulted in that station being catapulted to glory. It also maintained that between the 1950s and the 1970s, no Indian listener's day was complete without tuning in to Radio Ceylon.

21

Our Stories

Nearly all of us who worked on Radio SEAC's transmitters were conscripts. Apart from the radio mechanics at the centre of this story, there were drivers, riggers, linemen and clerks. Few will have been called up without some reluctance or doubts about what the future would hold.

They had come from a great variety of home backgrounds. Some were from loving families; some may have been brought up in institutions and thought army life was great because the food was better. So while the majority were impatiently waiting for their demob number to come up, there were some who were quite content with life as it was. Some were going back to a secure job, and others faced a bleak outlook in a country made poor by the financial burden of the war, and the destruction of much of its industrial base.

So we were all sharing the same life, but every man's future was different. This section attempts to go some way towards providing an answer, but it is a very partial one because many of us are no longer in touch, and some have died. Not everyone would want to be involved, for one reason or another. The main idea has been to try to answer the question 'how did the person use what they had learnt in the army?' If they had a lifetime in radio or electronics, the details of the jobs they did will be central to it. In other cases radio will have been just a hobby, and for some that meant amateur radio. Some readers may feel that more information about personal lives would make the stories more interesting, but this seemed to make the whole thing too open-ended.

Under the chosen definition, Denis Stenning, who was the first of us to die as far as we know, would have had little to say. When, happily, we did finally contact him, it emerged that he had had a lifetime career with Prudential Assurance, and did not do anything much with radio as a hobby. Nevertheless he was a great character with an infectious sense of humour.

Andy Whetstone was at the other extreme. He simply moved from Radio SEAC's studios in Colombo to a studio in Bond Street and carried on sound recording for the rest of his life. As if that was not enough he was also a keen radio amateur. A very rough sketch of his story is included in this section.

HAROLD'S STORY

(As Harold told it on cassette tape)

I guess my early interest in radio was kindled by my father, who, whilst he did nothing in that line as a job, had a good hobby of building quite a few of the Scott Taggart receivers. I think they were published in a magazine *Popular Wireless*, or something like that, and they used to put a blueprint in. They were all straight sets, of course. I think the last one he made was just before the war – the ST 800, I think. Maybe watching him build those, and the little crystal set I used to have, got me interested. I left school at Easter in 1940, and my ambitions at that time were in engineering, and I wanted to be a centre lathe turner. This arose because I had a school friend who had a small lathe, and his father bought him a larger one. This meant the small lathe was for sale, so I bought it off him. I didn't pay an awful lot for it. Less than a pound, I think. It was a small 'Adept'. It didn't turn large diameter things. It was about six inches between centres. I still have it, and it's used occasionally, mainly to make wooden wheels for various models, and other things I've done for the grandchildren.

I didn't get a job as an apprentice centre lathe turner. I heard there weren't many vacancies for those, but there were plenty of vacancies for apprentice fitters. Of course, this didn't require a lathe; just a vice and a bench. I did that for twelve months, but it consisted mainly of just filing castings, and so on, so after a time I wanted something a bit more interesting, so I went in a local radio and electrical shop. I had a word with the owner of what was a family business, and he took me on as an apprentice electrician. That was quite interesting, and the salary went from 13/4d a week to 15 shillings a week, which I thought was pretty good in those days. That was one of the reasons I went to work for him. It included house wiring and repairs, and general things like putting new elements in electric irons and charging up the 2 volt accumulators which were used in radios in those days.

This went on for some time, and then there was a change of scene, and I went to work at Barton airport. This may seem a surprising change, but that was what I did, and I stayed there about eighteen months. I have two main interests in life (as Audrey will tell you) one is aircraft and the other is radio.

The work was on Avro Ansons, which used to come in for 1000 hour overhauls. The work was very interesting, and we used to have to separate the wing from the fuselage. They used to go away to another factory and come back on those long lorries they used to call Queen May lorries. They were then re-assembled; new engines fitted and propellers put on and the undercarriage done, and then they would be flown back into service in the air force. Quite interesting. That was where I had my first flight or two, because if you were lucky and worked a bit of overtime when you could get a flight because the company had a pilot of its own, and he used to take it up for about three-quarters of an hour's test flight. The job I had to do, as a young fellow, was to wind up the undercarriage. I think it was one of the first planes (in the RAF) to have a retractable undercarriage, but it had to be wound up by hand; something like 120 turns on the handle beneath the pilot's seat. That was one thing I did to get a flight. At that time I was in the local Air Training Corps at Eccles. I went on a couple of camps, which were good because you got flights. These again were usually in Ansons. I had a triangular flight from a station in Cheshire past the Midlands to Bicester and Cirencester, and back again. Ansons were used a lot as navigational trainers, mainly, during the war. Another time I went to a camp at Blackpool. This was a naval air station and the planes I managed to get a flight in were Fairey Swordfish. That was quite an experience. We went up, and round Blackpool tower; over the Lake District and back again. I was in the rear cockpit. Quite good.

When it came to calling up time I wanted to get in the air force. I knew it wouldn't be on flying. I fancied the radio side, so I went to volunteer in Manchester, but at that time they were not accepting anyone for the RAF. It was either Bevin Boys (miners) or the army. So luckily I went in the army.

I should have mentioned that I had done a bit of radio servicing. I'd read one or two books, and I had repaired a few radios part time, in addition to my job.

I was called up on 19 October 1944, and went to a place called Alexandria, a barracks near Loch Lomond. We used to march up to Lock Lomond, on a route march, and back again. After the primary training of six weeks I went to Catterick for about three days and did some exams and tests, and so on. I was lucky then to be posted to Huddersfield, where I did the nine month radio course. This was only about twenty miles away from my home town, so I used to nip over to Rochdale now and again. The next thing was Radio SEAC.

Interestingly enough, I met a chap at a local radio club who was called up on the same day as me, and did the primary training at the same time. He was trained at Catterick as a wireless operator. He flew out to Mhow in India, and he used to listen to Radio SEAC. So that is another person I have found who used to listen to us.

I returned home on the *Empress of Scotland* just before Christmas in 1947; landed at Liverpool, and was demobbed at York, I think.

I forgot to mention that, before I went into the army, I worked at a firm that were distributors for Philco Radio for the whole of Lancashire and the north-west. A fair sized firm, in Rochdale, but they are no longer there. I went to work for them, and did quite a bit of radio servicing there, and television, when Sutton Coldfield transmitter opened. I worked at that firm for a number of years; I would say something like twelve or sixteen years. I was on radio and TV servicing for most of that time. I did a little bit of Night School work. For three or four years I taught the Radio Amateurs examination. Then, as now, there was a written examination and the Morse code. I didn't teach the Morse code because there wasn't the time in the course.

Then I decided I wanted a change. Television was changing to 625 lines (from 405). I wanted some industrial experience so went to work locally at a fairly large textile factory. They had an electronics workshop there, and we built pieces of equipment that were used in various parts of the factory. I was there for only about six months because I saw an advert for a radio and TV instructor at a government training centre. That was where the real work came in, I guess. The GTC's were set up for people to be retrained in various jobs. There were about twelve trades at Hindley, where I started. It was a Civil Service Job, the centres being run by the Ministry of Labour. After an interview in Manchester, there were practical and written tests down at the government training centre at Letchworth, Hertforshire. As a result I was appointed to a new centre which opened at Wigan.

It was quite demanding at first. The course was on radio and TV. Most of the other courses (on welding, engineering, joinery etc.,) were usually for six months, but the Radio & TV course was for forty five weeks. There was one instructor and twelve trainees in a class. So you were kept pretty busy. We started at 8.30 and went on until 4.30, with a break for lunch. Practical work was in the afternoons. In the early days this consisted of building a superhet, so that was right up my street. The trainees had to make an aluminium chassis, and make the holes for valveholders etc. They went on to make a four valve superhet receiver (6K8, 6K7, 6Q7, and 6V6 output). There were Wearite coils, and the usual two gang tuning capacitor. They had to get them working and align them, and it was quite a good receiver.

I used to get them to put faults on them, and then exchange the set with someone else, so that they learnt something about fault-finding. It was a highly practical course. The CTCs all followed the same pattern, and were very good. The name was changed to Skill Centres later on. Later in the course we went on to TVs, because colour had not come out at that time, as far as I remember. When they left, from my class, about ten of the twelve had jobs, which was pretty good. I did four or five courses like that, covering four or five years of course.

Then I got promoted to be a Chief Instructor, but this necessitated a move to Runcorn. A Chief Instructor didn't really do any instructing, but was involved with discipline and overall supervision. Keeping an eye on trainees and instructors, I guess. I did the forty mile journey from Rochdale to Runcorn every day for about eighteen months, so I did quite a lot of miles every week on that job, which lasted for about twelve months. I think I was late on about three occasions, and that was due to fog.

Then there was a vacancy for Chief Instructor at Hindley, which is only about twenty miles away, so I applied for that and was accepted. That was alright.

The next promotion meant going down to London to work at the head office in Victoria. So this was when I met up again with Andy and Eric. I am not sure, but I think it was in the seventies. The job (with two other instructors) was to re-write the syllabus of training. Of course, there are lots of changes in the radio and TV business, servicing-wise anyway. They said it was only going to be for six months, but it lasted for two years. I used to travel down on the Monday, and back on the Friday afternoon.

Whilst I was down there, after about a year and a half, they decided to build a new Skill Centre about a mile from my home, just near the centre of town. It was a completely new building. I obviously applied for that, and got the Assistant Manager job there, when the centre opened. It was nice to be back at home again. I was there for two or three years (maybe more) and then the next move was to the Regional Office.

The training was extended to various factories, and other establishments, and paid for by the Ministry. The job I had then was monitoring the training being done for us by other people, so that was quite interesting. It entailed going to various technical colleges and other training centres, to see that things were running smoothly.

At that time, quite a lot of the Training Centres were closing, so as I was getting on for retirement time, I took a little bit of early retirement.

So that has been the history of my working life.

I went recently to see an old school friend who had been in my class at school. He had been in the army and went to Singapore and Malaya. He was another one that listened to Radio SEAC, so what with the man in Scotland I worked from Canada, and the one in the Rochdale (radio) club, that makes three. ['Worked' means he made amateur radio contact].

PETER'S STORY

Being a member of a large family in the 1930s (a time of high unemployment and little money) my ears twitched when my older sister told me her friend's brother had built a radio which did not need electricity or batteries to run it. Needless to say, I wangled an invitation to see and hear it. I was about ten rears old, and this kindled my interest in radio and the many other electronic developments.

We had an old radio in the cellar from which I removed the basket-wound coils, holders and tuning capacitor. I cut the baseboard from the end of an orange box, and the front upright panel from the lid of a tea chest. I earned a little money from running errands which enabled me to buy second-hand headphones and a crystal detector. There were two types – a fixed detector (two crystals in contact with each other in a glass tube) or the type I favoured, a crystal in a holder with a cat's whisker. This I found to be superior; there were sensitive hotspots which produced 100% increase in volume. I made many types, but the best one had a very long aerial and drove an Amplion horn loudspeaker which my mother could hear downstairs. I was often in trouble for falling asleep with it playing away.

I proceeded to build one, two and three-valve sets, all TRF; and in the early 1940s, a short wave radio using Wyvern or Wearite plug-in coils. I used to listen to 'Lord Haw-Haw' and another German propaganda station – Radio Brazaville. It is only in recent years I realised it was a German colony in West Africa. They both came through at strength five.

I left school in 1940, aged fourteen – a school manned by 50% sadistic teachers, most of whom, in this day and age, would be in jail.

After a short time, a local firm advertised for an apprentice radio engineer. I applied, and started work a week later. I was used as a general dogsbody, with only brief tuition in the workshop in a practical way. No theory was taught, and what little I learnt came from *Popular Wireless* and *Practical Wireless.* I learnt to apply my limited knowledge to circuit diagrams of superhets.

Eventually, the manager of the workshop was called up, and I, and a much older man, had to run the workshop. It soon became obvious to me that many faults were repetitive and were concerned with the HT line. Open circuit, short circuit, or leaking capacitors were the most common faults. Valves failed, and resistors in high current circuits changed value. Silver/mica capacitors in tuned circuits would go open circuit, and dry joints would cause many intermittent faults. These faults applied to all makes of radios, so that, with time and a good memory, dozens of faults were stored away. By the time I was sixteen or so I was doing 90% of the radio repairs.

The practical experience I gained stood me in good stead in my future years. I volunteered for RAF aircrew at seventeen and a quarter, but, like many others, was called up into the army. In November 1944 I did eight weeks square-bashing at Squires Gate. Holiday camp? Try running at the double with rifle and full pack over the sand dunes. It had its compensations. Blackpool was just down the road, with the Winter Gardens, and the Tower Ballroom, and no shortage of partners.

From there it was on to Catterick, north Yorkshire; bleak and miserable. We were given aptitude tests to decide which type of training we were suitable for. Imagine how shocked I was to be told I would be trained as a linesman. Talking among ourselves, I found a GPO trained linesman had been chosen to go on the Radio Mechanics course. We requested an interview with the CO, who listened to what we had to say and agreed to change the listing.

I started on the thirty two weeks course, and soaked up the AC, and radio theory like a sponge. One of the weeks was radio receiver theory. The instructor approached me on the first morning and said:

> 'I see you were a radio mechanic before coming into the army. There is not much I can teach you. Instead, will you have a go at getting this captured German radio working?'

In response to my protests about passing the weekly exam, he assured me he would give me a pass mark. So I set to work in tracing the circuit. It had strange looking valves. I had it working in about three and a half days. The only signals we received were in Morse code, so I suggested we find a radio operator to translate the signals, but he seemed quite happy that it was an operational radio, complete with circuit diagram. I sat the exam, and was only stuck on a question about band pass coupling; something that was unknown in commercial radios. When I left the army I checked all the circuit diagrams at our workshop, and found only one set that incorporated it. It was an HMV 'Rolls Royce' of a radiogram, at some fantastic price.

From Catterick, I joined the other eleven of our party at Skelton, near Penrith, Northumberland, to be trained in the operation of 100 kW Marconi transmitters. This was a most enjoyable experience; lovely countryside, good food, friendly locals, and best of all a summer with plenty of sunshine. We even went to a local barn dance, after having plenty to drink in the local inn. Eric gave us an impromptu on the pub piano, from which I had removed the front panels. (Re-fitted when we left). We had a bit of a singsong (not recommended for ENSA) and trooped into the village hall and joined in the dancing. A wonderful night.

After training we went to Osset, near Wakefield, and then to London, and on to an airfield down south. There we were split into two groups. Ours flew to Sardinia or Sicily, direct. The other group landed at Brest before continuing their flight. It is only in recent years I realised the significance of this. As with royalty, if one plane had crashed there would still have been trained personnel to carry on.

Somewhere along the line our movement orders disappeared, so there was quite a delay at Lydda, and Karachi. In desperation they sent us to Mhow, where we heard the Radio SEAC test signal on a local radio (strength five). After a further delay we had a three day train trip to southern India (complete with iron rations). We threw these to the local natives who seemed to enjoy them. At the embarkation point we threw our 'Bombay bowlers' over the side of the ship. Who knows, they may still be floating in the Indian or Pacific oceans.

After reaching Ekala we soon settled into the camp routine. A short time after we arrived, the 100 kW transmitter became operational, and we worked three-man shifts; a duty sergeant and two operators. The shifts were four days on, two days off.

After a few weeks on the air, we were on duty, with the sergeant in the office, Harold at the control desk, and I was taking the readings. The transmitter crashed, the HSR tripped three times, and there was a momentary deathly silence. The other staff wanted to call the officers' bungalow, but I said 'No, leave it to me'. There was a circuit and AVO meter in the office, which was quickly produced. I asked Harold to keep running up the HT, whilst I rapidly checked the ammeters in all the sections along the cabinets, to see if I could isolate the section where the problem was. This was rapidly found. It was in one of the RF driver stages; the one driving the penultimate amplifier. It was a 2 μF condenser (now called a capacitor) which was a dead short. I quickly electrically disconnected it, and checked it with the AVO to confirm the diagnosis. The sergeant dashed to the stores and returned very quickly with a spare, which I set alongside the old one, connected up, and resumed transmission. I thought I would be put on a charge as I was bossing everyone about, but nothing happened. I felt quite pleased with myself, as we had been off the air only twenty minutes, and we had worked well as a team.

A few weeks later the monitor developed a fault. As it did not play a major role in the operation of the transmitter I thought some other engineer would like to repair it. It was still out of action three days later, so I got permission to try to find the fault. I did this in my own time, and it took quite a few hours to repair. All valves and voltages were within normal limits. It turned out to be a dead short of a 100 pf. silver/mica capacitor between grid and earth in an amplifier stage. With the aid of an oscilloscope it would have been quickly traced, but at the time I had only an AVO and the circuit diagram, not realising that other gear was in the officers' bungalow.

The third major problem the station had was the six loudspeakers, only one of which was still working. The shift sergeant asked if I could repair them, having had experience of doing this in civvy street. I set about putting them back in working order which was quite a fiddly job as it meant replacing bits of very thin wire between the speech coil and the solder studs on the cone.

Another major problem was the collapse of an aerial rig (not the mast), so I suggested using the other array of the same frequency but aimed in another direction. My reasoning was that with such a powerful transmitter it would still reach a large audience. It took two days to repair the array; transmission still carried on, and to my knowledge there were no adverse comments.

All this was in 1946. Just after Christmas I was called to the company office and told that if I stayed at Ekela I would soon become a sergeant. However, they had problems at Hora Hena with the receiving station which needed to be sorted out. They would supply me with any equipment I needed to reorganise the whole set-up. The snag was that it only carried the rank of corporal. As rank and money did not count for much, I agreed to accept the challenge.

I first set up the receivers into two racks, and fitted a bank of switches so that (apart from external aerial or mains power failure) any receiver in either bank could be switched out, and any of the others could be switched in. Both banks were tuned into the incoming BBC signal. As a result, if any faults developed in the bank of receivers feeding the signal to the studio, we could, with a click of the switch, put the stand-by rack into circuit.

The frequencies changed during the day, and about two minutes before the changeover the group of receivers not on line were re-tuned to the new frequency.

I never experienced frequency drift on the AR88s, and the settings, using the vernier dials, never seemed to need adjusting. In fact, they were the 'Rolls Royce' of receivers. We had only one breakdown in the time I was there, and a quick flick of a switch immediately brought in the spare rack which was already tuned in. The fault was an IF amplifier valve. There were plenty of spares in the stores so the whole thing was soon back in good working order.

They had a superb workshop in the high speed wireless station to which we were attached. RF generators down to a microvolt, AF audio generators, AF signal strength meters, a Cossor double-beam oscilloscope and FM generator – a radio engineer's dream workshop. I checked all the AR88s for alignment, and also for sensitivity. They varied from .5 μvolt to 1 μvolt for a 600 mW AF output. Quite impressive.

At the end of 1947 my 'demob number' was up, and I looked forward to going home. I was luckier than most. My father worked at Negombo, only a few miles away, and was with the Air Ministry. They were extending the air force base runway which was to have been used by the very large American bombers to bomb Japan. By this time, the atomic bomb had been dropped, and the war was over. As with all things, you cannot stop a large machine instantly, it has to be wound down slowly, so his return to UK was six months after mine.

On returning to civilian life, my old firm offered me my old job back, which I accepted. After two years I decided to go it on my own, which I did for a further forty years. Retirement came when my eyesight deteriorated, and reliability improved on all electronic equipment. Costs of new equipment (e.g. TV) actually fell over twenty years, but all other costs rose. This was time to hang up my boots and do other things.

I considered I was lucky in having worked in a most interesting career which gave me job satisfaction to the end. The best years, career wise, were my army days. I learnt a great deal and had some very good comrades.

ANDY'S STORY

Nothing is known of Andy's life before his army service, except that his family lived in the Weston-Super-Mare area. He was one of the party of ten men who spent some weeks at the BBC's Skelton transmitting station. At the Osset transit camp he shared a concrete hut with another member of the party and a No.12 set transmitter which was part of a local high speed wireless link. He could practice on the higher register of his clarinet without disturbing the camp's other 2,000 residents who were over one hundred yards away. He flew to India with the others in our party, and found life rather boring watching the 100 kW transmitter.

He felt he was very fortunate when he was moved to the studio centre in Colombo, where he eventually became a studio manager. He particularly liked the fact that there was very little there to remind you that you were in the forces; rank counted for next to nothing.

Unlike the great majority of men being demobilised, he carried on with the same job in civvie street, moving from a studio in Colombo, Ceylon to a studio in Bond Street, London. This had been set up by his brother, and was in the forefront of recording technology, having German open reel tape recorders running at fifteen inches/second. Some of the equipment (amplifiers etc.) was built in the studio. They could record an orchestra, and they also did off-air recordings for artists wishing to have a record of their broadcasts. As the years went by the technology kept up with the times. Mono went to stereo, and then up through eight track, sixteen track, and so on.

There were changes in the ownership and management, and the title of the company became 'Advision', which reflected the fact that they were involved with television commercials. They moved to new premises. Andy became a director of the company, but he was not very interested in the business side of things. His interest continued to be in technical developments. This was reflected in his hobbies. He enjoyed cine photography, stereo photography, amateur radio and private flying.

Towards the end of his life he left the company and became a freelance recording engineer. He said he wished that he had made the move sooner, because he so thoroughly enjoyed going out and about with camera teams to record interviews with people. He found that there was plenty of work, and it was very well paid. He was, by that time, hugely experienced, so it is not surprising he was in demand.

The fact that he was very interested in music was undoubtedly of great benefit in the studio. His enthusiasm for certain kinds of jazz was a source of enduring pleasure. The tape he provided of a few fragments of off-air recording of Radio SEAC is the only known audio record of the station's existence. A copy is in the Imperial War Museum.

ERIC'S STORY

My interest in radio began at school, in the Electricity and Magnetism part of the Physics classes. The teacher caught our interest with practical work, such as making an electric motor with a cork, some insulated wire, two pins for a commutator, two bare copper wires for brushes, and a horseshoe magnet.

Soon after leaving school in July 1942, I acquired a copy of the *Practical Wireless Encyclopaedia.* It included a circuit for a two-valve battery operated short wave receiver which I built from parts, most of which came from junk shops. I joined the Air Training Corps in West Hampstead; did a lot of square bashing, and learned a bit of Morse. I wanted to be a radio mechanic in the RAF, but it was the army which needed people when I was called up, and I was very lucky in being given the same job in the army. After some basic training at Maidstone (more square bashing) and a physical development course at Kingston, I was posted to Catterick, on the Yorkshire moors in about January 1945. The Radio Mechanics course lasted seven months, and covered theory and practice. The practical bit was a revelation. We had a few simple woodworking tools at home, so I had no idea that if you had a hacksaw you could cut metal. After some basic metalwork training we were each given a slab of metal, and told to make a pair of tin-snips. I don't think mine cut very well but they did look a bit like tin-snips. We also had to assemble a radio, which was more up my street.

The main part of the course, after the radio theory, covered the sets we were likely to have to repair, especially the No.19 transceiver (for tanks) and the No.22 transceiver, used by the infantry.

I returned from SEAC with a letter of introduction to the BBC, but they no doubt had plenty of former staff returning from the forces, and my interview did not lead to a job offer. I tried for and was offered a job at Marconi, but I settled for a return to Lloyds Bank, because I was twenty three years old and did not like the prospect of missing even more of my youth by having to do a lot of evening study.

So Lloyds Bank it was, for the rest of my working life. Radio became a very important hobby, and although I never became a radio amateur I did a lot of construction, including the television set, with a VCR97 green radar tube, which thousands of *Practical Wireless* readers must have built.

Two friends and I formed a trio to play dance music semi-professionally, for 21st birthdays, weddings, and so on. I built an amplifier to play records at home, and we also used this on jobs. Strange to recall now, I also built an AC/DC amplifier, because there was a chance we might get a band job in an area still on direct current.

In the early fifties a *Practical Wireless* article gave the basic theoretical circuit for an electronic organ. It showed a triode master oscillator and neon indicator lamps used as frequency dividers. Twelve of these circuits were needed – one for each note of the scale. My effort had three octaves, so it meant acquiring thirty six of many of the components. Fortunately cheap war surplus components were still around. I had to smash up a very old piano to get the keyboard. The organ was transportable, but too much to carry about for most band jobs, and the lower notes tended to be unstable. So the couple of years I spent building it were a waste of my spare time.

Meanwhile, my career in Lloyds Bank followed the usual branch bank pattern, until (in about 1959) I read a book on office automation. I asked if I could be considered for something in that line, which led to a move to Worthing, and to the bank's share registration department, which used punched card machines. After a year or two the first computer arrived, an IBM 1401 with four tape drives and 16K of random access memory. I was not involved in system design until it was decided to computerise and centralise the staff payroll of the whole bank. There were many teething troubles as the system was well ahead of its time in some respects. I left the design team when the system went live in April 1966, and was the manager of the pay section for some time before returning to other system development work on customer payrolls.

So banking eventually turned into an interesting career, because it involved pioneering work, which is often exciting to do. Working on Radio SEAC's transmitters had been a unique adventure, and working on early computer applications had something of the same flavour.

Appendix A

SEAC Forces' Radio Times December 1946

Issued free

DECEMBER 1946

SEAC FORCES' RADIO TIMES

A COMPLETE GUIDE TO PROGRAMMES BROADCAST BY YOUR OWN ENTERTAINMENT STATION—RADIO SEAC

PRODUCED MONTHLY BY RADIO SEAC, C/o G.P.O. COLOMBO, CEYLON

Editor: Ronald George

Distribution: Aden, India, Burma, Ceylon, China, Malaya, Borneo, New Zealand, Australia, Japan, British Pacific and East Indies Fleets, and selected listening posts throughout the world.

GREETINGS FROM THE STATION DIRECTOR

WHAT a year! I repeat.... WHAT a year! Let's take a glance at what 1946 has meant to Radio Seac. Most important of all, of course, has been the vast increase in power when our new 100 kilowatt transmitter opened in May. At the same time we stepped up broadcasting hours from 9 hours a day to 16½ hours, and announcers and technicians had to learn to get out of bed at five able mother. A year of change in every way. Look at the staff we've lost. Lieut-Col. "Benjie" McNabb, whose shoes I am endeavouring to fill, left early this year after having guided Radio Seac ever since it was no bigger than a crystal set: Ray Hudson, Paul Froshaugh, Macdonald Hobley, Jack Read, Tito Burns, Dennis Gregory, Martin Roth, Di St. Clair, Sybil Tufnell, Bob Caro, Peter Albrecht, John Smith, each one of them key-blokes, and irreplaceable, or so it seemed at the time—yet somehow we've not merely carried on but (if we believe all we are told in your letters) we've kept up the standard. The thanks for that, of course, must go to our newcomers, who are rapidly making names for themselves.

So we come now to the end of annus mirabilis 1946, in which 70,000 records have been played by Radio Seac, 9,000 original scripts (including 100 original plays and sketches) have been written by the servicemen of our staff, 2,000 news bulletins broadcasts: a year in which Ross Parker has said "er" 7,000 times, Joy Allen cooed "Goodni-i-ght" 250 times and received 39,000 letters, a year in which the Station Director has consumed 1,400 aspirins.

Still and all—WE LOVE THE GAME, WE'RE HAVING FUN! Merry Christmas!

A. E. SMITH

"Just because it's Christmas", they said, "don't think you won't be on the air", they said, "because you will", they said. And how very right they were—because here I am!"

DECEMBER JAZZ

GREETINGS, hep-cats, for the festive season which is upon us, but if anyone dares to ask me to play the Squadronaire's version of "Jingle Bells", there'll be trouble! This is the time of the year when all good jazzmen follow in the traditions of their idols and eat, drink and make merry. Are you wondering what has brought all this on? I'll tell you. I've had a couple of letters from new jazz enthusiasts who state that they are fascinated by the loose lives which the old jazz men led—wine, women and song and all that,—and they think that a good jazz lover should try to re-create the old environment—so here I go. Seriously, my statement in the last issue that jazz was fading from popularity brought a host of indignant denials from the purist boys, plus many more requests for jazz. Well, I can only judge by results and if jazz requests equal those of swing I'll apologise to the purists. It is true that the majority of regular requestees are jazz-fans, but the casuals, who form the greatest part of my listeners, are overwhelmingly in favour of Swing. Anyway, I do think that both factions are satisfied with their respective lots and they know that a line to me will bring them what they want to hear—most times anyway.

This month I'm getting together with Swingman Scotty to arrange a Three O'clock Special on the life of the King of Swing, Benny Goodman. His life is an epic in jazz and swing so I hope you'll all listen out for it.

Space doesn't permit me to say more, but if there's anything you want to know on the subject of jazz or swing or any discs you'd like to hear, well—you know my address. Keep listening, keep requesting and—stay hep!

BERNIE MILTON

From Joy to You

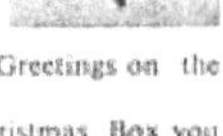

There is no accident ab ut my omission from the Christmas Greetings on the [illegible]

If you want *my* Christmas Box you must tune in at 1200 I.S.T. on Christmas Day.

Thank you—all of you—for your thousands of nice letters.

Love to you, and R.O.T.B.

Keep writing.

JOY

RADIO SEAC'S WAVELENGTHS AND FREQUENCIES

MAIN PROGRAMME

0600—0900—15.12 Mcs., 19.84 M.
6.075 Mcs., 49.38 M.

0900—1000—15.12 Mcs., 19.84 M.
1000—1630—15.12 Mcs., 19.84 M.
6.075 Mcs., 49.38 M.

16.30—1730 15.12Mcs., 19.84 M.

17.30—22.30 11.77 Mcs. 25.48 M.*
6.075 Mcs., 49.38 M.

*There will be a break in this transmission from 17.30 to 18.00

INDIAN FORCES PROGRAMME

09.00—10.00—17.77 Mcs., 16.88 M.
6.075 Mcs., 49.38 M.

16.30—17.30 -11.77 Mcs., 25.48 M.
-6.075 Mcs., 49.38 M.

NOTE—All the above are subject to change, of which the only warning will be preliminary microphone announcements. All times given are in Indian Standard Time.

SUNDAYS

December 1st, 8th, 15th, 22nd & 29th

0600 Music on the Air
0630 *News and Home News*
0645 Morning Star
0700 Soldier Serenade*
0730 *Dance Music*
0800 *News and From Today's Papers*
0810 Programme Announcements
0815 *Shipmates Ashore*
0845 *Forces Favourites*
0930 Cotton Pickin' Time
1000 ITMA**
1030 Film and Theatre Music
1100 Radio Seac's World News Flashes
1102 You've Got It Coming
1130 Vignette
1200 Radio Seac's World News Flashes
1202 Football Results
1215 Yours for the Asking
1300 Top Billing
1330 *News from London*
1340 Top Billing (Continued)
1400 Best Sellers*
1430 Appointment With Fear**
1500 Sunday Symphony
1600 30 to 1
1630 *News and Home News from Britain*
1645 Out of the Blue*
1700 Swing With Scott
1730 In the Interval............*(Frequency Change)*
1800 Radio Seac's News and Home News
1803 Answering Back
1810 Yours for the Asking
1855 Chief Engineer Calling
1900 SEAC Theatre
2000 Song at Twilight
2030 *Radio Newsreel*
2045 Hotel Suite
2115 Round the Fireside
2130 *News and From Today's Papers*
2145 *Spotlight on the Stars**
2200 Music from the Mirammar*
2230 Close Down

3 O'CLOCK SPECIAL

Every Friday

Dec. 6th....THE STORY OF THE PROMS
„ 13th....THE KING OF SWING
„ 20th....NEGRO SPIRITUAL
„ 27th....HIT PARADE OF 1946

SUNDAY SYMPHONY

Dec. 1st Variations on a theme by Haydn,....Brahms,
Vlatava, from ' My Country '.......Smetena.

Dec. 8th Symphony No. 4 in G.........Dvorak
Symphony No. 88 in G....major, Haydn

Dec. 15th Violin Concerto,..........Tchaikowsky
Symphony No. 100 in G major,....Haydn

Dec. 22nd Symphony No. 3 in E. flat ' Erioca '....Beethoven
Symphony No. 101 in D minor ' The ' Clock ' ....Haydn

Dec. 29th Piano Concerto No. 3 in C minor....Beethoven

INDIAN FORCES PROGRAMME

WE are now operating two networks. The additional network will carry the Indian Forces Programme at the following times :—
Daily 09.00 to 10.00
Daily 16.30 to 17.30

MONDAYS

December 2nd, 9th, 16th, 23rd & 30th

0600 Music on the Air
0630 *News and Home News*
0645 Morning Star
0700 Radio Seac's Hit Parade
0730 *BBC Midland Light Orchestra*
0800 *News and From Today's Papers*
0810 Programme Announcements
0815 *Beggin' Yours*
0845 Ridn' Up the Canyon
0900 Forces Educational Broadcast
0920 Musical Interlude..." B...B...V."
0930 Echoes from the Shows
1000 Theme song
1030 Band of the Week
1100 Radio Seac's World News Flashes
1102 Bright Idea
1115 A to Z
1145 Fiesta
1200 Radio Seac's World News Flashes
1202 Yours for the Asking
1240 Pluggin' Time
1300 Comedienne
1315 Piano Playtime*
1330 *News from London*
1340 Bandstand
1400 Chorale
1430 Pot Pourri
1500 Poets Corner
1530 The Hate Parade
1600 30 to 1
1630 *News and Home News*
1645 Sporting World
1700 The Larker Club
1730 Hawaiian Paradise*......*(Frequency Change)*
1745 Overture Beginners
1800 Radio Seac's News and Home News
1803 Heard Melodies Are Sweet
1900 *Navy Mixture**
1930 *Radio Rhythm Club*
2000 From You To Us
2030 *Radio Newsreel*
2045 Programme Announcements
2050 *Forces Favourites*
2130 *News and From Today's Papers*
2145 Waltz Time
2200 *Welsh Half Hour*
2230 Close Down

SEAC THEATRE

19.00 Hours Every Sunday

Dec. 1st

THE COLONEL'S BEEN MURDERED AT LAST..A crazy comedy by H. R. Jeans.
and
BRIEF CANDLE..A play about a night raid on Berlin. (By very kind permission of the author Frank Gabb and Radio Malaya)

Dec. 8th

FRENCH WITHOUT TEARS....Terence Rattigan's famous comedy.

Dec. 15th

THE SHINING HOUR....The well known drama by Keith Winter.

Dec. 22nd

THE PLOT TO OVERTHROW CHRISTMAS....A brilliant comedy by Norman Corwin.
and
RENOVATIONS AT MERRETS....From the story by Honore de Balzac.

Dec. 29th

TO THE PUBLIC DANGER....Patrick Hamilton's drama of a drunken joy ride and its results for the occupants of the car. A man is killed on the road and the car does not stop. If it had....

*Produced by the Overseas Recorded Broadcasting Service **London Transcription Service BBC Relays in Italics 3

RADIO SEAC'S WAVELENGTHS AND FREQUENCIES

MAIN PROGRAMME

0600—0900—15.12 Mcs., 19.84 M.
6.075 Mcs., 49.38 M.

0900—1000—15.12 Mcs., 19.84 M.
1000—1630—15.12 Mcs., 19.84 M.
6.075 Mcs., 49.38 M.

16.30—1730 15.12 Mcs., 19.84M.

17.30—22.30 11.77 Mcs. 25.48 M.*
6.075 Mcs., 49.38 M.

*There will be a break in this transmission from 17.50 to 18.00

INDIAN FORCES PROGRAMME

09.00—10.00—17.77 Mcs., 16.88 M.
6.075 Mcs., 49.38 M.

16.30—17.30 -11.77 Mcs., 25.48 M.
-6.075 Mcs., 49.38 M.

NOTE—All the above are subject to change, of which the only warning will be preliminary microphone announcements. All times given are in Indian Standard Time.

TUESDAYS

December 3rd, 10th, 17th & 31st

(For Christmas Eve and New Year's Eve Programmes See Page 7)

0600 Music on the Air
0630 *News and Home News from Britain*
0645 Morning Star
0700 Singing for You**
0730 *Tip Top Tunes*
0800 *News and From Today's Papers*
0810 Programme Announcements
0815 *In Town Tonight*
0845 Songs my Mother Taught Me*
0900 Forces Educational Broadcast**
0920 Musical Interlude..." B...B...V."
0930 Swingtime*
1000 Something For the Boys
1015 Strictly Odd
1030 Composer Cavalcade*
1100 Radio Seac's World News Flashes
1102 Old Acquaintance
1130 Over To You*
1200 Radio Seac's World News Flashes
1202 Heard Melodies Are Sweet
1300 Those Were the Hits
1330 *News from London*
1340 Bandstand
1400 Flip Over
1430 Personal Choice
1500 Strictly Sentimental
1530 Music from the Ballet
1600 30 to 1
1630 *News and Home News from Britain*
1645 Going Solo
1700 The Larker Club
1730 Tea at the Corner House......... *(Frequency Change)*
1800 Radio Seac's News and Home News
1803 Yours for the Asking
1900 SEAC Revue
1930 Swing Session
2000 Show Lowdown
2030 *Radio Newsreel*
2045 Interlude in Blue*
2100 Floor Show
2130 *News and from Today's Papers*
2145 Off Duty*
2200 When Day is Done
2230 Close Down

WEDNESDAY SYMPHONY

Dec. 4th....Symphony No. 5 in E minor......Tchaikowsky

Dec. 11th....Piano Concerto No. 3 in D minor Rachmaninoff

Dec. 18th ....Symphony No. 5...... Shostakovitch

Dec. 25th....The Messiah.......... Handel

"—and as usual at this time we invite you to Swing with Scott—"

TOP BILLING

Every Sunday at 13.00 to 14.00 Hours

Dec. 1st

Lily Pons, Kenny Baker
The Delta Rhythm Boys
Guest Pianist—Mayer Rosenstein (Playing part of Tchaikowski's Piano Concerto)
The Concert Orchestra of the United Services conducted by Lynn Murray (from the Forum Theatre)

Dec. 8th

Jo Stafford, Robert Merrill
An All-Services' Choir
Guest Pianist—Earl Wilde (Playing Chopin's Fantasie Impromptu)
Paul Whiteman and His Concert Orchestra (from the Rienzi Theatre)

Dec. 15th

Maggie Teyte, Perry Como
The Three Suns
Guest Pianist—Victor Borge (Playing The Warsaw Concerto) and
The Concert Orchestra of Britain's Overseas Forces conducted by Howard Barlow (from a Garrison Theatre)

Dec. 22nd

Kate Smith, Richard Tauber
Guest Pianist—Hubert Richards (Playing The Waltz in Swingtime)
Ethyl Smith at the Hammond Organ
Andre Kostelanetz and his Orchestra (from the Rienzi Theatre)

Dec. 29th

Georgia Gibbs, Nelson Eddy
An All-Services' Choir
Guest Pianist—Peggy Cochrane (Playing The El Alamein concerto)
The Concert Orchestra conducted by Sigmund Romberg (from he Rienzi Theatre)

WEDNESDAYS

December 4th, 11th & 18th

(For Christmas Day Programme See Page 7)

0600 Music on the Air
0630 *News and Home News from Britain*
0645 Morning Star
0700 Ivor Pye*
0715 Out of the Blue*
0730 Light Music
0800 *News and From Today's Papers*
0810 Programme Announcements
0815 *Have A Go...... (4th)* '*All Hole*' *(11th and 18th)*
0845 Piano Playtime*
0900 Forces Educational Broadcast**
0920 Musical Interlude..." B...B...V."
0930 Music from the Mirammar*
1000 And the Next Gentleman
1030 Band of the Week
1100 Radio Seac's World News Flashes
1102 Melody Makers*
1130 Musical Appreciation
1200 Radio Seac's World News Flashes
1202 Yours for the Asking
1300 Something For You
1315 Interlude in Blue*
1330 *News from London*
1340 Bandstand
1400 Show Piece
1430 Swing With Scott
1500 Shake Down the Stars
1530 Their Music Lives
1600 30 to 1
1630 *News and Home News from Britain*
1645 At the Console
1700 The Larker Club
1730 Cotton Pickin' Time......*(Frequency Change)*
1800 Radio Seac's News and Home News
1803 Yours for the Asking
1900 *Swing Club*
1930 Wednesday Symphony
2015 Old and New Book Review
2030 *Radio Newsreel*
2045 Press Button "A"
2100 Words and Music
2130 *News and From Today's Papers*
2145 Ridin' Down the Canyon
2200 *Scottish Half Hour*
2230 Close Down

"AND THE NEXT GENTLEMAN"

Every Wednesday at 10.00 Hours

Dec. 4th....JACK HULBERT
,, 11th....JEAN SABLON
,, 18th....NELSON EDDY
,, 25th....JACK BUCHANAN

AT THE CONSOLE

Wednesdays at 16.45 Hours

Dec. 4th....FREDERICK BAYCO
,, 11th....REGINALD DIXON
,, 18th....JACK DOWLE
,, 25th....REGINALD FOORT

4 *Produced by the Overseas Recorded Broadcasting Service **London Transcription Service BBC Relays in Italics

RADIO SEAC'S WAVELENGTHS AND FREQUENCIES

MAIN PROGRAMME

0600—0900—15.12 Mcs., 19.84 M.
6.075 Mcs., 49.38 M.

0900—1000—15.12 Mcs., 19.84 M.
1000—1630—15.12 Mcs., 19.84 M.
6.075 Mcs., 49.38 M.

16.30—17.30 15.12 Mcs., 19.84 M.

17.30—22.30 11.77 Mcs. 25.48 M.*
6.075 Mcs., 49.38 M.

*There will be a break in this transmission from 17.50 to 18.00

INDIAN FORCES PROGRAMME

09.00—10.00—17.77 Mcs., 16.88 M.
6.075 Mcs., 49.38 M.

16.30—17.30 -11.77 Mcs., 25.48 M,
-6.075 Mcs., 49.38 M.

NOTE—All the above are subject to change, of which the only warning will be preliminary microphone announcements. All times given are in Indian Standard Time.

THURSDAYS

December 5th, 12th & 19th

(For Boxing Day Programme See Page 7)

0600 **Music on the Air**
0630 *News and Home News*
0645 **Morning Star**
0700 **Melody Makers***
0730 *Dance Music*
0800 *News and From Today's Papers*
0810 **Programme Announcements**
0815 *Grand Hotel*
0845 **Spotlight on the Stars***
0900 **Forces Educational Broadcast****
0920 **Musical Interlude..." B...B...V."**
0930 **Floor Show**
1000 **Out of the Attic**
1030 **Chorale**
1100 **Radio Seac's World News Flashes**
1102 **Musical Name Place**
1130 **Marching and Waltzing**
1200 **Radio Seac's World News Flashes**
1202 **Yours for the Asking**
1300 **In the Interval**
1330 *News from London*
1340 **Bandstand**
1400 **Conducted By**
1430 **Soldier Serenade***
1500 **Poles Apart**
1515 **Band of the Week**
1545 **Songtime***
1600 **30 to 1**
1630 *News and Home News from Britain*
1645 **Sporting World**
1700 **The Larker Club**
1730 **Tea Time Tunes**......*(Frequency Change)*
1800 **Radio Seac's News and Home News**
1803 **Heard Melodies Are Sweet**
1845 **Rhythm in the Sun**
1900 **ITMA****
1930 **Film and Theatre Music**
2000 **Rhythm Club**
2030 *Radio Newsreel*
2045 **Here's Wishing You Well Again**
2130 *News and From Today's Papers*
2145 **Thursday Story**
2200 **Moonlight Theme**
2230 **Close Down**

BAND OF THE WEEK

Mondays, Wednesdays and Thursdays

Week commencing :—
Dec. 2nd Harry Roy
" 9th Tommy Dorsey
" 16th Jack Payne
" 23rd Louis Armstrong
" 30th Mantovani

FOLLOW THE LEADERS

Saturdays at 10.30 Hours

Dec. 7th Ted Heath..Charlie Spivak..Rita Williams
" 14th Carlo Kramer..Xavier Cugat..Jo Stafford
" 21st Paul Fenhoulet..Benny Carter..Betty Kent
" 28th Carrol Gibbons..Charlie Barnet..Marlyn Maxwell

FRIDAYS

December 6th, 13th, 20th & 27th

0600 **Music on the Air**
0630 *News and Home News from Britain*
0645 **Morning Star**
0700 **Best Sellers***
0730 *Light Orchestral Programme*
0800 *News and From Today's Papers*
0810 **Programme Announcements**
0815 *Vic Oliver Programme*
0845 **Off Duty***
0900 **Forces Educational Broadcast****
0920 **Musical Interlude..." B...B...V."**
0930 **Over to You***
1000 **Old Acquaintance**
1030 **Music Brings Memories**
1100 **Radio Seac's World News Flashes**
1102 **Music from the Opera**
1130 **The Savoyards**
1200 **Radio Seac's World News Flashes**
1202 **Football Fixture**
1215 **Heard Melodies Are Sweet**
1300 **Black and White**
1315 **All Together Now**
1330 *News from London*
1340 **Bandstand**
1400 **Swingtime***
1430 **3 O'clock Special**
1500 **Lucky Dip**
1530 **The Hate Parade**
1600 **30 to 1**
1630 *News and Home News from Britain*
1645 **Military Band**
1700 **The Larker Club**
1730 **March of the Movies** ...*(Frequency Change)*
1800 **Radio Seac's News and Home News**
1803 **Yours for the Asking**
1900 **Hospital Magazine**
1945 **Swing Session**
2015 **Sleepy Lagoon***
2030 *Radio Newsreel*
2045 **Programme Announcements**
2050 **Forces Prom**
2130 *News and From Today's Papers*
2145 *World Affairs*
2200 *Shipmates Ashore*
2230 **Close Down**

BLACK and WHITE

Fridays at 13.00 Hours

Dec. 6th ARTHUR DAVSON
" 13th ROGER HAGGER
" 20th ROSS PARKER
" 27th GUEST PIANIST

MILITARY BANDS

Fridays at 16.45 Hours

Dec. 6th R.A.F. (FIGHTER COMMAND)
" 13th R.A.F. CENTRAL BAND
" 20th R.C.A.F. MILITARY BAND
" 27th H.M. GRENADIER GUARDS

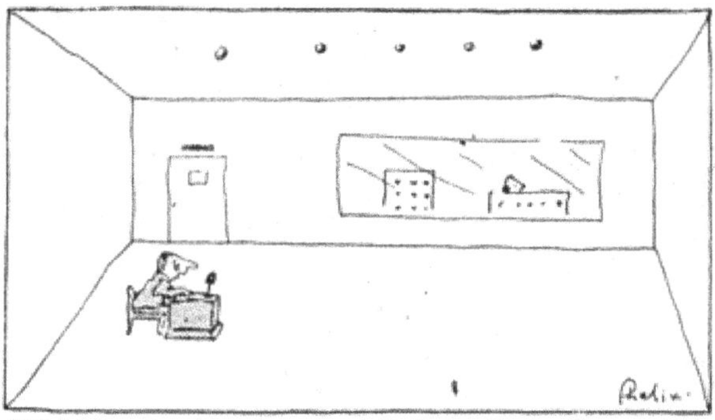

" Well, ladies and gentlemen, here we are in the Garrison Theatre. You can probably hear the orchestra tuning up—and ah ! Here comes the first of the soloists for this afternoon—"

*Produced by the Overseas Recorded Broadcasting Service. **London Transmission Service. BBC Relays in Italics. 5

RADIO SEAC'S WAVELENGTHS AND FREQUENCIES

MAIN PROGRAMME

0600—0900—15.12 Mcs., 19.84 M.
6.075 Mcs., 49.38 M.

0900—1000—15.12 Mcs., 19.84 M.
1000—1630—15.12 Mcs., 19.84 M.
6.075 Mcs., 49.38 M.

16.30—1730 15.12 Mcs., 19.84M.

17.30—22.30 11.77 Mcs. 25.48 M.*
6.075 Mcs., 49.38M.

*There will be a break in this transmission from 17.50 to 18.00

INDIAN FORCES PROGRAMME

09.00—10.00—17.77 Mcs., 16.88 M.
6.075 Mcs., 49.38 M.

16.30—17.30 11.77 Mcs., 25.48 M.
6.075 Mcs., 49.38 M.

NOTE—All the above are subject to change, of which the only warning will be preliminary microphone announcements. All times given are in Indian Standard Time.

SATURDAYS

December 7th, 14th, 21st & 28th

0600 Music on the Air
0630 *News and Home News from Britain*
0645 Morning Star
0700 March of the Movies*
0730 *I'll Play to You*
0800 *News and From Today's Papers*
0810 Programme Announcements
0815 *Jazz Society*
0845 Hawaiian Paradise*
0900 Forces Educational Broadcast
0920 Musical Interlude..."B...B...V."
0930 Song at Twilight
1000 Vaudeville
1030 Follow the Leaders
1100 Radio Seac's World News Flashes
1102 Intermission**
1130 Light Orchestral Concert
1200 Radio Seac's World News Flashes
1202 Yours for the Asking
1300 What am I Here For ?
1330 *News from London*
1340 Bandstand
1400 Composer Cavalcade*
1430 Echoes From the Shows
1500 Singing For You**
1530 The Hit Parade
1600 30 to 1
1630 *News and Home News from Britain*
1645 Comix Corner
1700 The Larker Club
1730 Cafe Spain......*(Frequency Change)*
1800 Radio Seac's News and Home News
1803 Yours for the Asking
1845 Tzigane
1900 Appointment With Fear**
1930 *Sports and Music*
2130 *News and From Today's Papers*
2145 Sports and Music
2230 Close Down

VAUDEVILLE

Saturdays at 10.00 Hours

Dec. 7th....VIC OLIVER
,, 14th....TESSIE O'SHEA
,, 21st....GEORGE FORMBY
,, 28th....TOMMY TRINDER

ECHOES FROM THE SHOWS

Saturdays at 14.30 Hours

Dec. 7th....THE COCHRAN SHOWS
,, 14th....THE NOEL COWARD SHOWS
,, 21st....THE HIPPODROME SHOWS
,, 28th....THE PALACE SHOWS

AUSTRALIAN TESTS

LISTEN for microphone announcements [illegible] as programmes may be interrupted for commentaries between 12.30 and 13.45 on the following days :—

Dec. 1st to 5th (inclusive)
Dec. 13th to 19th (inclusive)

DECEMBER SPORT

TIMES may be troublesome, wars may come and go but the British public still demands its Sport. Never has such a boom in sport of all kinds been known, and events have shown that it isn't merely a flash-in-the-pan while civilians spend their Income Tax refunds or troops their gratuities. There is a wholesome enthusiasm, both among the players and the fans, which is fast taking the Mother Country to the forefront.

Soccer is at its height and even the most lowly clubs are reporting attendances larger than ever. Continental teams have pitted their skill against ours and failed. We have shown that we still lead the world in soccer, and if further proof were needed there's the fact that foreign countries are putting forward huge and attractive offers to our players to leave Britain and to take up posts as coaches and trainers with them. This first normal season was destined to be a success, but the success has exceeded all expectations. The same is true of every sport. Speedway racing has finished for the season—and what a season. Crowds attending ordinary meetings were as large as Cup Final attendances, and fans of this sport are eagerly anticipating next season, when there'll be many more tracks open and competition even more keen. Bristol, for instance, opened a track towards the end of this last season, and despite the fact that the only matches staged there were "friendlies" attendances were incredibly large.

Yes, Speedway has finished, but something new has taken its place—ice hockey. Since the advent of Canadian troops into the British Ice-hockey arenas, the sport has found its niche in British popularity. Some teams, such as Wembley, are including British born and trained players, others prefer to import Canadian experts and have sent representatives over to the land of the Maple Leaf for that purpose. Already the stadiums are full and the game—reputed to be the fastest indoor sport in the world—is bound to flourish.

From the Turf to the boxing ring, from the ice rink to the soccer field, Sport is at its height and it's going to stay that way. As long as it does, I'll try to keep you as well informed as possible through the medium of my bulletins plus B.B.C. Sports Relays. Until the time when you can go along and see for yourselves, keep listening and—play hard.

AL BERNERS

TALKS FOR DECEMBER

Answering Back—
Sundays at 1803
Chief Engineer Calling—
Sundays at 1855
Old and New Book Reviews—
Wednesdays at 2015
World Affairs, by Wickham Steed (*BBC*)
Fridays at 2145

MORNING STARS FOR DECEMBER

Sun.	1st	Malcolm Sargent
Mon.	2nd	Roger Edens
Tue.	3rd	Doreen Villiers
Wed.	4th	Nelson Eddy
Thu.	5th	Ray Noble
Fri.	6th	Max and Harry Nesbitt
Sat.	7th	Jose Iturbi
Sun.	8th	Dennis Noble
Mon.	9th	Marriott Edgar
Tue.	10th	Bob Zurke
Wed.	11th	"Enoch"
Thu.	12th	Oscar Rabin
Fri.	13th	Vic Oliver
Sat.	14th	Reginald Foort
Sun.	15th	Mark Hambourg
Mon.	16th	Joe Venuti
Tue.	17th	"Emilie"
Wed.	18th	George Formby
Thu.	19th	Roberto Inglez
Fri.	20th	Elizabeth Welch
Sat.	21st	Fred Elizalde
Sun.	22nd	Eugene Ormandy
Mon.	23rd	Michael North
[illegible]	[illegible]	[illegible]
Wed.	25th	Western Brothers
Thu.	26th	Eric Winstone
Fri.	27th	Beryl Orde
Sat.	28th	Hoagy Carmichael
Sun.	29th	Derek Oldham
Mon.	30th	Ted Ray
Tue.	31st	Phil Park

" Game and first set to Bokj..Bokjyl..Bok..anyway Crabtree loses it."

 *Produced by the Overseas Recorded Broadcasting Service **London Transcription Service BBC Relays in Italics

CHRISTMAS PROGRAMMES

CHRISTMAS EVE

0600 Music on the Air.
0630 *News and Home News from Britain*
0645 Morning Star : Featuring Duke Ellington
0700 Singing for You**.........Adele Dixon with Jack Cooper and the Augmented Dance Orchestra conducted by Stanley Black.
0730 *Tip Top Tunes.........played by Geraldo and His Orchestra*
0800 *News and From Today's Papers*
0810 Programme Announcements
0815 *In Town Tonight*
0845 *Melody Fair*
0900 Forces Educational Broadcast
0920 Musical Interlude..." B...B...V." ....Benny, Bing and Victor
0930 Swingtime.*.........Britains No. 1. Band of the Year featured in the Ted Heath Show
1000 Something For the Boys
1015 Strictly Odd......Strange Facts and Figures connected with Christmas
1030 Composer Cavalcade*
1100 News from Radio Seac
1102 Old Acquaintance......The songs of yesterday which are the songs of today and tomorrow
1130 Flip Over......the numbers on the back of the Hit Parade
1200 News Flashes from Radio Seac.
1202 Heard Melodies are Sweet......a repeat of Monday's Broadcast
1300 Those Were the Hits
1330 *News from London*
1340 Christmas & Boxing Day Football Fixtures : Bandstand
1400 Over To You*
1430 Personal Choice.........Contribution from All-Station Staff gratefully accepted
1500 The MESSIAH...Part I. (Second Half to be broadcast on Boxing Day)
1600 30 to 1
1630 *News and Home News from Britain*
1645 Going Solo
1700 The Larker Club
1730 *Christmas Variety Bandbox*
1830 Dance Music
1900 ITMA......It's That Man Again. Tommy Handley with his usual 30 minutes of non stop nonsense
1930 Swing Session presented by Bernie Milton
2000 Show Lowdown......The Inside Information on the Entertainment World
2030 *Radio Newsreel*
2045 Interlude in Blue*
2100 Floor Show......when we take you over to the Blue Room where Bernard Freedman Introduces the stars of the Cabaret
2130 *News and From Today's Papers*
2145 *Talk*
2200 Music for Dancing......The Slow-foxtrot to the Eightsome
2345 Carols
2355 Happy Christmas
2359 Close Down

CHRISTMAS DAY

0600 Music for Christmas morning
0630 *News and Home News*
0645 Music for Christmas Morning
0730 *Carols*
0800 *News and From Today's Papers*
0810 Programme Announcements
0815 *All Hale*
0845 *Music for Dancing*
0930 Far East Round Up
1000 Christmas Service
1020 Musical Interlude
1030 And the Next Gentleman
1100 *Anne Shelton*
1130 Christmas Crackers or 'Nuts to You.'
1200 Joy Allen's Christmas Box
1300 Background for Blowout...Feast your fill and relax...
1330 *News from London*
1340 Announcements
1345 *Carols*
1400 Show Piece
1430 Swing With Scott...Scotty with a Special Bag of discs for Swing fans
1500 *All Star Variety*
1600 *Command Performance*
1700 The Larker Club
1730 Cotton Pickin' Time...Wot ? On Christmas Day !—I'll say
1800 Radio Seac's News and Home News
1803 Yours for the Asking
1900 Radio Seac's Christmas Party
1930 Christmas Greetings from the Commander In Chief, Allied Land Forces, South East Asia
1935 *Christmas Feature...Round the World with the BBC*
2045 *Radio Newsreel*
2100 Words and Music...the Spirit of Christmas
2130 *News and From Today's Papers*
2145 *Talk*
2200 *Joyce Grenfell Revenue*
2230 Jack in the Box......And who know's what's coming out ! We don't.........yet
2359 Close Down

BOXING DAY

0600 Music for the Morning After...... Parker plus Alka-seltzer.
0630 *News and Home News from Britain*
0645 Morning Star. Featuring Eric Winstone
0700 Melody Makers*
0730 *Music for Dancing*
0800 *News and From Today's Papers*
0810 Programme Announcements
0815 *Grand Hotel*
0845 *The Kentucky Minstrels*
0930 Floor Show. A repeat of Tuesday's Broadcast
1000 The MESSIAH. Part 2
1100 *It's up to You*
1130 Radio Seac's News Flashes
1132 Marching and Waltzing
1200 Command Performance
1330 *News from London*
1300 In the Interval
1340 Christmas Day Football Results : Bandstand
1400 Sentimental Greeting
1430 Soldier Serenade*
1500 Ali Parker and the 40 Thieves...... Radio Seac presents it's unabridged version of the famous Yuletide Fable as it really happened
1600 30 to 1
1630 *News and Home News from Britain*
1645 Sporting World
1700 The Larker Club
1730 Tea Time Tunes
1800 Radio Seac's News and Home News
18 1 Heard Melodies are Sweet
1 4 Rhythm in the Sun......The music of Latin America
1900 *Jazz Society*
1 30 Film and Theatre Music
2 00 R ythm Club
2030 *Sport*
2130 *News and From Today's Papers*
2145 Thursday Story.........A Radio Adaptation of "A Christmas Carol" by Charles Dickens, presented by Desmond Carrington
2215 Moonlight Themes
2230 Close Down

NEW YEAR'S EVE

0600 to 2230 As detailed in Routine Schedule
2230 Music for Dancing
2300 Mealie Pudding......with Peter Sinclair and a host of other Scottish Comedians and artistes
2330 Hogmanay Beat Up......a programme of Scottish Reels and Dances played by the Scottish Variety Orchestra
2359 Big Ben Chimes Midnight, and Radio Seac sends New Year Greetings to all our listeners

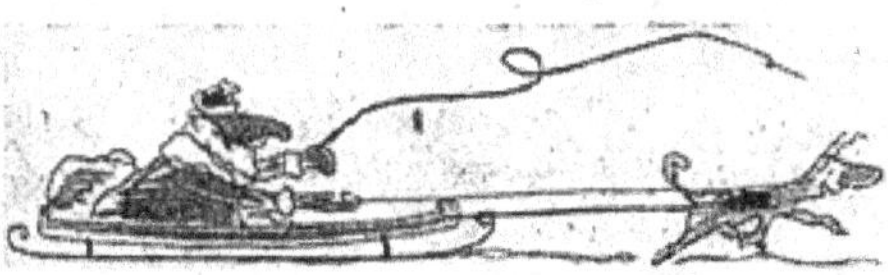

0005 Prayer for Peace
0015 Music for Dancing
0030 Close Down

During the course of the evening Radio Seac will be sending New Year Greetings to all our listeners every where as midnight chimes for them.

*Produced by the Overseas Recorded Broadcasting Service **London Transcription Service BBC Relays in Italics 7

DON'T SHOOT THE ANNOUNCER...

YOU think it's easy, don't you, to spin a disc and announce the title over the air? So did I—once. Money for jam, really. Just walk into the studio, slap the disc on to the turn-table and switch down the needle. So very simple.

Let me introduce to you a little panel of switches, turn-tables that revolve only when they feel like it, and an array of coloured lights that wink insinuatingly as soon as you sit down in front of them. *This* switch, for instance, represents the whole of South East Asia, India Command, the Far East, and probably most of the world. If you say, with the switch down, all the things you usually say with the switch up, you are quietly led away to an unknown fate. We've lost several announcers that way already. Or if you sneeze or cough with that switch down, maybe a dear old lady up in the top corner of Sweden or Australia jumps clean out of her rocking chair and is speeded on her way into the Great Beyond. Just a cough, that's all.

"This is the Forces Broadcasting Service—Radio Seac, Ceylon. The time is four forty—"

I was going to say five, but it's not. The BBC News has finished a minute early......

"The time is four forty—"

Just suppose I said four forty five and it was four forty four. Many of the clocks around the world might have been altered—certainly many in SEAC. That *could* have international repercussions.

"I beg your pardon. The time is four forty four, p.m. Indian Standard Time.

Thank Heaven that's right. Somebody might have been checking.

"We present now—"

Well, what the devil do we present now? Frankly, I haven't a clue. And where is that continuity sheet? Ah—!

"We present now a programme of Light Orchestral music".

Yes, but I haven't got the disc, and they weren't in the library shelf. Maybe they're being spun from the other studio.

A silent prayer, up go the switches, a terrible two second silence, and the cool sweet notes of a violin slip gently out of the loud speaker. Announcing? There's nothing in it, really.

Have you ever come across that interesting piece of scientific phenomena, the repeating groove? It creeps up swiftly, when you suddenly realise that the recording of the Forces Educational Broadcast is hic-coughing away merrily, with the Duty Controller gesticulating like a tick-tack man with a beetle down his back.

"—and what do you think—think—think—......"

A noise like cloth tearing crunches out of the loud speaker.

"—it's all a matter of nuts-nuts-nuts.. ....."

It's the pick-up at fault. Glory, Hallelujah. Why don't those technicians put these things right? The technician stalks into the studio with a frown creasing his fevered brow. He eyes you up and down as you explain, and wave a finger towards the turn table. But does it happen while he's there? Obviously not. If it did that would spoil one of the main peaks of this article. But as soon as he closes the door, up it comes again.

"And that was the works-works-works-manager, speaking on production-production-production...."

Repeating grooves are infuriating things. But they can be good clean fun.

Have you ever had the singularly odd experience of hearing the Station Close Theme when the Station Opening should be playing? Neither have I, but any day now. Can you imagine switching to another studio, waiting eagerly for the expected burst of chords, only to be greeted by a very pregnant silence? Or pushed the wrong switch and tuned in to Ross Parker singing at a rehearsal, instead of going over to the News Room for the News? It's an experience, believe me.

And then there are the scripts one has thrust into one's hand, at unexpected moments. I think one day I must write a book on Scripts—'The Thin Red Line' or 'Kitten on the Keys'.

"Hello hep-cats......"

What a greeting! I believe it is derived from the ancient Egyptian—or possibly it was an old Biblical saying, a form of greeting as boiling oil was poured over the battlements. Whether that was before or after the city walls collapsed, I couldn't say.

"—and as we fade slowly into the sombre finally......"

How does one fade slowly into a sombre finally?

"Er, sorry. As we fade slowly into the sombre finale......"

"Listen now to Il Duce fillestc in Rudus Chordeo......"

My Italian needs some very obvious attention.

"—sung by Benjamino Giggly"

Anybody knows it's Beniamino Jeely. Then why did I say Benjamino Giggly?

Yes, it's really very easy being an announcer. Money for jam, really. Really? Well, it's rather fun, you must admit

HUGH BURNETT

" *I'm a repeating groove—!*
I'm a repeating groove—!"

FORCES EDUCATIONAL BROADCASTS FOR DECEMBER

Dec. 2 RUSSIA AND AMERICA TODAY: "Agriculture in the U. S. A."
3 WORLD OF WORK: "Another edition of Service Magazine"
4 SCIENCE OF RATIONING: "Talk by F. Le Gros Clark"
5 PLAIN ENGLISH: "Request week"
6 SCIENCE: "Questions in Television"
7 BIOGRAPHY: "Do Great Men make History"
9 RUSSIA AND AMERICA TODAY: "Funnies: Footnote to America"
10 WORLD OF WORK: "Resettlement Survey"
11 CURRENT AFFAIRS: "Position of the British Zone in Germany"
12 HISTORY BACKWARDS: "[illegible] ridge"
13 THIS HAD TO HAPPEN: "Synthetic Rubber"
14 PLAIN ENGLISH: "The Story behind Language"
16 RUSSIA AND AMERICA TODAY: "The American Century"
17 THIS HAD TO HAPPEN: "Nylon"
18 OFF DUTY: "At the Dogs"
19 WORLD OF WORK: "Services Industrial Magazine"
20 SCIENCE OF CRIME DETECTION: "The Luton Sack Murder"
21 PLAIN ENGLISH: "Dog Bites Man"
23 JOURNAL OF THE PLAGUE YEAR: Speaker—S. P. B. Mais
24 THIS HAD TO HAPPEN FIRST: "Perspex"
27 WORLD OF WORK: "Services Industrial Magazine"
28 HISTORY BACKWARDS: "Conscription for All"
30 SCIENCE OF CRIME AND DETECTION: "The Trial of Mrs. Maybrick"
31 ENGLISH APPRECIATION: "Huckleberry Finn"

Printed at the Daily News Press, Lake House, McCallum Road, Colombo, by Bernard de Silva, for RADIO SEAC, c/o G.P.O. Ceylon.—Dec., 1946

Bibliography

Archival Sources

Hansard

HC Deb 20 December 1944, vol 406, cc1786-93

HC Deb 21 February 1945, vol 408, cc794-5

Imperial War Museum Library

SEAC All Services Daily Newspaper, 7 May 1946 edition.

National Archives

Annual Register 1945

CAB 78 - 27

IOR/L/PO/4/24

PREM4 13/1

PREM4 13/2 Part 1

PREM 4 13/2 Part 2

WO 163 200

WO 163 260

WO 165 111

WO 172 9361

WO 203 2118

WO 203 3217

WO 203 3218

WO 203 4410

WO 203 4869

WO 203 5207

Mountbatten's Diaries

WO 172 1732, 1733, 1734 (7-31 October 1944)

WO 172 1804-10, and 1811 (6-15 May 1946)

Published Sources

Baker, W. J., *A History of the Marconi Company*, London, Methuen, 1970.

Beachcroft, T. O., *Calling All Nations*, London, BBC, circa 1943.

Bennington, T. W., *Radio Waves and the Ionosphere*, London, Iliffe, 1944.

Berg, J. S., *On the Short Waves 1923-1945*, Jefferson, North Carolina, McFarland, 1999.

BBC, *Engineering Division Training Manual*, London, BBC, 1942.

Christman, T., *Brass Button Broadcasters*, Paduka, Kentucky, Turner Publishing, 1992.

Clarricoats, J., *World at their Fingertips*, Bedford, Radio Society of Great Britain, 1967.

Grace, A., *This is the British Forces Network*, Stroud, Alan Sutton Publishing, 1996.

Hill, J., *The Cat's Whisker, 50 years of wireless design*, London, Oresko Books, 1978.

Joubert de la Ferté, Sir P., *The Fated Sky*, London, White Line, 1977.

Ladner, A. W. & C. R. Stoner, *Short Wave Wireless Communication*, London, Chapman & Hall, 1938.

Lord, C. and G. Watson, *The Royal Corps of Signals, Unit Histories of the Corps (1920-2001) and its Antecedents*, Solihull, Helion, 2003.

Lunt, J., *A Hell of a Licking — The retreat from Burma (1941-42)*, London, Collins, 1986.

Morley, P., *"This is the American Forces Network"*, Westport, Praeger, 2001.

Mountbatten, Earl, *Report to the Combined Chiefs of Staff by the Supreme Allied Commander South East Asia 1943-45*, HMSO, 1951. (Especially Annexure 8, Public Relations and Service Relations).

Pedrick, G., *Battledress Broadcasters, A History of the British Forces Broadcasting Service*, London, British Forces Broadcasting Service, 1964.

Reyner, J. H., *Short-Wave Radio*, London, Sir Isaac Pitman & Sons Ltd, 1939.

Sollom, P. H., 'The Station Behind the Call – VS7PS', *Radio Society of Great Britain - Bulletin*, May 1949.

—'Skybeams, Moonbeams and Howitzers - Part 1', *Radio Society of Great Britain - Bulletin*, July 1952.

Taylor, D., *A Microphone and a Frequency - Forty Years of Forces Broadcasting*, London, Heinemann, 1983.

Terraine, J., *The Life and Times of Lord Mountbatten*, London, Hutchinson, 1968.

Wood, J., *History of International Broadcasting*, London, Peter Peregrinus, 1992.

Ziegler, P., *Mountbatten — The Official Biography*, London, Collins, 1985.

— (Editor), *Personal Diary of Admiral The Lord Louis Mountbatten, Supreme Allied Commander, South-East Asia, 1943-1946*, London, Collins, 1988.

Index

Other titles published by Helion & Company

THE ROYAL CORPS OF SIGNALS. UNIT HISTORIES OF THE CORPS (1920-2001) AND ITS ANTECEDENTS
Cliff Lord
416pp
Paperback

ISBN 9781874622925

DESTINATION D-DAY: PREPARATIONS FOR THE INVASION OF NORTH-WEST EUROPE 1944

D. Rogers
328pp
Paperback

ISBN 9781909982055

MEN AMIDST THE MADNESS: BRITISH TECHNOLOGY DEVELOPMENT IN WORLD WAR II

D. Rogers
304pp
Paperback

ISBN 9781909982086

BATTLEFIELD RATIONS. THE FOOD GIVEN TO THE BRITISH SOLDIER FOR MARCHING AND FIGHTING 1900-2011

Anthony Clayton
120pp
Paperback

ISBN 9781909384187